Dancin
An
Weary Blues

Dancing Fools
And
Weary Blues:
The Great Escape
Of The Twenties

Edited by
Lawrence R. Broer
and
John D. Walther

Bowling Green State University Popular Press
Bowling Green, Ohio 43403

Acknowledgements

The editors wish to express particular thanks to the English Department of the University of South Florida for originally providing the forum for many of these essays. We are especially grateful to former Chairman John R. Clark for inspiring the revels and sustaining the harmony of meaningful dialogue.

Except for the selection by Malcolm Cowley, all selections in this volume were prepared exclusively for this anthology.

Copyright © 1990 Bowling Green State University Popular Press

Library of Congress Catalog Card Number: 89-061587
ISBN: 0-87972-457-9 Clothbound
      0-87972-458-7 Paperback

Cover design by Laura Darnell-Dumm

This book is for
Jim Spillane and John W. Parker

Contents

Introduction

This book is offered in the conviction that it represents a definitive, scholarly researched anthology dealing with the decade of the 1920s in America. All too often productive exploration of that vital period of our national experience has drowned in a sea of antithesis. No decade in our cultural history has accrued such an explosion of contradictory slogans and orotund pronouncements—often at the expense of both common sense and consistency. Convenient clichés and tags may be useful, and in fact contain a degree of mythological truth, but more often such stereotypes obscure the diversity, complexity, and paradox they pretend to illuminate. Inevitably this single-minded approach undermines honest evaluation, leading instead to what might be defined as an excess of unreconciled historical and cultural formulation.

For too long the decade has been stereotyped with such convenient labels as "The Roaring Twenties," "The gayest, gaudiest spree in history," "The Jazz Age," or "The Lost Generation." While such definitions may be verifiable in the eye of the beholder, depending upon his point of view or emphasis, historical perspective has forced considerable reevaluation of a generation that appears to have spun off shibboleths at a faster pace than they could be questioned or verified. How, for example, does one reconcile Harding's "Return to Normalcy" with Fitzgerald's documentation of "Babylon"? Such sloganeering has gravitated into the folklore of the Twenties where it tends to persist as popular nostalgia. The fact is that Harding's call for "Normalcy" is hardly consistent with the Teapot Dome scandals of his own administration; and Fitzgerald's "Babylon" produced as much moral outrage in the hinterland as hedonism in Bohemia. In his comprehensive survey of the period (Chapter 1) Amos St. Germain remarks on the dualities and myths of the decade: "It is very easy to think of the '20s in terms of popular images. But such stereotypes were created and endured because they contained some truth. However, to see the 1920s only as the period of the 'flappers' or of the 'lost generation' or to sum up the period with terms such as 'big business domination' and 'isolation' is to ignore the complexity of the time."

Virtually every one of the contributors to this anthology has begun by putting aside stereotypes and balancing particulars against popular mythology. Thus Elizabeth Stevenson weighs the Flappers in the Twenties with "Some Who Were Not Flappers" and she contrasts the "world of the speakeasies and flappers and gangsters" with "a great, dull, small-town space labeled Main Street or Middletown where the generation just older than the Flappers...are occupying the foreground and doing a respectable fox

1

trot at a comfortable country club." More restrictive in her approach, Patricia Erens identifies the Flappers as a full-scale Hollywood production, as visible as tickets to spicy domestic movies, but hardly more unseemly than "an outraged public" and The Hays Office would allow.

Roderick Nash, in a more subjective if not polemical view, perceives the avant garde segment of "The Nervous Generation 1920s" more or less as a 1960s style counter-culture, alienated from the mainstream, but nevertheless worthy of prophetic respectability. It is obvious that Nash's contribution to this anthology provides ample opportunity for vigorous, stimulating counterpoint, which may well invite conflicting and informative perspectives.

Certainly Alfred Kazin would find Nash's remarks challenging. Kazin is seriously disturbed by "the *unformed* mass taste" of the pleasure-seeking beat generation. To Kazin the true modernist tradition, "now our only real tradition in the arts, is the poetry of Eliot, Pound, Frost, Stevens, Cummings, the novels of Hemingway and Fitzgerald and Faulkner, the plays of O'Neill, the architecture of Frank Lloyd Wright, the movies as a major narrative form, the modern dance, ballet, the comic strip, the musical comedy"— all with roots at the beginning of the century and in many instances representing "the *technical* breakthrough in language, style, form of a [creative] elite essentially conservative and even traditionalist." Kazin contends that this essentially anti-democratic, modernist revolution "...and many of its forms became national only in the twenties," and since "became popularized and academized" by an assortment of mid-cult consumers and academic sophisticates. Thus Kazin finds it "chilling to see how little the increasingly despotic, over-organized society of the 1970s resembles the 'careless' society of the 1920s." Having created this critical centerpiece and forecasting a Spenglerian demise for the remainder of this destructive century, Mr. Kazin bids a sympathetic farewell to the Twenties—the last decade of innocence and pleasure: "A world in which a few with better eyes than most saw that one day the whole gorgeous machine could go smash." Right or wrong we are grateful for his perception.

While the essays in this anthology say many things in common about the culture of the Twenties, each writer's contribution provides a perspective that is uniquely informative about some salient feature of the age. Conflicting points of view, as between Kazin and Nash, Aldridge and Cowley, make for stimulating counterpoint—often incidentally arbitrated by a third party. Malcolm Cowley, for example, elaborates on Kazin's contention that the late, great writers of the Twenties regarded themselves (with Cowley's blessing) as a talented "elite." Yet even as Cowley honors the passing of Hemingway, Fitzgerald, Dos Passos, Cummings, Wilder, Faulkner, Wolfe, Hart Crane and others he has so often celebrated in a final tribute—"Taps for the Lost Generation"—he would not agree with Kazin's dire prophecy that another great generation of writers is impossible. While Cowley does, in fact, share Kazin's lament for the passing of innocence, and after confessing a weakness for "living too much in the past," Cowley is moved to say of the Twenties: " 'But we had such good times then'...We thought of ourselves as being wise, disillusioned, cynical, but we were wide-eyed children with a child's capacity for enjoyment. Did other generations ever laugh so hard together, drink and dance so hard, or do crazier things just for the hell of it? Perhaps some did—but they did not leave behind such vivid records of their crazy parties and their mornings after."

The "crazy parties" would seem to move Cowley closer to Nash's analogy of counter cultures. But except for some noteworthy "vivid records" of the beat generation by such commentators as Jack Kerouac and Tom Wolfe the 1960s seem to have faded with the popular media. Nevertheless, Cowley's cyclical approach to cultural phenomena appears to welcome such youth revolutions as a possible prelude to yet another period of literary activity, "for a new [literary] generation does not appear every thirty years...it appears when writers of the same age join in a common revolt against the fathers and when, in the process of adopting a new life style, they find their own models and spokesmen."

Yet, one hears echoes of Kazin's dismay that the "unformed mass taste" of the '60s and beyond produced so many hippies and so few "traditional modernists" who might have become writers and artists. Cowley would agree that creative art demands more of life than lifestyle. The protests of the 60s had more to do with manners, morals and vocal political activism than with recording artistic archetypes for the edification of posterity. Despite legitimate displays of political idealism, it was heavily weighted with narcissism—leading eventually to its characterization in the '70s as "the me generation." It seems axiomatic to reflect that any youth culture that does not authenticate itself in the enduring arts is doomed to sustain its image primarily as a variety of historical curiosity—just as inevitably as hairlines recede, hemlines expand and the last hoorah fades away. Such a fate would surely have awaited Fitzgerald's Flappers or Hemingway's "Lost Generation" if they and their talented associates had not possessed the creative urgency to render themselves into the mosaic of legend. Thus Cowley contends that the writers of his generation "were all working together to produce a cycle of myths for a new century which—so they had felt from the beginning— was to be partly a creation of their own." If Kazin's apocalypse prevails, however, Cowley's "Lost Generation" may indeed be "Lost"—and last.

John W. Aldridge is skeptical of the myth-making capacity of the ego-centric writers of the '20s. Aldridge's attitude toward this "aristocratic fraternity of talent," though not devoid of concessions to what he considers genuine artistry, appears iconoclastic when set beside Cowley's general bias toward the "Lost Generation" writers. In Aldridge's view their novels and poems suffered all too frequently from a variety of youth-centered narcissism, resulting in a pseudo-elitist incapacity to see themselves, their traditions, their world in a coherent, synthesizing, emotional maturity and enduring cultural or moral perspective. Aldridge builds his premise from a traditional point of view, insisting that the artist should assume at least as much responsibility for universality of experience as for his own dislocated sensibilities. Thus what Aldridge perceives as solipsism in the '20s is put down as artistic lapse. Excessive preoccupation with one's own experience—Hemingway's preoccupations with Paris or Pamplona, Fitzgerald's profligate plunges into the Plaza Fountain or the French Riviera, Wolfe's inchoate laments for Old Catawba or New York—are all suspect.

Aldridge reminds us that "The act of moral reclamation may be a necessity for every literary generation." And in one of his strongest indictments of the Twenties' writers he charges that they were misled or self-deluded into thinking that "their own experience was indeed unprecedented, and that the older modes of literary statement were inadequate to describe it. They, therefore, became excessively preoccupied *with* experience and, in both their writing and their lives, with the innovative and the defiant. For reasons of temperament and historical position they were fixated permanently at the level of *rite de passage*, where they were condemned forever to play the roles of rebellious sons and wayward daughters, able to find their identity only in the degree of their opposition to the literary and social conventions of the past."

There is brilliance and considerable verity in Aldridge's exegesis, though in his attempt to defoliate Cowley's characterization of the Twenties as "A Second Flowering"—commensurate with the period of the 1840s and 1850s termed by F. O. Matthiessen and others as "The American Renaissance"—one suspects a degree of nostalgic empathy on Cowley's part and, ironically, a critical and generational revolt on the part of Aldridge, not too far removed from the expatriate writers' erstwhile revolt against the fathers.

Malcolm Cowley was there; and he knew them all. He had the advantage of immediacy, if not intimacy. He might well contend that great writers *must* write from their own experience, even as they convert that experience into a "cycle of myth." He might also insist that while writers like Hemingway, Fitzgerald, and Wolfe did indeed revolt against post-Victorian social conventions they had enough respect for honest literary craftsmanship to "go to school" on past greats like Flaubert, Twain, Dostoevsky, and Tolstoy. Hemingway, for one, may have felt equal to Flaubert, though he declined to "step into the ring with Mr. Tolstoy." While such arguments might well impress John Aldridge he would no doubt continue to suspect that Malcolm Cowley's predisposition to define and defend the literary merits of his own generation suggest more of camaraderie than of cultural detachment—a prime requisite for qualitative criticism.

Philip Young, in a satirical and often brilliantly witty contribution to this anthology, is not so sure that Cowley's use of the terms "Exile," "Lost," and even "Generation" to describe a select group of American writers is historically or critically justifiable. Cowley used these terms in working titles, subtitles or internal premises for his books; *Exiles Return* (1934, revised 1951) and *A Second Flowering: Works and Days of the Lost Generation* (1973). The word "Exile" in the context of American expatriate writers was apparently Cowley's own invention. The phrase "Lost Generation" had been bequeathed to him by Hemingway, who used it as a belated epigraph for

The Sun Also Rises just before the book went to press in 1926. Hemingway apparently used the phrase with tongue-in-cheek because it is ascribed to "Gertrude Stein in conversation." She in turn had acknowledged her debt to a French garage mechanic for having described the whole American colony in Paris as *"Perdu."* Mr. Young thinks the sobriquet does not fit Mr. Hemingway's generation and therefore should not be taken seriously. Although Mr. Cowley has confessed to using the term "Lost Generation" only as a convenient tag for a group of writers who shared common experiences or interests (as previously defined in this introduction) he apparently used the term often enough to have generated a serious critical controversy. One can imagine endowing a chair in literary history with the proceeds from books, articles and rejoinders that have kept the disputations alive—and interesting.

According to Philip Young the whole issue might have long since dissolved in semantics if Mr. Cowley had not lately blown "Taps for the Lost Generation"—and in print! Furthermore, Mr. Young can find only one "authoritative, probably definitive definition" of the "Lost Generation" in the encyclopedias, which (though no doubt lifted from *Exile's Return*) begins; "A common but misleading designation...Origin is something Stein told Hemingway in Paris...etc." And as if that were not enough to inflame Mr. Young's pen, Mr. Cowley has insisted upon extending his original compilation of 224 qualified *losers* which he began in 1951 to 385 in *The Second Flowering*. To make matters worse, Mr. Young has never even heard of most of them. If ever there was a "Lost Generation" Mr. Young has rediscovered it. Mr. Cowley knew them all. And so it goes.

A similar semantical controversy surrounds the term,"The Jazz Age." John (Knocky) Parker, internationally renowned jazz pianist and silent film scholar, has the credentials to know. His three-score and more years lend a chronological ear-witness credibility to a career devoted to the study, if not the resurrection, of the era. Most jazz buffs who have heard Knocky beat-out "Basin Street" and other tunes of the decade that won't go away venerate him as a kind of one man Preservation Hall. When he accompanies his collection of silent films with all that jazz his audience "knows" that the jazz age not only was, but still is. Furthermore he keeps in musical contact with a cluster of performers who themselves remain legendary. As if that were not enough to establish the validity of an era, Knocky can also resurrect the dead—those player-musicians who strutted their stuff in New Orleans, Chicago, or on hot or cool wax, or on sheet music for subsequent consumption from Fort Worth to Tin Pan Alley.

Why then, after restoring such pioneer virtuosos as King Oliver, Jelly-Roll Morton, Louie Armstrong and Bessie Smith to their rightful place as pied pipers of the '20s does Mr. Parker conclude his essay with a lament for the ultimate perishability of the jazz age? Surely not because the music of the Twenties lacked artistry or authenticity or life—but because, like the stock market crash of 1929, the art of its purist originators gave way to manipulation by imitative composers, portentous promoters, and a public that increasingly demanded compromise and cliché. King Oliver, who might well serve as a metaphor of public neglect was left to die in Savannah with high blood pressure, $1.60 in savings, and a janitorial job working from 9 A.M. to midnight. And the Great Jelly Roll Morton, who had made a fortune for such distributors as The Music Corporation of America, died penniless and friendless in the forties.

Thus, as John "Knocky" Parker suggests "The art of the jazz age could no longer conceal, like the picture of Dorian Gray, the ravages of corruption. When the buying on time fell due and the payment on demand was ordered, the twenties' imitation of life—the concept of a paper moon sailing over a cardboard sea, or the paper doll that one could call one's own—changed abruptly." The public had replaced the authentic timber of jazz with a sententious house of cards that could hardly have withstood the tempestuous forces of its own ephemeral culture.

Was all that jazz real? At the risk of constructing a relativistic merry-go-round, it seems to depend on the perspective of the beholder—or listener. To those who were there, it lingers like a blue note wafting along Basin Street at night or drifting out of speakeasies in Chicago or Harlem. Commingled with illegal booze the sounds and capers of the Twenties blend in the minds of the nostalgic to produce a degree of intoxication that simultaneously suggests the chromatic scale of reality and myth. There is Louie Armstrong wiping real sweat from his brow while filling a hall with honest improvisation. Yet even illusion becomes real to Jay Gatsby waiting for the green light of romance—even as the beautiful and the damned, the cynical, become drunk on his ill-begotten liquor and ultimately forget to attend his funeral.

Edward George Lueders has made the rewarding discovery that the next best thing to living through an era is to know someone who has. In the present case Lueders has selected Carl Van Vechten, author of nineteen books as music critic, photographer, essayist and novelist—a man who not only lived in the jazz age—but who helped to define it in the public imagination. Besides, Van Vechten had the forethought to become a personal friend of Scott and Zelda Fitzgerald. Finally, Lueders himself modestly claims an introduction to that remarkable era by virtue of having been born into it.

The claim is not extravagant. When Lueders arrived on the scene in Chicago, February 4, 1923, the party was already in full swing. And though the immediate sights and sounds of the Twenties were destined to end when he was still a child of seven, one might justifiably say that both the memory and the melody lingered on. It was as he puts it, a natural interest—"My parents' generation—the one whose ways were passed quite directly along to me." No wonder then that he recalls so vividly a spectrum of cultural touchstones ranging form LUCKY LINDY through a catalogue of sports heroes to "the marvelous jazz music of the Twenties that captured me body and soul." Like the guest who came to the party and could not bring himself to leave, his interest in this vast assortment of memorabilia has never flagged.

That is why Lueders has subsequently devoted his life and his work to the fiercely elusive era of the Twenties. Like "Knocky" Parker, Lueders has maintained musical contact with the Twenties via his devotion to the keyboard of his jazz piano. This musical proclivity, combined with his abiding interest in literary studies of the period, amount to an attempt at cultural restoration. Professor Lueders maintains musical affinity with the Twenties as "a jazz pianist on a Brubeck kick." Unlike Professor Parker, who also contributes his share to the musical preservation of jazz, Lueders appears more unwilling to acknowledge its demise in the Thirties and beyond. He is highly selective in his artistry, though he evokes and even romanticizes a degree of behavioral high-jinx and period piece eccentricity. Thus he tends to balance critical disillusionment with a fairly eclectic celebration of nostalgic reminiscence of friends who might well qualify as real characters at Gatsby's imaginary garden party: those who came equipped with such sentimental or cynical verbal "valentines" as "Kiss Me," "My Pet," "Be Mine" and his personal favorite—now rare—"Pa's Wild," Lueders appears to tolerate the "nonsense" of the period as an integral part of its essential adolescent innocence. Furthermore, he believes "the Twenties are legitimately Romantic for us because the lasting writers of the period—...Fitzgerald Sherwood Anderson, O'Neill and Hemingway as against, say, Sinclair Lewis—were themselves true romantics: half-way, you might say, between the valentines of Gertrude Stein and those of H. L. Menchen." Not until the modern media spawned a host of bush-league pop imitators such as Winchell and Cosell does Lueders consider the authentically innocent and idealized expressions of the Twenties to have given way to decadence. If such self-serving duplicity and stylish excess appeared in the Twenties, they encroached upon a garden of innocence. After all, Lueders reminds us, F. Scott Fitzgerald and Carl Van Vechten have already identified and recorded the era's "fatally misplaced idealism" and consigned Jay Gatsby to an empty edifice just down the road from Dr. Eckleburg's ashen landscape.

Darwin Turner's contribution to this anthology is heroic. From his vantage point as Professor of English at the University of Wisconsin, he has undertaken the considerable task of placing Black literary experience into the analogue of the Twenties. His title, "The Harlem Renaissance: One Facet of an Untwisted Kaleidoscope," is appropriate because it suggests a multiplicity of cultural perspectives and literary points of view. Although Turner tends to focus his critical attention on Harlem writers, his cultural geography is disbursed throughout the whole of Black experience in America, including characterizations of multi-hued Negroes by White as well as Black writers, poets, and dramatists. While Turner is generous in giving credit to accurate and qualitative artistry on both sides of the color line, he is understandably chagrined by what he perceives as an excess of literary stereotyping by writers who might have known better. Some are simply victims of their own facile preconceptions; others apparently wrote to please white-dominated publishing houses or delivered melodramatic or local colorist clichés to the paying public. The inevitable result of such compromises proved to be a variety of Black cultural neglect.

Now Darwin Turner asks us to adjust the kaleidoscope in order to restore the full spectrum of Black culture to our latent, inquiring consciousness: "A knowledgeable individual twists the instrument to view the primitivism depicted by such White authors as Julia Peterkin, Eugene O'Neill, Sherwood Anderson, Dubose Heyward, Mary Wilborg and William Faulkner, or the exotic abandon simulated by Carl Van Vechten. But a slight adjustment reshapes those images into the cultural elitism revealed by Van Vechten and cherished by W. E. B. DuBois." Turner would remind White interpreters of Black culture, that despite their artistry, or lack of it, there was more to Harlem than glittering speakeasies; more to generalized Black experience than urban Catfish Row crap games or rural Dilseyesque endurance.

Nor do Black artists, partisan propagandists, or sentimentalists escape the changing perspectives of Turner's kaleidoscope: "Another adjustment reveals the integrationist optimism of Langston Hughes, or the pan-Africanism of W. E. B. DuBois, or the Black nationalism of Marcus Garvey...Scrutinize the urban Northeners of Toomer, Claude McKay, Rudolph Fisher, Langston Hughes, and Countee Cullen. Smile at the enthusiastic and naive Carl Van Vechtens, Mabel Dodges and other white patrons as they prance about with their trophies collected on safaris into Black jungles; then scowl at the lynchers painted by Claude McKay and photographed by Walter White...Consider the African nationalism vaguely sketched by Cullen, Hughes, and McKay; but compare it with Hughes' poetic demands for American integration and McKay's impressionistic sketches of the damnable siren, America, that fascinates, challenges, and captivates Blacks."

There are many more colors in Turner's montage. But does his constantly shifting kaleidoscope constitute a picture of a neglected "Harlem Renaissance?" Perhaps, in a relativistic and somewhat futuristic sense. It is now clear that a nucleus of Black writers used their considerable talents to restructure many dormant shibboleths of Black experience that had for too long confused the vital distinction between local color and reality. Turner himself says that in the traditional sense, "the Renaissance was not a rebirth, but in very significant ways, a first birth for Blacks in literature." Furthermore, his own penetrating scholarship has enlarged our perception and focused our attention upon Black writers of the Twenties who overcame two centuries of cultural neglect to produce a more distinctive and authentic literature than many students of Americana have hitherto perceived.

While Lueders has chosen to emphasize the lighthearted, eccentric lyricism of the Twenties and Turner has explored the panoply of dissonance behind the dark laughter of Harlem, Norman H. Hostetler, outstanding Professor-Critic at the University of Nebraska examines the tragic cultural destruction inherent in a decade that remained too long at an irresponsible, hedonistic party. Hostetler's critical terrain is not restricted to the Bacchic bash at Gatsby's enchanted palace; Hostetler presents convincing evidence from Fitzgerald's own commentaries as well as his fiction that the ambivalent and insubstantial icons of the party-goers produced a variety of moral disintegration from the moment Fitzgerald began to record his social milieu.

In a perceptive article entitled "From Mayday to Babylon: Disaster, Violence, and Identity in Fitzgerald's Portrait of the 1920's," Hostetler verifies his premise by quoting from Fitzgerald's essay "Early Success" wherein the generally acknowledged "Chronicler of the Jazz Age" comments on his first published fiction:

All the stories that came into my head had a touch of disaster in them—the lovely young creatures in my novels went to ruin, the diamond mountains of my short stories blew up, my millionaires were as beautiful and damned as Hardy's peasants. In life these things hadn't happened yet, but I was pretty sure living wasn't the reckless, careless business these people thought.

Hostetler, a distinguished scholar, whose interests range from Hawthorne to American naturalism, traces such ominous premises through the sub-strata of Fitzgerald's fiction and commentaries with the patience and acumen of an anthropologist sifting the cultural ruins of a Babylonian twilight. It is a realm uncharted by assorted nostalgia seekers and souvenir hunters who languish in more "innocent, sentimental, idealized, yet worldly, dissipated" artifacts of the Twenties.

What sets Hostetler apart, therefore, is his effective explorations of the labyrinthian *violence* in Fitzgerald's fiction not always apparent to the secular realist of today or yesterday. Like most good critics, he is curious about literary symbols primarily as they serve cultural analysis and insight. His distillation of psychological, spiritual and naturalistic approaches to Fitzgerald's rendition of the Twenties lends Hostetler's own explorations of the dark side of Babylon an impact that often approaches revelation. Was the "Age of Wonderful Nonsense," then, played out at the expense of the American Dream?

If Lawrence E. Mintz, who has contributed a brilliant essay to this anthology entitled "American Humor in the 1920's," were to arbitrate the cultural duality inherent in Lueders' emphasis upon optimistic refrains and Hostetler's vision of the dark side of Babylon both viewpoints would be vindicated.

On the basis of his specific contribution to this anthology Professor Mintz views the Twenties as "a transitional period in which the evolution of American humor toward darker, more serious self-criticism becomes clear and defined." Thus he dismisses such shibboleths as "The Roaring Twenties" and "The Golden Age of American Humor" as far too simplistic to define a post-war age that was rapidly assuming the complexities of an urbanized, industrialized, mass-production society. He does not suggest that humor did not figure prominently during the period, and he offers plenty of evidence to support his thesis that Americans had not lost the gift of laughing at themselves. Not only did the interwar humor represent a culmination of past comic traditions, but in many respects the humor of the period proved to be both ubiquitous and unique. To underscore this point, Mintz offers his readers a representative parade of comic genius in every genre from comic strips, silent film, vaudeville, theatrical reviews, the follies, radio, drama and literature—sufficient to make succeeding generations yearn for more carefree days.

But for Laurence Mintz, quantity is not enough. His ultimate critical floodlights are directed toward more qualitatively cultural criteria; and it is precisely in the latter arena that he perceives that all was not well in the Twenties—that laughter all too often serves as a mask for personal and social pathos. From this quantitative perspective Charlie Chaplin and his cohorts come to symbolize the "little man" too small for his equalitarian britches, not quite bereft of dignity and minor victories, but constantly tripping over the machinery of modern life.

The common sense philosopher of an agrarian past is often replaced by the ineptitude of his blue collar counterpart. And his white collar compatriots at every stage of the economic spectrum—from mid-cult Andy to parvenu Jiggs—somehow manage to entangle themselves in self-indulgent tomfoolery. Nor does the celebrated nineteenth century wise fool find a haven in the serious literature of the 1920s. Sinclair Lewis's George F. Babbitt is impaled on his own middle western clichés and exhibited before the world as a specimen of what Mencken would call *Boobus Americanus*—a metaphor for the weak-willed, socially dominated residue of the "American Dream."

Thus the "little man" of the "Golden Age of American Humor" is victimized by his production-line gadgets, his job, his boss, his friends, his family, his weak-willed incertitude: in sum, a social environment he usually survives with a resigned smile, a pathetic shrug, though at considerable cost to his self-esteem.

Only in the film comedies does Mintz discern "little men" characters who enjoy a degree of ironic victory over life. Apparently the *deus ex machina* possibilities of the film media combined with more complex character development in such artists as Chaplin, Keaton and Lloyd to produce a "God's fool" syndrome which enabled them—for all their ambivalent vulnerability—to demonstrate sufficient parodic cleverness, wit and basic courage to prevail.

But Professor Mintz reveals the Twenties as "much more than a decade of humor," just as it is more than "the roaring twenties or any other such simplistically designated period." His galaxy of men and women comic artists leaves little doubt that even in transition, the Twenties traversed low roads of cynicism, pessimism and cultural collapse—in ironic contrast to its well-deserved reputation as a high road of comic genius and "wonderful nonsense." Of major significance, however, is Mintz's revelation of the humor of the 1920s as a vital and reflective theater of America's diverse culture.

Dr. Ralph Von Treschow Napp, a highly respected practicing psychologist associated with Winston-Salem State University studied Freudian psychoanalysis at the University of Munich from 1951 until 1957. His numerous publications, including a book entitled *Breaking Down the*

Barrier, have led to considerable and diverse expertise in such interrelated subjects as sociology, American studies, and modern history.

As a Freudian psychologist Dr. Napp is, as one might expect, a defender of his own discipline and the general principles of its founder. Yet he is perplexed at the extent of its misapplication, not only in the "enlightened" past, but especially in terms of pervasive public misunderstanding and misuse of Freudian tenets as a cultural rationale and moral panacea in the 1920's. Napp hastens to point out that the "Revolution in Morals" that followed A. A. Brill's emphatically sexual translation of Freud would have amazed the oracle himself: first at the initial susceptibility of American intellectuals who dispersed themes of uninhibited sexual freedom to the public and finally at the mass indulgence of sensuality and promiscuity that swept the general culture. Napp records that "In the early Twenties" Brill gambled on the acceptance or rejection of Freud's teachings in America when he lectured to women on masterbation, until that day a strongly forbidden subject for public conversation. Instead of being shocked by such public disclosures on sex, Americans broke out into a sweat of sexual mania. By the end of the Twenties there was hardly anyone "in the know" who had not heard of Freud and his new terminology. The four letter words were rapidly replaced with intellectual gusto by such terms as *ego, superego, id, libido, coitus,* etc...So far, Freud's objectivist stance may have weathered the storm. But Napp insists that Freud would not have taken kindly to more activist corollaries such as widespread pre-marital license, extra-marital sex, women relegated to sex objects and a cornucopia of forbidden fruit that too often overburdened family relationships. According to Dr. Napp, "What the people of the Twenties failed to grasp from the pages of Freud was that sex is a moral responsibility in all cultures. All cultures control sex to survive..."

So ubiquitous was the "liberated" sexual appetite in the Twenties that Napp laments that notable authors: "Hemingway, O'Neill, Anderson, Lawrence and others became increasingly popular as they were read with a kind of mutual lust for the legendary 'forbidden fruit'." Paradoxically, in Hemingway's *The Sun Also Rises* (1926) a pair of expatriate "initiates" scoff at the notion that "sex explains it all." Fitzgerald portrays Jay Gatsby as substantially victimized by a profligate society, and Thomas Wolfe, in *The Web and the Rock,* satirizes a group of New York cocktail party cultists for neglecting their spiritual dimensions in order to embrace the latest psychological fashions:

Were they not released by the miracle of the age and science from all the blights of hatred, love, and jealousy, of passion and belief, which had been rooted in the structure of man's life and soul for twenty thousand years? Oh, could they not tell you who were made of baser earth the place where you might take your packed and over-laden hearts (if only you were rich enough!), the physician who could analyse your error, medicine your woe in forty stylish treatments, instruct you in deep damnation of an ancient grief three times a week, mend and repair your sorrowful and overladen spirits out of chaos of their grief and folly in eight months' alchemy of fashionable redemption?

Dr. Napp may well suspect a degree of psychodrama in this prose; yet on a more objective level it reflects a basic consistency with his own analysis of the psychomania that swept through America in the Twenties. Notwithstanding the profound and beneficial impact of Freud on the world of psychotherapy and cultural understanding, Napp nevertheless concedes that despite the plethora of surface gaiety, bath-tub-gin and extravagant behavior, "...America became a tragic society in the Twenties, tragic in that it expected so much, for so many, from so few." So the author confronts us once more with the unsettling image of escape that emerges so frequently in these essays—a picture of all the sad young men and women whose frenetic search for pleasure and beauty dropped them far this side of paradise. But despite the vulnerability of the American Dream during a time of major crisis, we believe that our cultural reassessment of the Twenties offers us a picture of the continual redemption and revitalization of that dream, and reasserts its basic democratic values.

The Flowering of Mass Society:
An Historical Overview of the 1920s

Amos St. Germain

Amos St. Germain is a distinguished teacher and scholar of American Civilization on the faculty of Wentworth Institute of Technology where he is Professor and Head of the Department of Humanities and Social Sciences. Author of numerous essays on American Culture, he is a regular participant in such scholarly organizations as the American Culture Association, the Popular Culture Association and the Humanities and Technology Association, and teaches a variety of courses in humanities. His degrees include a B.A. in History from Fordham University, an M.A. in American Studies from Purdue University, and Ph.D. in American Civilization from the University of Iowa.

Professor St. Germain's historical overview of the period of "revolutionary agitation" that he calls perhaps the most stressful in American history has been strategically placed at the beginning of this volume for two reasons. It evinces the cultural "future shock" of the 1920s that called for human readjustments more stupendous than any made before in American society, and it looks forward in substance and method to the more specialized critical revaluations that follow. That is, it constantly challenges the clichés and half-truths that surround the major personalities, values, and institutions of the age and deny its true complexity, and it explains what the newly surfaced imperfections in our American democracy tell us about our problems then and now. In probing the ever quickening patterns of stress and change that contributed to disaster at the end of the decade, Professor St. Germain asks us not only to consider the crisis of faith accompanying the imminent failure of the American dream, but whether the values such failure called into question deserved to endure.

* * *

To some perhaps the 1920s is the period portrayed by Dorothy Provine in *The Roaring '20s,* or it is Robert Stack pursuing the "untouchables" in Chicago during Prohibition. Or maybe it is the home run swing of Babe Ruth frozen forever in the memory's eye or the vaudeville immortalized in *The Night They Raided Minsky's.* It is very easy to think of the '20s in terms of popular images. But such stereotypes were created and endured because they contained some truth. However, to see the 1920's only as the period of the "flappers" or of the "lost generation" or to sum up the period with terms such as "big business domination" and "isolation" is to ignore the complexity of the time.

If one were to seek a more complete descriptive summary of the 1920s, perhaps the best thing would be to say that the period was the flowering of modern mass society in America. Historian David Shannon has noted, "By 1929 the typical American had become a mass man. He worked for a huge industrial corporation; he more than likely lived in an apartment house or in a small residence that differed little from thousands of others; he read a mass newspaper; he attended Metro-Goldwyn-Mayer movies and listened to national radio programs; he avidly followed the athletic exploits of Babe Ruth and Red Grange—and, wonderously, he voted for Herbert Hoover because the Great Engineer praised 'rugged individualism.' "

In the 1920s the United States faced both political and cultural changes. We faced the problems of regulating the economy, forming a coherent agricultural policy, and determining the correct role of government in the lives of the business community and individuals. The country also had to endure political scandals which would be unrivaled until the Nixon administration. Some people thought that the country's problems were the result of dark conspiracies. As far as foreign affairs were concerned, we had to choose between a desire to be a world power and a desire to keep all foreign policy options unencumbered. America and the world debated an arms race.

In the '20s America was also faced with a new technological society similar to today's. The roles of family and community in governing behavior were questioned and changed. We had become more of an urban than a rural society. There were great changes in the ways we worked, in our standard of living, and in our methods of transportation and communication. More and more, American society came to be controlled by functional elites who could make the society work. Along with the changes there were many signs of strain. Large groups within the economy failed to share in the general prosperity of the times.

During this period Americans also had new sources of information available to them. The new mass media exploited, mirrored, questioned, and affirmed our styles of living. For the first time many Americans became aware of the richness of their ethnic heritage. A whole generation of American writers and thinkers now demanded a useful and independent cultural life. As can be seen, changes had taken place in all areas of Americans' lifestyle, and more and more change became the constant condition of American life.

A Return to "Normalcy"—To What?

In May of 1920 in Boston, Massachusetts, Senator Warren G. Harding, who was to be the Republican presidential nominee, would tell an audience that what America needed was "not heroism but healing, not nostrums but normalcy, not revolution but restoration, not agitation but adjustment, not surgery but serenity, not the dramatic but the dispassionate, not experiment but equipoise, not submergence in internationality but sustainment of triumphant nationality." Harding's style of speech, which has been described as the march of pompous phrases in search of an idea, may have pleased his audience; but events had transpired to make a "return to normalcy" an impossibility. There was no one to say what normalcy was and no way to bring it forth from the conditions of American society.

"Normalcy" was a land that never was. The universal presumptions of Western Civilization—beliefs in progress, order, and culture—had been blown to pieces by the World War. It had truly been a world-wide conflict. By war's end some 56 declarations of war had been made. Theologian Paul Tillich spoke rightly when he said that those who had seen the troop trains pull out and the burial trains return would never be the same again. The flowers still grow well in the fields of Verdun for there's so much human bone meal in the ground.

When the war that could not have occurred came to an end at 11 a.m. on November 11, 1918, the '20s truly began (and would last until October 29, 1929). By this time tremendous personal and economic strains were felt in the United States. World War I was America's first experience with universal conscription. Some 2,800,000 men had been drafted into the Army alone. At war's end the War Department had more than $4 billion in outstanding and unfilled orders. The Wilson administration did surprisingly little in planning an efficient demobilization aside from earnestly requesting governors and mayors to do something for the boys when they came home. Some reformers argued that the moral energy of America's military crusade could not be allowed to go to waste. Felix Adler, a pioneer in social work, maintained that the war had to be taken as a sign for a peacetime domestic effort for social welfare and against vice. Progressive lawyer Donald Richberg argued that reforms had to be made in the management and regulation of business or else the returning workers would be exploited by the "vain and stupid" ways of industry.

The dreams of these reformers did not come true, however, as the Wilson administration did not embark on any domestic reform crusades. The Wilson administration rejected as too radical the Plumb Plan which would have called for continued government management of the railroads as had been the case during the war. The Transportation Act of 1920 allowed for a substantial increase in freight and passenger rates, but even by the government's figures the railroads would not make sufficient profit. In two moves, which many might associate with the "Republican business domination" of the '20s, the Wilson administration passed the Webb-Pomerene Act which exempted foreign units of American corporations from anti-trust actions and the Edge Act which did the same for foreign bank branches. The end of the war then presented a variety of economic problems and expectations.

But there were other problems that had developed in the field of civil liberties and labor that would further guarantee that "normalcy" could not be a happy return to a simple past. Conscientious objectors, even those who chose to serve in non-combat capacity, had been treated miserably during the war. In 1917 Congress had given the Bureau of Labor the power to deport aliens advocating the destruction of law, property, or government. In 1918 in a speech in Ohio, Eugene V. Debs, leader of the Socialist Party, would be critical of the war. He would be indicted and convicted. In 1920 Debs would run for President from prison and get almost a million votes. Debs would be freed, not by the Wilson administration, but by a pardon from Warren G. Harding. The Wilson administration had come down hard on both dissenters and free speech.

The public concluded that dissenters and radicals were threats to public safety. In March of 1919 the Russian Bolsheviks created the Communist International for the purpose of exporting revolution. They boasted that Europe would be Communist by May 1920. Some Americans were all too willing to interpret their own problems as part of a Communist plot, even though in 1919 less than .001% of the population was in the party. In 1918 the mayor of New York City, equating radicals, labor unrest, and nascent Bolshevism, had given orders to the city police to not allow red flags to be flown at public demonstrations. In 1919 eighteen bombs were sent by anarchists in time for May Day to assorted notables such as Justice Holmes, John D. Rockefeller, and the Commissioner of Immigration at Ellis Island. In June of 1919 an Italian national anarchist accidentally blew himself up while attempting to murder A. Mitchell Palmer, Wilson's Attorney General. Late in 1919 Senator Kenneth McKellar of Tennessee asked for the expulsion of native-born "radicals" to a penal colony in Guam, and Senator James F. Byrnes of South Carolina asked federal assistance to avert a violent uprising by Southern Blacks which was being planned by the Communists. Bolshevism, radicalism, and the German enemy were all part of the same foreign evil in the public mind.

Sensing the possibility of riding the "Red Scare" into the White House, A. Mitchell Palmer engineered a political persecution. In December of 1919 249 aliens who had committed no offense, and most of whom had no criminal records, were deported to Russia on the transport U.S.S. *Buford*. The "Red raids" were on a nation-wide scale in 1920. In Detroit 300 people were held in jail for a week without charges. Palmer predicted an attempted revolution on May 1, 1920. There was no revolution. The hysteria spent itself and people came to see terrorist activities as the acts of a violent few, not a nation-wide movement.

There was, however, one long-lasting "red" issue. In May of 1920 Nicola Sacco and Bartolo..neo Vanzetti were arrested for robbery and murder in a shoe company holdup in Massachusetts. They were convicted and sentenced to death in 1921. The process of appeal would go on till their execution in 1927. Sacco and Vanzetti would become an international cause for there was at the time, and there has continued to be, the belief that these men were convicted not for any crime but because they were anarchists.

In addition to the Red Scare, 1919-1920 was a period of labor unrest. There were approximately 3600 strikes in 1919, and they were in a variety of regions and occupations. The Tampa cigar workers went out as did the Willys auto workers in Ohio. Shipyard workers went out in Seattle, and they were eventually backed by other unionized workers. Seattle's Mayor, Ole Hanson, broke the strike. A strike against U.S. Steel in September of 1919 involved 365,000 workers, and the coal strike of the winter of 1919-20 involved 394,000. In all, some 4 million workers were involved in strikes that year. There was even a strike among the Boston police. The Governor of Massachusetts, Calvin Coolidge, got a great deal of favorable publicity by bluntly stating that public employees had no right to strike against the public safety. Labor wanted to insure itself a share in the post-war prosperity and to seek adjustment of wages to meet post-war job pressures and price increases. Many industrial leaders labelled the union demands as "radical" or refused to even recognize the existence of the unions. Unions, they argued, were not "the American way." The unions violated the "personal relationship" between employer and employee. The strikes were directed by Trotsky and Lenin. The wartime solidarity and truce over wages and working conditions were depicted by employers as the natural labor-management relationship.

By 1920 Americans had to make decisions as to where they would direct their material and political energies. They had to decide if they would continue the policies of governmental reform that had characterized the years 1900-1917. The shock of war and readjustment, strikes, price increases, a fear of foreigners and radicals, flagrant violation of constitutional rights, a fear that American idealism might be adrift—all these made up the period immediately preceding Harding's attempt to "return to normalcy."

Harding, Coolidge, Hoover—The Just Government for a Burgeoning Society

Warren G. Harding, with sixty per cent of the popular vote, was an easy winner in the presidential election of 1920. The senator from Ohio had been chosen by the Republicans because he was an "available" man. Legend has it that he was the choice of a group in a smoke-filled hotel room prior to the balloting, but it would be more accurate to say that he was the eventual choice of several important Republicans at the convention. Thirteen of the sixteen Republican senators present as delegates had not voted for Harding in the early ballots.

As President, Harding's main virtue and flaw was his uncritical sociability linked with a thoroughly mediocre political mind. It has been said that he attempted to dismantle the accomplishments of his Progressive predecessors, Theodore Roosevelt, William Howard Taft, and Woodrow Wilson, by appointing foxes to mind the hen house. He appointed V.W. Fleet to the Federal Trade Commission. Fleet was a close associate of Senator James E. Watson of Indiana who had referred to Woodrow Wilson's supporters and appointees as "anarchists and seditionists." In a similar move, Harding appointed T.O. Marvin, editor of *The Protectionist* (a pro-tariff magazine), to the Tariff Commission. Harding surrounded himself with friends who later would prove to be dishonest. Harding made a boyhood friend governor of the Federal Reserve System; he chose a chance acquaintance to be head of the Veteran's Bureau; he made an Ohio sheriff the Director of the Mint; and he made his brother-in-law Supervisor of Federal Prisons. Alice Roosevelt Longworth, daughter of Teddy and wife of the Speaker of the House, recalled that the White House had an informal, collar unbuttoned, men's club atmosphere about it during the Harding days. Yet defenders of Harding might answer that he could claim credit for choosing Andrew Mellon as Secretary of the Treasury, perhaps the most influential Secretary since Alexander Hamilton; Herbert Hoover as Secretary of Commerce, perhaps the single most important man in American government in the 1920s; and Charles Evans Hughes as Secretary of State, a post wherein Hughes acquitted himself admirably.

However, what people remember most about Harding is the scandals. They were banal compared to the Watergate episode, for the Harding people only took money; they did not attempt to perpetuate power. The Secretary of the Interior became the first cabinet member to go to jail for deeds committed during his tenure for giving over Naval Oil Reserve lands to private interests. The head of the Veteran's Bureau, Charles R. Forbes, had cost the country over $200 million. Jess Smith of the Justice Department, an intimate associate of Attorney General Harry Daugherty and the reputed bag man for the Harding gang, killed himself. In March of 1924 the now former Attorney General Daugherty was tried for selling German chemical patents.

Overweight, overworked, and overworried about the intimations of disaster within his administration, Harding died of a heart attack on August 2, 1923. His sudden death brought Calvin Coolidge to the Presidency. From outward appearances Coolidge was a man who was a prime subject for caricature. The ever irrepressible Alice Roosevelt Longworth remarked that he looked as if he had been weaned on a pickle. As a result of the caricatures and idiosyncrasies he was often thought to be the least impressive president America ever had. The man himself helped these caricatures along with several undying Coolidgeisms such as: "The man who builds a factory builds a temple; the man who works there worships there." and "The business of America is business."

But in retrospect Coolidge appears neither callous nor simple minded. He attempted to retire the national debt, balance the budget, cut the functions of government, and simply let the country run itself unimpeded. Transcripts of his press conferences reveal him as a man who could think on his feet and see the complexity of an issue, and enjoyed doing so. Coolidge was not merely the agent of business selfishness. Of a flood relief bill in 1928 Coolidge observed that there was something in it for everyone: for the railroads, the banks, the investors, and the lumbermen—for everyone, that is, except for the little man whose way of life was washed away. What Coolidge attempted to do was to apply sound principles of business to the problems of government. And there were many in government and industry who were more than willing to help. Of course many questions remain. Does success in business wash away the tendencies of original sin? Was there a real chance that America would have developed other than it did? Does the adoption of any set strategy in administration, be it ecclesiastical, industrial, or governmental, make people forget about other important human needs?

A true judgment of the Harding and Coolidge administrations cannot be made without considering the important role played by their Secretary of the Treasury, Andrew Mellon. Mellon, Pittsburgh banker and heavy investor in the Aluminum Corporation of America and Gulf Oil, served in that influential position under all three Republican presidents in the '20s. He was one of the wealthiest men in America and became the willing agent of American wealth and industry.

Secretary Mellon did not go so far as to say, as some of the 19th century capitalists did, that God in his goodness had placed the affairs of mankind in the hands of the wealthy; but he did pursue a program dedicated to letting wealth work. Expenditures on public works, health, and welfare were reduced while funds for the Department of Commerce, law enforcement (Prohibition), and the subsidizing of shipping were increased. The Budget and Accounting Act of 1921 provided for the systematic planning of overall federal expenditures and receipts rather than the endless parade of supplicant departments. The passage of the Fordney-McCumber tariff in 1922, which was at the time the highest tariff in American history, showed that business has a firm position. There were also provisions made for tariff revisions but the few rate revisions were mostly upward. The tariff had an unfavorable effect on America's foreign trade.

Mellon also attempted to have the excess profits tax repealed, to reduce the surtax on large personal incomes, to repeal the gift tax, and to reduce estate taxes. He was successful in most of his programs. In 1926 a person with an annual income of $1 million paid less than 1/3 the tax he paid in 1921. Some individuals such as J.P. Morgan sometimes paid no income tax at all. Mellon wanted the burden of taxation reduced for those in the upper brackets and the financial weight shifted to the middle and lower brackets. It was argued that these people were the ones who could least afford to pay, but Mellon envisioned a trickle-down theory. The rich don't put their money into mattresses—they invest it. These investments make the economy grow. This growth provides more jobs and money. The middle and lower income groups who don't have either the resources or the skill to invest eventually profit. Of course Mellon's theory was based ideally on productive investment and not just on speculative investment that doesn't employ people or produce goods and services. Anti-trust indictments declined in the '20s. Illegalities were usually resolved by consultation between the Justice Department and the offending company. As a result of this informal friendly extra-legal procedure the company would hopefully cease and desist.

Although Harding, Coolidge, and Mellon had a great effect on politics in the 1920s, the one man who embodied Republican principles and economics of the '20s the most was Secretary of Commerce (under Harding and Coolidge) and later President Herbert Hoover. Hoover (always the engineer) wanted to continue the efficiency that he had seen during the war in the efforts of the War Industries Board. It was not the function of government to manage business, but government could collect and distribute economic information. It could investigate economic and scientific problems and point out remedies. Hoover saw the collecting and distributing of economic information as the chief duty of the Department of Commerce. A great deal was accomplished through the Department's Bureau of Standards and its Bureau of Foreign and Domestic Commerce. The Department employed many economic and technical experts. Advances were made in the simplification of industrial machinery and processes. With the assistance of the Department, auto manufacturers, for example, were able to develop and mass produce engines with new, narrower tolerances which displayed a degree of efficiency only previously obtainable in hand-tooled engines.

Hoover was particularly active in stimulating the organization of trade associations and energizing and strengthening existing ones. By 1920 there were roughly 2000 such associations with periodic meetings and in many cases a trade publication. Under Hoover, the Department of Commerce encouraged the formation of hundreds more. It sponsored conferences for industries that stressed the benefits of such associations and even produced a publication that told how to set one up. The Department also urged the adoption of uniform cost accounting systems. In competitive bid industries this almost inevitably resulted in decreased competition. In the American Linseed Oil Association case of 1923 the Supreme Court prohibited them from punishing noncompliance in pricing or from enforcing a mandatory interpretation of cost and price data. But in the Maple Flooring Manufacturing Association case the Court held that it was perfectly permissible to publish and distribute all relevant cost and price information.

The government's benevolent gaze on business in the '20s resulted in the consolidation of economic wealth in the hands of corporations. By 1929 the 200 largest American corporations controlled 20% of the national wealth and 50% of the corporate wealth. Concentration occurred in many fields such as mining, manufacturing, public utilities, and banking. The large corporations were growing about three times as fast as new competitors in their fields. The problems caused by the misuse of wealth as well as the problems involved in big industry were present in the 1920s. Management became a matter of "teams" and "units" rather than of personalities. The worker became an ever more highly skilled machine.

In a way, Herbert Hoover was the successor of Theodore Roosevelt. Roosevelt had not feared either bigness or concentration in industry. Neither did Hoover fear it. It had been Roosevelt who created the Department of Commerce, and it was Hoover who was its greatest Secretary. In the name of efficiency and prosperity Hoover would make government assist private initiative. Roosevelt had raged only against the "arrogant stupidity" of some business leaders who thought only of their own profits. The methods of Hoover, Coolidge, and Mellon seemed to be bringing prosperity. Woodrow Wilson had argued that the individual's right to compete had to be maintained, but there seemed (at least until 1929) to be no large argument with Republican prosperity.

This is not to say that interest in governmental reform, in health, in safety, in decent working conditions, and in government protection of individual opportunity vanished completely in the 1920's under Harding, Coolidge, and Hoover in face of a flood of pro-business sentiment. The Esch-Cummins Act and the Water Power Act were passed in 1920 which gave the federal government a significant role in the regulation of railroad rates and utilities. In 1921 the Packers and Stockyard Act and the Grain Futures Act gave the Secretary of Agriculture the power to issue cease and desist orders to end unfair practices. Senator Norris was able to keep the Muscle Shoals Dam from being sold to private interests, and this dam was to become one of the lynch pins of the TVA electrification program. A sizeable and varied group of reformers attended the Conference for Progressive Political Action called in Chicago in 1920, and the candidates backed by the Conference did well in the elections of 1922.

In February 1924 the Conference called for a nominating convention to meet in Cleveland in July since it was disgruntled with both the Democratic frontrunners for the presidential nomination, William G. McAdoo and Al Smith. A variety of reform groups attended: left of center farm organizations, representatives of the Socialist Party, Wisconsin Progressive Republicans, members of the railroad union brotherhoods, and other union representatives. The delegates were an odd mixture indeed. Some wanted to smash the "monopolistic" power of big business. Others, such as the Socialists, wanted the federal government to run the monopolies on behalf of the people. The convention settled on Robert M. La Follette, the old Progressive, as its presidential nominee. The platform they finally produced called for a reduction of the power and influence of big business, the nationalization of railroads and the power industry, guarantees of collective bargaining for unions, and a lessening of the use of injunctions against union activities.

Businessmen labelled this platform "Wisconsin Bolshevism," and the honorable old political warrior, La Follette, was pictured as the candidate of Moscow. La Follette captured only 16% of the popular vote in 1924 as Coolidge won the election in his own right, but in eleven states La Follette drew more votes than did the eventual Democratic nominee, John W. Davis. The message would not be lost on the Democratic Party in the elections in 1928 and 1932. Sentiments of La Follette's platform would find an audience with the Democrats. But in the election of 1924 there was little argument with Coolidge prosperity. And even the old social crusader Lincoln Steffens would declare in 1928, "Big business in America is producing what the Socialists held up as a goal: food, shelter, and clothing for all. You will see it during the Hoover administration."

American Foreign Policy-Insulationism

The conventional view of the foreign policy of American mass society in the 1920s was that we vigorously pursued a policy of isolation. No generation ever followed the advice of Washington's Farewell Address better. We wanted no part of foreign controversies and no part of "entangling" alliances. At first glance, this view appears to be correct. But perhaps a better term for American foreign policy during the period would be "insulationism." We wished to insulate ourselves from international problems and particularly from any situation that we could not control, but we wanted the fruits of certain international involvements. The United States was very conscious of itself as a world power. We were aware of international affairs and at times acted vigorously in them.

When Warren Harding became President, America was technically still at war. We had rejected the Peace of Paris, and Woodrow Wilson had refused to sign a joint resolution of Congress ending the War. Harding did so however, and we ended the war on July 2, 1921, claiming all the privileges of the Paris Peace package regarding Germany, Austria, and Hungary but accepting none of the responsibilities. This action certainly seems to support the "isolation" viewpoint. In a similar vein, we collectively told Miss Liberty to throw her torch into New York harbor. We decided in the early 1920s that we really didn't want the "huddled masses of your teeming shore" that the poetess Emma Lazarus had spoken of. The Emergency Quota Act of May 1921 restricted each country's immigration to 3% of that immigrant population in America according to the census of 1910. Some 700,000 people a year emigrated to the United States from 1921 to 1924. The Immigration Act of 1924 went even further. The number of immigrants was limited to 2% of those populations in America according to the census of 1890. This deliberately cut down the number of immigrants from southern and eastern Europe. In addition, the law of 1924 virtually excluded all Asians. This was a measure particularly aimed at the Japanese. In 1922, the Supreme Court had already declared that the Japanese might be ruled permanently ineligible for citizenship. The tone of this legislation was not lost on the Japanese government.

Also supporting the isolation viewpoint was the steadfast refusal of the United States to subscribe to the protocols of the World Court. The Court, which had been created by the charter of the League of Nations, had its first sessions in June of 1922. President Harding recommended to the Senate in February of 1923 that we join this new international judicial agency, but the Senate did not concur. President Coolidge submitted a similar proposal in December of 1923, but the Senate demurred on the grounds that the power of the Court's "advisory opinions" was unclear. In February 1926 another proposal was put forth in which the United States demanded that the World Court give notice well in advance of considering any case involving any question that touched the vital aims of the United States. When the World Court asked for a clarification of this "everything but mine" position, Coolidge interpreted their inquiry as a rejection of terms. Later efforts to enroll the U.S. under Herbert Hoover and Franklin Roosevelt would also fail. And of course, the nation that was the homeland of the architect of the League of Nations never did join the League.

Rejection of the peace treaty, refusal to join the League, refusal to take part in the proceedings of the World Court, claim of victory without responsibility, immigration restriction—all these tended to support the view that America wanted to be isolated; she wanted to be left alone. But this is far from being the whole picture of the '20s foreign policy. A wider consideration of events would make the term "insulation" more desirable than isolation. The United States, in fact, was very active in the economic and military aspects of foreign policy. But we wanted to be active in the areas we chose, to avoid entangling agreements, and to keep all our options open.

In the '20s America was active in the field of oil diplomacy in Latin America. Our rejection of the Versailles Treaty did not prevent us from ratifying the Thompson-Urrutia Treaty with Colombia in 1922. We faced competition from the British for Colombian oil. In the treaty we admitted that we had been less than proper in our enthusiastic backing of Panama's break with its mother country. American oil investment in Colombia in 1912 was $2 million, and it was almost that low in 1920. By 1925 United States investment had increased to $17 million, and by 1929 it stood at around $124 million. The United States also engaged in oil diplomacy on other fronts. We were able to press successfully our claims for a cut of the investment in Mideast oil. Under steady economic pressure the British discreetly retired from investments in Mexico and South America.

The United States was active in foreign relations with Mexico. Mexico had changed its policies concerning land holdings, manufacturing interests, and oil deposits after the 1917 revolution, and the United States feared Mexican nationalization of our industrial holdings there. We were more optimistic when Alvara Obregon became President of Mexico in 1920. He proposed only the regulation and taxation of foreign industries and their mineral rights and granted concessions for improved properties. America was pleased with his position to the point of selling him arms, which some might interpret as interference in the internal affairs of Mexico. The hopes of the United States waned again when Plutarco Elias Calles became Mexico's president in 1925. Calles declared Mexico's mineral rights, particularly oil, to be inalienable, and he proposed new regulations. He also contended that if you operated businesses in Mexico you should fully expect to accept all the privileges and responsibilities of a Mexican, not of a foreign national. Most of the 380 U.S. companies in Mexico agreed with the Calles rules but some 22 did not, and they included such oil giants as Doheny, Standard, Sinclair, and Gulf. Undersecretary of State Dwight Morrow intervened and was able to persuade Calles to soften his position on oil and his anti-Catholic Church policy, another issue that disturbed many Americans.

The United States was also active in the affairs of Nicaragua. In 1916 we had negotiated the right to construct a canal and to fortify the approaches to it. With this policy in mind a token military force had been stationed there. In 1925 that force was removed because everything seemed fine. But immediately the Nicaraguan government embarked on disastrous financial policies. President Coolidge sent 5000 Marines to Nicaragua, and the United States supervised the elections in that country in 1928, '30, and '32.

Some might call our hemispheric self-interest as interference in the internal affairs of other countries, but the U.S. had claimed broad powers in Latin American affairs. Until the 1920s the United States had Platt Amendment-type privileges (namely, the right to interfere when necessary) in the constitutions of Cuba, Panama, Haiti, and the Dominican Republic. At the Fifth Pan American Conference in 1923 the United States began to back away from this position. We agreed that diplomacy and arbitration were proper recourses before war. More specifically, in the Clark Memorandum of Undersecretary of State J. Reuben Clark issued in December 1928, the United States disavowed its role as policeman of the Hemisphere. By the end of the 1920s the United States had replaced Great Britain as the primary source of capital for Latin America. We bought their government bonds and were their best customers. We sent Latin America machinery and autos, and they sent us coffee, rubber, tin, copper, bananas, and oil. The basic "Good Neighbor" tone of American foreign policy toward Latin America was set in the 1920s. Yet some of the more serious problems were potentially there too. Would we consider their agricultural production in dealing with our agricultural surplus? How much would we pay for their raw materials? What would our attitudes be if they opted for forms of government greatly different from our own? What was the future of our relations with the one-crop agricultural countries?

American foreign policy extended to Europe as well as to Latin America. In 1924 Secretary of State Charles Evans Hughes, in a speech in London, declared that the United States was a non-aggressor nation devoted to peace. We would cooperate fully in the promotion of international public health and other humanistic projects. The United States would support institutions of international justice and help to rehabilitate Europe short of direct economic aid. The relations of the United States and Europe became quite complex in the 1920s with or without our approval of the League of Nations, with or without our membership in the World Court. The United States had gone into World War I owing other nations money, but she emerged from the war a creditor nation. We had loaned some $7 billion to the Allies, and by 1920 we had loaned $3 billion more to Finland, Poland, Estonia, Yugoslavia, and Czechoslovakia. We wanted our money back with 5% interest. The Europeans felt that it was unjust as the war had been fought in their countries, not ours; they had borne far more damages and casualties; and the United States had emerged from the war as a major power. Besides, where would they get the money? Uncle Sam renegotiated the debts in the

'20s. Great Britain, for instance, was given 62 years instead of 25 in which to pay, and her rate of interest was reduced.

The United States became intimately involved in the financial affairs of Germany also. Germany had been assessed a staggering $33 billion in reparations. She was to pay $375 million from 1921 to 1925 and some $900 million each year thereafter. Such payments were highly punitive and impossible. Secretary Hughes, in a speech in New Haven in 1922, remarked that something would have to be done. In 1923 Belgium and France declared Germany willfully in default and so occupied the Ruhr Valley. Finally the American Hughes-Dawes-Young plans rescued Germany. The U.S. made loans to Germany. Germany used a part of the money to get credit from the Allies. What was happening a good deal during the 1920s was that the United States' money (taxpayers') was going to Germany who gave it to the Allies who gave it back to the United States.

Besides Latin America and Europe, the United States' insulationism extended to Asia. The Japanese objected to the Open Door policy in China advocated by the United States. They wanted economic domination of the Chinese province of Shantung and of Siberia. They wanted to be the heirs to former German possessions in the Pacific. In short, the Japanese wanted to dominate the East. The potential problem with Japan was not lost on the Navy Department. In the '20s the United States reorganized its fleet, sending a good portion of it to the Pacific for the first time. The Navy managed its building and funding with an eye to a possible eventual clash with the Japanese in the East.

But perhaps more important than any preparation for war was the United States' involvement in idealistic attempts to prevent future wars. In 1921 the United States proposed a "Conference on the Limitation of Armaments." Great Britain, France, Japan, Italy, and the United States were to attend. Later China, the Netherlands, Belgium, and Portugal were added to the list. The United States' delegation included Democratic Senator Underwood, Republican Senator Lodge, Secretary of State Hughes, and former Secretary Elihu Root. This would be the Harding administration's blow for peace and the correct answer to Woodrow Wilson's one-man peace crusade. The Conference, called the Washington Naval Conference, subsequently began on November 12, 1921, three years and one day after the armistice. (As a solemn reminder of duty the delegates had attended the interring of the unknown soldier the previous day.) Out of the talks came the now famous "5:5:3..." ratio of naval armaments intended to prevent an arms race and consequent war.

By 1927 there was need for another conference. The idea was proposed, but France and Italy flatly vetoed it. The arms race had occurred. The United States, for example, was building 26 light cruisers, 3 aircraft carriers, 18 destroyers, and 5 submarines—precisely those types of arms not mentioned in the Washington agreement. Instead of an arms conference the United States and France made a symbolic legal gesture. In Paris on August 27, 1928 the Kellogg-Briand Peace Pact was signed. Eventually fifteen nations signed it. The Pact declared war illegal. It was the child of Undersecretary of State Frank B. Kellogg and French Foreign Minister Aristide Briand. It attempted to marshal world opinion and international law against war as a legitimate tool of diplomacy. The United States inserted a disclaimer in its signing, again always wishing to keep its options open. In retrospect, the Pact was a failure but it was nonetheless a hopeful gesture.

International monetary policy, war debts, reparation, disarmament, military preparedness, and the promotion of peace and economic recovery were all part of United States-Europe foreign policy. The '20s was the period of insulation. We wanted no crusades. We wanted no entanglements. We wanted no situation that we could not control. But we also wanted to maintain the military and economic influence of a major world power.

Changes in the Lifestyle of Mass Society—America in the '20s

In terms of everyday experience, the commonly felt stresses on individuals and families, public communication, entertainment, and patterns of consumption, the United States in the 1920s was a mass society. America presented its citizens with a constant display of change that contained issues and problems which are still very much with us today.

The "we" of the American population of 1920 had come to include a remarkable number of "them," those of immigrant birth. The 1920 census revealed that there were more Americans who were of a mixture of native American with immigrant stock than there were citizens who were exclusively of one or the other. In terms of religion, the census revealed that 41% of the population claimed some sectarian Christian affiliation with 64% of the group identifying themselves as Protestants and 36% as Catholics.

The census of 1920 also revealed that for the first time the United States was more of an urban than a rural nation. The 1920 census announced that there were 54,318,032 urban Americans as opposed to 51,390,739 rural Americans. For every 46 people engaged in agriculture there were 54 in manufacturing and mechanical industries. The Gross National Product of manufactured products was three times that of agricultural production. During the 1920s the number of farmers increased, but the number of farms decreased by 2.5%. Tenant farms increased from 38.1% in 1920 to 42.4% in 1929 and the mortgaged farms from 37.2% to 42%. With the boom of wartime food production and the immediate recovery gone, the value of farm exports fell from $21.4 billion in 1920 to $11.8 billion in 1929.

But while the farmer did not share in the general prosperity of the '20s, there was abundant prosperity in other areas of the economy. The quality of business in America was changing. There was more diffusion of ownership, and management was becoming the function of a team or unit rather than a matter of personality. Management as a profession was growing, and the "personnel" department with its definitions and functions was becoming increasingly the focus of contact between labor and employers. Henry Ford, with his efficiency in production and his reduction of costs, seemed to many to exemplify the new model for American industry. Ford's famous "Model

T'' had been in production since 1909. Over the years Ford had steadily brought the price down. His auto cost $1500 in 1913, $760 in 1920, and $600 or less in 1929. Despite Ford's predilection for hiring and firing by whim, his contempt for labor unions, and his high-handed ways in making allocations to dealers, there were those in 1924 who even went so far as to entertain thoughts of him as a presidential candidate!

The prosperity of the 1920s could be calculated in some very impressive figures. Net corporate income increased from 1923 till 1929 from $8.3 billion to $10.6 billion. Savings increased from $19.7 billion to $28.4 billion. The value of life insurance policies rose from $9.4 billion to $15.9 billion, and the assets of building and loan companies increased from $3.9 billion to $8 billion. From 1919 to 1929 gross wages rose 26%. Real wages rose 8% from 1923 to 1929, and workers found the average work week shortened from 47.3 to 45.7 hours.

Many of these workers were employed by new and growing industries. The most visible new industry of the 1920s was the auto industry. Perhaps the automobile has shaped America in the first 3 quarters of this century more than any other institution, invention, or event. At the beginning of this century in the state of Tennessee a motorist, by law, had to advertise by newspaper his taking to the road at least one week in advance. Similarly in Vermont, motorists had to have a flagman advancing an eighth of a mile before them as a warning.

Such was not the case in the 1920s. Ford, the early giant of the industry, was joined by two others. William C. Durant founded General Motors. It was Durant's idea to produce cars that were both attractive and comfortable. Competition from Durant forced Ford to abandon his famous Model T (You could have any color you wanted—as long as it was black.) and retool to produce the classic Model A. By the time Ford had retooled, Durant had firmly established himself in the market. A man by the name of Walter P. Chrysler revived the Maxwell Motor Company in 1923 and renamed it the Chrysler Motor Company. Then he bought out the Dodge Brother auto business and eventually added the Plymouth line. Like Ford and unlike the promotional Durant, Chrysler came from the mechanical side of the industry. By 1929 the Chrysler Building dominated the New York City skyline as its tallest building and symbol of the company's success. Auto registrations rose in the '20's from 6,771,074 to 23,122,000, and truck registrations rose from 794,372 to 3,380,000.

But of course just the huge increase in auto registrations does not give the machine's full social and economic impact. By 1929, 19% of the steel and iron produced in the country and 27% of the lead was consumed by the auto industry. The popularity of the closed car gave the glass, leather, and textile industries a boost. If anything, the manufacture of rubber tires and inner tubes grew faster than the auto industry. By 1929 the car consumed 18% of hardwood production, 67% of the plate glass production, and 85% of the rubber production. There was a corresponding boom in the petroleum and refining businesses with 80% of gasoline sales going to autos. There was a rapid increase of sales agencies for both used and new cars. And of course you had to have filling stations, garages, and fast food emporiums. The impact of the auto on tourism and the motel trade almost defies calculation. The auto enabled new factories to be started. City railway and streetcar companies disappeared. By 1920 the trend was already apparent. America would have its great metropolitan centers, such as New York City, encircled by satellite suburbs. The auto meant an end to the one-room schoolhouse and the beginning of the consolidated school district. In 1922 the National Department Store in St. Louis took the gamble of opening a branch three miles from the center of town. The day of the branch store had arrived; the shopping center and the mall would follow.

The existence and continuing improvement of the auto demanded good roads. Every year during the '20s Americans spent over $1 billion on the construction of roads and at least $400 million on the paving of city streets. Trucking and bus lines sprang up almost immediately and quickly began to establish themselves as very serious competition to the railroads in moving freight and people. Country clubs, golf courses, road houses, and suburbs came to every sizeable city in America due to good cars and good roads.

Some of the most serious questions of public policy of the 1970s were born with the spread of the auto in the '20s: urban planning (or the lack of it), the allocation of energy resources, pollution, and the time spent each day in the process of commuting. We began to do some other things too. We created suburbs with their rows of salt boxes or tract houses. We created a new and problematic domain for the American mother and housewife. Neighborhoods were disrupted. We separated the work of many men in both space and time from their homes. With the use of the car, no longer did children grow up seeing people of all types and varying economic states. The mobility provided by the auto put pressure on the extended family. It became less and less likely that three generations of a family would be living together in one locality. We began to create ghettos, be they inner city ghettos of the poor or golden or gold-plated ghettos of the rich and the middle class called suburbs. We began to create communities stratified by income. Lastly, but not of least importance to young Americans, possession of a car and a driver's license became part of the American rites of puberty.

In the area of fashion, hemlines were shortened as long skirts made driving too difficult. The automobile also caused changes in the most intimate sorts of behavior. It has been said that one of the bulwarks of pre-auto American morality was the inability to find the privacy for misconduct. Now young women were no longer chaperoned. A judge of juvenile court estimated that a third of the sex cases that came before him involved misconduct in cars. In 1926 the Secretary of Princeton University declared that the ownership of a car was probably detrimental to satisfactory academic progress. In 1927 a New York City policeman was embarrassed by arresting a newlywed couple for petting in the back of their car.

Besides affecting the lifestyle, the car affected the building industry. Urbanization meant a need for new housing and for offices, stores, hotel accommodations, schools, churches, hospitals, and public buildings of every kind. The great demand for housing set off by the returning veterans in 1922 accounted for more than 40% of the construction each year. Industrial and commercial building accounted for only about half as much expenditure. Residential construction peaked in the mid-1920s, but speculation would continue well into 1929. The growth of construction carried over into the brick, stone, steel, glass, tile, and plumbing industries. All this growth encouraged speculation in land. The value of all land in cities of over 30,000 increased from $25 billion in 1920 to $50 billion in 1926, while at the same time the value of all farmland decreased from $55 billion to $37 billion. The most dramatic example of land speculation was the Florida land boom (burst by a devastating hurricane in 1926). Miami, a city of 30,000 in 1920, was a city of 75,000 in 1925; and it is estimated that the population was easily double that during tourist season. If you had a car you could get to Florida and make money selling and investing in lots or in the options on them.

The automobile industry was not the only rapidly growing venture of the 1920s. The electric power industry had perhaps the most dramatic growth in that decade save for the automobile. The increased availability of cheap electric power had a tremendous effect on American industry. One can look to the '20s for the beginnings of such questions as who should control the utilities and energy policy and whether bigger and more is necessarily better. Improvements were made in electronic technology, in the procedures of transmission, and in the network of power stations. These changes were very expensive. Power companies spent at least $750 million each year on improvements. For reasons of economy and efficiency there were many mergers in the industry. In 1926 alone there were 1000 mergers in the power industry.

American industry made modern advertising a necessity in the 1920s. The annual budgets for advertising doubled during the decade. Some $1.5 billion was spent in 1927. Businessmen discovered that their task was not merely to satisfy demand but to create demand. They also discovered that any well advertised product would sell. In an effort to police themselves the businessmen in many cities waged campaigns for "Truth in Advertising" and formed "Better Business Bureaus." A new premium was placed on the craft of salesmanship. Employees became more salesmen than clerks. College and university programs in business administration now offered courses in advertising and salesmanship, and a myriad of books appeared on the subject.

Advertising urged Americans to spend money whether they had it or not. This led to an increase in installment buying. By the end of the decade the majority of autos were bought on time, and the network of dealer-loan company-commercial bank was a sizeable economic commodity. In the mid-1920's credit sales reached some $5 billion per year.

What Americans could buy with their new credit included a wide variety of products which had been recently developed or which were now easier and cheaper to produce: oil furnaces, wrist watches, cigarette lighters, antifreeze fluids, reenforced concrete, paint sprayers, book matches, pyrex glass, and motion picture film. The chemical industry benefitted greatly from the government acquisitions of German patents and from government assistance in converting wartime facilities such as coke plants to peacetime production. Bakelite, developed for military purposes, would be very important in postwar electronics and radio. In 1923 lacquers were introduced. They were easier and faster to apply than paint and came in a variety of colors. The production of synthetic fibers boomed. The output of rayon multiplied 69 times between 1914 and 1923. In 1925 celanese, an artificial silk superior to rayon, was introduced. In 1924 the DuPont Company opened its first cellophane plant in Buffalo, New York. Cellophane revolutionized packaging. It was used for everything. Every year during the decade cellophane doubled in sales.

American patterns of buying underwent a change in the 1920's also. Consolidation in industry was not limited to banks and power companies. The 1920's saw great growth in chain stores. The F.W. Woolworth 5-and-10-cent stores put the older notion shops out of business. By the end of the decade Drug Incorporated was running a network of over 10,000 Rexall stores. The outlets of the Great Atlantic and Pacific Tea Company increased from 400 in 1912 to 15,500 in 1932. Figures for sales were equally impressive. From 1917 to 1927 sales increased 124% in drug outlets, 287% in chain grocery stores, and 425% in clothing stores. The number of chain store units of all kinds had grown from 29,000 in 1918 to 160,000 in 1929.

Americans even began to eat differently. In the 1920's a New York City dweller might breakfast on Arizona melon and have an afternoon snack of Louisiana cherries. Improved shipping made more products available "out of season." Americans also got more variety. In 1920 we consumed 13,800 carloads of lettuce. By 1928 demand required the shipping of 51,500 carloads. And this growth was certainly not limited to fresh produce. The canning industry had been given an impetus by the war and doubled from 1914 to 1929. The output of canned milk trebled. In many a home in the '20s it was not unusual to sit down to a dinner of canned soup, canned meat, and canned vegetables. Of course there were canned peaches for desert.

The pattern of American education also underwent a change. It struggled mightily to keep up with the new demands made upon it. Every year in the '20s 50,000 more students than the year before went to college, and the proportion of people in the population with some college experience to those without it increased greatly. Higher education, which had previously been looked upon as a stepping stone to the professions, was now a preparation for a good job in business. The needs of business caused changes in the college curricula. There were new programs and new schools of business administration. There also was an increase in the number of Ph.D. programs. The universities of America tended to become more and more centers for research. The gap between the quality of European and American scholarship was greatly narrowed. For the undergraduate the division, tension, and stress between the research needs of the university and the teaching emphasis of the colleges presented a diversity of both opportunities and problems.

In the 1920s Americans experienced changes in the way they lived and where they lived. Average life span in America had increased from 49 years in 1901 to 59 years in 1927. There were changes in where Americans worked and in their means of transportation. The interlocking complexity of transportation, construction, manufacturing, and advertising helped to give rise to the mega-cities and the technological lifestyle that endures to this day with both its problems and its opportunities.

Signs of Strain

Undoubtedly the 1920s was a period of change in lifestyle, and these changes caused tension for many. It is these signs of strain which are often rightly or wrongly remembered as the outstanding characteristics of the period. They have earned the 1920s and its people the appellations "jazz age," "lost generation," and "roaring '20s."

One of the tensions of the period was that the worker, especially union members, did not share equally in business prosperity. While wages increased 11% from 1923 to 1929, corporate profits increased 62%; and corporate dividends to stockholders increased 65%. Unionized workers suffered a setback in that the Supreme Court in the 1920s upheld the validity of "yellow dog" contracts whereby workers promised under pain of termination not to associate with union people or to organize. Similarly in 1922 the Court struck down laws attempting to regulate child labor in the coal, glass, and steel industries. In 1923 the Court found unconstitutional a Washington, D.C. minimum wage statute. A Massachusetts study also termed a proposal for old age insurance "a counsel of despair." In addition to unfavorable decisions in the courts, the trade union movement in the '20s was not blessed with aggressive, dynamic leadership. In 1920, Bethlehem Steel refused to ship steel to New York and Philadelphia contractors because those contractors allowed union shops. Individually and in association, employers depicted union activity as "un-American" and often countered the benefits offered by unions with their own programs of "welfare capitalism." The employers offered the workers a variety of benefits ranging from improved restrooms and lounges to plant athletic programs and even to generous stock purchase plans—all achieved without a union.

Another group who shared little in the prosperity of the period was the unemployed, and there was a good deal of unemployment in the '20s. Technological unemployment, which resulted when workers were replaced by machines, was often looked upon as a necessary (and hopefully temporary) by-product of progress. There were also a number of "sick industries" such as cotton mills and coal mining that did not share in the prosperity. The Secretary of the Gastonia, North Carolina Chamber of Commerce boasted that children of fourteen could only work eleven hours a day in the mills. The average pay scale for mill work in Gastonia was $18 a week for men and $9 a week for women in exchange for a mere seventy-hour week. The bituminous coal industry found new and growing rivals in oil and hydro-electric power. The price of coal fell from $3.75 a ton in 1920 to $1.78 a ton in 1929, and many mines and miners found themselves idle. The share of prosperity allotted to the laboring man did not keep pace with the new "necessities" of radios, telephones, well-appointed bathrooms, and kitchen equipment. Similarly, white collar workers and professionals often found themselves lagging behind their neighbors in the accumulation of signs of affluence. Prosperity favored the Middle Atlantic states, the East North Central states, and the Pacific states. The soft spots in prosperity included New England, the West North Central states, and the South. New England was hit particularly hard by the defection of textile mills to the lower-paying South.

Farmers were another group who felt that the prosperity of the '20s had passed them by. The use of motorized machinery dramatically increased during the '20s. In 1920 there were 230,000 tractors on American farms; by 1930 there were 920,000. Wheat growing had been revolutionized by the development of disk plows, power drills, and small combines. Cotton production was enhanced by the opening of new lands for cultivation in Oklahoma and Texas. All phases of corn production were changed, and both acreages and yields per acre increased. In 1922 the Congress had passed the Capper-Volstead Act which exempted farm cooperatives from anti-trust laws and defined their role in interstate commerce. But the underlying problems remained. America produced more than we could sell. Demand had declined from wartime highs. With changes in technology American farmers were producing even more. Recovering Europe no longer needed American surpluses. Moreover, American products had to compete with increased production from Canada, Argentina, and Australia. The manufacturer could control his production. The farmer lacked such precision. One solution would be to "dump" excess production on the world market and hope that a profit could be made or at worst losses would be minimized. But who would coordinate such a plan? The national government refused to do so. The farmer had less profits yet had a higher capital investment, higher taxes, high freight rates, higher wage expenditures, and higher distribution costs each year. Something had to be done.

A solution to the farmers' dilemma was offered by Senator Charles L. McNary of Oregon and Representative Gilbert N. Haugen of Iowa. The Secretaries of Agriculture and Labor would compute a price ratio whereby the government would give the farmer a portion of a predetermined "fair" price for his excess crops. An Agricultural Export Corporation supervised by the Secretary of Agriculture and appointees would sell excess farm products on the world market. The farmer got something immediately and with luck might make additional profits. If the Corporation sold products at a loss the difference would be made up by a special tax on the farmer called an equalization fee. There were various modifications of this plan proposed. A program such as this, loosely called McNary-Haugenism, passed the

Congress twice in 1926 and 1927 but was vetoed each time by President Coolidge. He complained bitterly in one veto message that the bills proposed to put the government into private business, specifically agriculture; this was something that the government simply did not have the power to do.

Besides the problem of unequal prosperity, there were three more highly publicized causes for tension. One of the major flaws in normalcy in the '20s was the national attempt at prohibition. It might be wise to point out that prohibition was neither a new nor a uniquely American experiment. There had been temperance laws passed in this country in the 1840s and again in the late 19th and early 20th centuries; the French banned the use of absinthe; the Scandinavians passed prohibition laws; and even the English, for whom the pub was an aspect of a normal social life, attempted to regulate the hours of pubs. Prohibition was looked upon by its advocates with great hope. Rural Americans often favored prohibition on the grounds that abuse of alcohol was one aspect of change which would not come to them from the city. In addition, many Evangelical Protestants looked upon the use of alcohol as immoral. Even those Americans today who do not see the use of alcohol as immoral would certainly agree that the abuse of alcohol is a serious drug abuse problem and that alcoholism is a dread, debilitating disease. Prohibition advocates contended that it would help reduce social tensions. Alcohol inflamed the passions of the poor against the rich, and stoked the fires of racial hatred. Whiskey dealers and saloon keepers were often linked in the popular mind with the corrupt big city political machines. Alcohol was what kept the poor and the workingman from improving their lot.

The prohibition of the 1920s was a result of a gradual series of events. In 1913 the Webb-Kenyon Act had been passed which prohibited the transport of alcoholic beverages into "dry" areas. by 1915 the Anti-Saloon League had chapters in all the states. In 1917 the war brought about brief prohibition, since distilling diverted needed grain from the war food effort. The Eighteenth Amendment (1919) did not declare drinking illegal. It simply proposed to make the importation, sale, transport, and manufacture of alcoholic beverages illegal. The Amendment was ratified by thirty-six states. Congress passed the enabling legislation. The Volstead Act, passed over President Wilson's veto, declared January 1, 1920 to be the start of the "noble experiment."

Prohibition was perhaps the outstanding example of Americans voting for something that the other guy needed, not them. The government was faced almost immediately with the task of enforcing the law and curtailing smuggling attempts from Canada and the Caribbean. There probably was less drinking during Prohibition, but the difficulty was that it was all illegal. The law enforcers had the additional problem of law officers, politicians, and otherwise good citizens who declared prohibition at best ridiculous and at worst an infringement on personal liberty and honored the law in the breech. Politician Jim Reed of Kansas City freely dispensed the recipe for apple jack and advised people on how to drill and plug pumpkins to make pumpkin gin. At one point the city police of Chicago were unable to bring anyone to justice in over one hundred and thirty gangland murders.

People who broke the law did not feel that they were morally wrong. Some answered the bootlegger's knock with all the self-righteousness of conductors on the Underground Railroad. Some raised John C. Calhoun's doctrine of concurrent majorities: local violation of the law affirmed the rights of local groups to rule on the validity of national laws. Senator Oscar Underwood of Alabama argued that just as his Northern friends were justified in declaring the Eighteenth Amendment inoperable, so too must they in turn recognize the right of the South to declare parts of the Fourteenth Amendment inoperable. Prohibition then was a noble experiment, but it was also a costly, impractical, corrupting, and divisive failure.

Another of the most famous phenomena of the '20s was the Ku Klux Klan. The modern Klan was founded in 1915 by Colonel William J. Simmons, a history professor at Lanier College, Georgia. The new Klan was to be a revival of the post-Civil War movement. The Klan expanded to a few chapters in Georgia and Alabama. In 1920 it began to grow dramatically under the leadership of Texan Hiram Wesley Evans, assisted by supersalesman Edward Y. Clarke and Mrs. Elizabeth Tyler. The Klan was merchandised with modern sales techniques. It was an emotionally satisfying organization with a ritual, robes, initiations, and ranks. A pyramiding scheme was even devised to allow members to keep $4 of the $10 initiation fee for new members brought in. The Klan grew to an estimated membership of four and a half million in 1924. To many it was a superpatriotic organization dedicated to preserving the traditional values of White Anglo-Saxon Protestant America from "them" and the changes they were bringing about. One only had to look at the cities to see how bad these changes were. Many probably joined the Klan with good intentions.

The Klan was wonderfully adaptable. In the South the Klan was anti-Black. In the West the Klan was anti-"wet." The Klan was consistently anti-immigrant and anti-sexual permissiveness. Regionally it was whatever people wanted: anti-Catholic, anti-Jew, or anti-political reform. The New York *World* of 1921 credited the Klan with 4 killings, 1 acid burning, 41 floggings, 27 tar and featherings, and 43 rail ridings. The Klan would temporarily yield great political power. In 1923 it succeeded in impeaching the governor of Oklahoma. In Oregon the Klan controlled the governorship and both houses of the state legislature. In Indiana the Klan would be very powerful in traditionally Republican areas.

Ultimately the Klan would self-destruct. In 1925 D.C. Stephenson, an Indianapolis Klan official, picked up a secretary at a party. He took her on board a train, fed her liquor, and then sexually assaulted her. The girl attempted suicide. Stephenson removed her from the train, and he and his friends kept the girl from medical attention. She died, and Stephenson stood trial for manslaughter. Such an episode discredited the Klan; and more and more people realized that it was no benevolent, protective, or patriotic organization.

The third event of the '20s that has generated great interest among students of the period is the evolution controversy. Anti-evolution laws had been passed in Oklahoma, Florida, and North Carolina. In 1925 a young biology teacher named John Scopes was humored into taking up the American Civil Liberties Union offer to defend anyone who violated the Tennessee evolution law that forbade instructors "to teach any theory that denies the story of divine creation as taught in the Bible." Scopes used *Civic Biology* as a text, taught evolution, and was arrested and brought to trial in Dayton, Tennessee.

The trial was a circus. William Jennings Bryan was the special prosecutor, and Clarence Darrow represented Scopes. Scopes lost. The trial has been great for fictional and dramatic treatment. Undoubtedly it had a carnival air. T.T. Martin, National Secretary of the Anti-Evolution League, greeted people with the slogan "Keep Hell out of the High Schools." H.L. Mencken of the *Baltimore Sun* treated the trial as a contest between freedom and ignorance; but for an "enlightened" man, he himself indulged in depicting Bryan and his followers as "anthropoids."

The Scopes trial was looked upon as a forum by religious fundamentalists. Fundamentalism however was not purely a theological opinion found only in the West and South, for there were fundamentalist pulpits in New York City and Boston too. But what the fundamentalist controversy seems to have been about, with the Scopes trial at the center, was the issue of local control and the rate of change rather than religion. No farmer who had raised cattle, poultry, pigs, or horses would deny that there was something to this evolution question. But what *Civic Biology* presented was the "doctrine" of evolution, and that was not acceptable. People felt they and their children were being talked at, not to. An old cherished, beautiful doctrine was being replaced by one that wasn't fully explained and by one that came from big city pulpits, big universities, and big city publishers. That was one change too many.

To be sure, there were other changes in the '20s. In 1904 a woman had been arrested for smoking on New York's Fifth Avenue, but by 1929 women could smoke in dining cars. If there was not more sex there was a lot more talk about it. Freud was in the livingroom. Divorces had increased from 100,000 a year in 1914 to 205,000 a year in 1929. By the end of the decade more women were working than ever before and at occupations once never considered. A Midwest conference of 800 college girls declared that moderation, not abstinence, was the proper course in petting. Necking and heavy necking seemed to be practices having nothing to do with the anatomy between the head and the shoulders. Thomas Watson's *Behaviorism*, which implied to some that anybody could be conditioned to do anything, became a best seller in 1925.

The 1920s then included both serious changes and fads. In the appearance of prosperity, which for many was undeniably true, there were some large, painful, and important exceptions that would contribute to prosperity's rapid dissolution. There were several movements in the '20s such as Prohibition, the Ku Klux Klan, and the Fundamentalist controversy where people, for a variety of reasons, tried to find an anchor in the river of social and technological change. People, sometimes wrongheadedly, sometimes with bad results, and sometimes even against the voice of their own votes, busily attempted to interpret and order their own times.

Mass Behavior—Popular Culture

The 1920s then was a complicated period with problems the same as or analogous to those which have troubled American society today. Patterns of working, eating, housing, transportation, and education were changing. Unsurprisingly, there were also great changes in entertainment and in opinion formation.

On November 2, 1920, station KDKA near Pittsburgh made a radio broadcast of the returns of the 1920 presidential election. A new era was being born. Radio developed spectacularly during the '20s. The outstanding pioneer in broadcasting and radio technology was the Radio Corporation of America, a subsidiary of General Electric-Westinghouse. In 1926 the National Broadcasting Company, an affiliation of stations, would be formed. The following year the Columbia Broadcasting Company was formed. By the year 1930 there were over 600 commercial stations broadcasting regularly. By necessity the Federal Radio Commission was formed in 1927 to license users and to assign broadcast frequencies.

The census of 1930 would reveal that 40% of American families owned radios; expenditures by the American public for radio sets and parts rose from $10 in 1921 to $400 million in 1929. Radio furnished a wide variety of programs: children's shows, church services, market information, dramatic readings, weather reports, educational broadcasting, and, of course, music. Radio singers crooned such spicy numbers as "Hot Lips," "Baby Face," and "Burning Kisses." Velvet-voiced announcers, the forefathers of those who minister to the clogged bowels, burning feet, and aching heads of America on today's television, explained the virtues of their products. Unquestionably, radio raised the cultural and educational level of Americans. People were exposed in great numbers to the same kinds of information. They were also exposed to music and entertainment that previously they perhaps did not have the inclination, time, or money to indulge in. A mass society is a society where public opinion is vital. Radio helped to produce increased homogeneity in American life. Now you could see things with your own two ears!

Another factor that perhaps made the Americans of the '20s the most informed in our history was the popularity of new tabloid newspapers. The New York *Daily News* was founded in 1919 and by 1924 had the largest circulation in the New York City area. The success of the *News* was copied in the founding of the Hearst-connected New York *Daily Mirror* in 1924. These papers were called by some the "daily pornographic" because of their emphasis on sensation stories, photojournalism, and a low reading level which made world, national, and local events available to many who had not previously formed the newspaper habit.

The '20s was also a period of maturity and change in the motion picture. By 1920 Hollywood was producing 300 feature films a year. The film industry had literally created the town. By 1931 there were 22,731 motion picture theaters in America; and some of them, such as the Roxy Theatre in New York City, were justifiably called palaces. These theaters had a combined seating capacity of 11.3 million, and they were built in response to a demand. In 1922 average weekly attendance at the movies was some 40 million. By 1929 95 million Americans were going to the movies every week. Despite the Depression this figure would rise to a weekly attendance of 115 million in 1930.

If the previous decade of filmmaking had been dominated in America by the brilliance of D.W. Griffith, the '20s can be called the era of Cecil B. De Mille. He brought the American middle class to the movies in droves. His crowd scenes ran into the thousands, and his budgets increased to millions of dollars. De Mille mined the Bible for sure popular hits. His epics always affirmed the good, but he often took time to show you in detail what evil was really like, and of course the Bible contains a wealth of sensual materials and crowd scenes. De Mille's three most famous epics were *The Ten Commandments* (1923), *Ben Hur* (1926), and *King of Kings* (1927).

The '20s also saw a new group of movie idols who exuded sexuality. Theda Bara was "the vamp," and Clara Bow was the "It" girl—and there was very little guessing as to what "It" was. In 1921 a sultry male actor appeared in the movie version of *The Four Horsemen of the Apocalypse*, and the cult of Rudolph Valentino was born. Valentino, as the Latin or Arab lover, left little doubt in the mind of the viewer that the character he depicted was as adept in the bedroom as he was at dispatching villains. Valentino's *The Sheik* would be a huge moneymaker for Paramount; his Arab lover would foster a whole stable of aspiring sheik-types. *The Sheik* would be such a box office draw that it would make money for Paramount when it was re-released in 1938.

Sexual connotations in films had become very explicit. Hollywood movie chiefs were disturbed when the public began to discover that the idols were prone, perhaps more so than the rest of the population, to infidelity, sexual hi-jinks, and forms of drug abuse. As a result, Will H. Hays resigned his post as Warren Harding's Postmaster General in order to head up an industry self-censorship office. Hollywood wanted the public to think of it as a place where moral stars, producers, and directors filmed equally moral stories.

As a result, the movies provided social commentary. As the popular arts in a mass society have traditionally done, they fulfilled three social functions. They asked questions of American society in a form that could be accepted; they affirmed the traditional values of American life, though most of the story might make transgressions appear very attractive; and they reflected what was going on in the society around them. A film such as *The Golden Bed* (1925) showed the disastrous results of high living and opulence. *Forbidden Fruit* (1922) dealt with the prospect of adultery. *Prodigal Daughters* (1923) deplored the changes in the role of women and the '20s version of the generation gap. Their dresses were too short; they were highly mobile; and they went out without chaperons. The wild behavior of the "flappers" was similarly exposed in *Our Dancing Daughters* (1928). *The Collegians* (1929) declared that young people went to college to learn how to pet, how to drink, and how to use people. Hollywood was even willing to use itself for material. *Show People* (1928) claimed to show both the public and private lives of Hollywood people.

In addition to social commentary, the film genres that we think of today were well represented. Tom Mix, in such films as *The Pioneer Scout, Deadline,* and *The Bearcat,* was the major Western star of the period. Comic Buster Keaton made several features including *Three Ages* (1923), a parody of the De Mille epics. Charlie Chaplin did not make many films in the '20s. Perhaps this was because his films were becoming less funny and more a personal, political, and philosophical statement. But Chaplin did turn out a classic in *The Gold Rush* (1925). The '20s also featured the great Harold Lloyd as the bespectacled common man bumbling his way through a technological maze in such films as *Safety Last* (1923) and *Speedy* (1928). There were a number of films made about the recent war. One of them, *Wings* (1927), would receive the first newly instituted American award for movie excellence, the Oscar.

Films in the '20s then had reached a considerable degree of both artistic maturity and variety. There was a huge revolution coming to films that arrived in the late '20s. With the development of talking motion pictures, the first one of which was *The Jazz Singer* (1927) with Al Jolson, there would be new problems of acting technique, production, distribution (Movie house piano players were left unemployed.), direction, and script writing. The modern era of motion pictures may rightly be said to have begun in the '20s.

The '20s also featured another phenomenon called "ballyhoo," which was the creation of celebrities and extravaganzas through broadcasting. The network of communication would create stars and make national news. The '20s was the beginning of modern-day mass sports. From November to December 1925 Red Grange, the great running back of the University of Illinois, would go through the following: his jersey was retired; he received $12,000 for signing with the Chicago Bears professional football team; he received $30,000 for playing a single professional football game in New York City; and last but not least, he was presented to President Coolidge. All this in two months. The media also discovered boxing in the '20s. National radio and press coverage lifted boxing out of the neighborhood clubs and put it on the front pages. In September 1926, 130,000 people would see Gene Tunney take the heavyweight title from Jack Dempsey, and some 145,000 would see the rematch in 1927. The gate for the second bout was an astronomical $2,600,000, and it was estimated that in addition to the live crowd some 40 million Americans heard the fight on radio. Tunney would retire after a brief three-year career with earnings of $1 3/4 million. Football and boxing were not the only major celebrity sports, of course. In 1920 the New York Yankees acquired a pitcher-turned-outfielder from Boston who had led the league in home runs. His name was George Herman "Babe" Ruth. Audiences all over America would also be aware of the deeds of Bobby Jones in golf and Big Bill Tilden in tennis.

Besides sports, the country had an interest in passing entertainments or fads. The parlor game Mah Jong swept the country. In 1923 the Mah Jong League of America was formed. The publishing house of Simon and Schuster would be founded in the '20s on the production of crossword puzzle books. As in our own times, the country was receptive to popularizers of knowledge and apostles of self-help and self-improvement. In 1923 the French guru Emil Coué would have a triumphal tour of America. A Coué Institute was formed. Coué gave this gospel to eager audiences, "Every day in every way, I am getting better and better." Sometimes the creation of celebrities bordered on the macabre as when an enterprising reporter named W.B. Miller brought fame and sympathy in February 1925 to a fatally trapped spelunker near Sand Cave, Kentucky, named Floyd Collins.

But the most significant media hero of the 1920s was the "Lone Eagle," Charles A. Lindbergh. Commercial aviation came into its own in the 1920s. In 1926 Congress had passed the Air Commerce Act, giving great powers to Secretary Hoover. By 1929 there had been 25,000 miles of improved runways finished, and some 25 million miles of commercial flights were being scheduled each year. By 1921 over half a million Americans were flying each year. Against such a background Lindbergh's achievement does not look that important. His feat, after all, was performed in order to win a $25,000 prize offered for the first non-stop trans-Atlantic flight. By making his flight on May 20-21, 1927, Lindbergh nosed out two other competing planes. Someone would have made it soon if it had not been Lindbergh. A longer flight in June 1927 by Clarence Chamberlin and C.A. Leon, one that landed bear Berlin, and the flight of explorer Richard E. Byrd to the South Pole in 1929 received less acclaim than Lindbergh's feat.

But of course, Lindbergh was the first. He was tall, quiet, pleasant, a farm boy, a Westerner, and looked younger than his twenty-five years. With the help of his Ryan monoplane, *The Spirit of St. Louis*, he went from barnstorming adventurer to national hero. He received a tumultuous welcome in Paris and the same in London. President Coolidge brought him home on the cruiser U.S.S. *Memphis*. He was commissioned a colonel and awarded both the Distinguished Flying Cross and the Medal of Honor. In later life Lindbergh would be an aviator consultant and would conduct himself with a gentleman's grace. In 1927 Lindbergh was our hero. We empathized with him. Not insignificantly, his work dealing with the flight was entitled *We*. Lindbergh was at once a blend of the old and new America. He was the rugged individualist, the pioneer, the lone scout, and at the same time he was the pilot, the manipulator of one aesthetic hunk of American technology. Forty thousand in Yankee Stadium did not think it strange to stand for a moment of silent prayer as the country had marked his progress. He was us. He was an American boy in an American machine. We would be all right for we made the planes and the Lindberghs.

In the 1920s America sought and created heroes in the air, on the gridiron, and at the plate. Their worlds were clearly defined, and we could live vicariously through them. They entertained us. They defied the complexity of modern life, and they were used to affirm traditional values. Fads and new amusements distracted people from the new complexity of their lives. Through the radio and the newspapers America swam in music and information as never before. The motion picture became sophisticated as an entertainment and as an art form. At the end of the decade this new art was revolutionized by the advent of sound. In the '20s man's exploits, his written and spoken word, and his music saturated the American public as never before in human history. Whole new vistas of subjects and vehicles now existed for discussion, entertainment, and education.

Literature in the 1920s—Creative Reaction to a Mass Society

The 1920s, in regard to American literary activity, has been referred to as the second American Renaissance, equalled only in our history by that period from 1836 (Emerson's *Nature*) to 1850 (Melville's *Moby Dick*). It was a period when new writers emerged before the public and when new publics were explored. It was a period of a great burst of activity that declared America's cultural independence and the possibilities of our own language once and for all. The American drama came to maturity in the '20s; American poets carried on the pre-war tradition of experimentation with language and also attempted epics. It was a period when our didactic literary form, the novel, both satirized our mores and sketched the loneliness of the modern condition.

One of the unique areas of the literary renaissance of the 1920s was the "Harlem Renaissance." Harlem had been the center of a land boom in 1904-05. By 1915 any anti-Black feelings among the populace had cooled, and Blacks began to move there in numbers. By 1917 there was a strong Black community in Harlem. Representatives of all the major Black cultural institutions and business concerns in New York City were centered there. In the 1920s Harlem would be the political and social capital of the Black world. Artistically speaking, what New York City was to America, what Paris was to France, Harlem was to the Blacks. With the publication of a book of essays called *The New Negro*, a group of writers—including Langston Hughes, Alain Locke, Countee Cullen, and Claude McKay—burst upon the American scenes. These Black writers addressed themselves to an ever wider public—to Harlem, to American Blacks, to all American whites, to all the colored races of the world. They were the literary flower of four hundred years of suppression. Their talents blended in the '20s with the Black pride preached by Marcus Garvey of the back-to-Africa plan to form the heady brew that was Harlem.

Literary achievement was not confined to only Black literature. During this period America saw significant works appear by many novelists, three of whom would eventually be awarded the Nobel Prize for literature. These writers would analyze and satirize American society and at the same time depict the modern condition. Theodore Dreiser, in *An American Tragedy* (1925), showed a kind of complicated naturalism. Dreiser hinted that people usually reacted to the circumstances in which they found themselves. This novel, thought by some to be his best, declared that there were people who were too dull or weak to rise in American life. In defiance of the American belief in upward mobility, they were doomed to lives of striving for material pleasures and security which would be forever beyond their reach.

The writer whom many people came to believe had both chronicled and created the "roaring '20s" and the "jazz age" was F. Scott Fitzgerald. In *This Side of Paradise* (1926), which was serialized in the New York *Daily News*, Fitzgerald depicted the bored, aimless college generation of the '20s. In *The Beautiful and the Damned* (1922) he depicted the spending, parties, trips, drinking, and gaiety that have come to many to symbolize the period. Readers vicariously experienced parties till dawn, conspicuous wealth, and a fortune based on bootleg liquor in *The Great Gatsby* (1925). For those not lost by Fitzgerald's clever romantic ending, the book also included the criticism that, even if you believed in the American dream of success with every fiber of your being, there were things that you still couldn't do. Will power and a belief in the maxims of Benjamin Franklin do not inevitably mean happiness.

The first writer of the 1920s to receive the Nobel Prize was Sinclair Lewis, who received that honor in 1930. He was at the time the symbol of the best in American literature. Lewis surgically dissected a variety of sacred American social types and institutions. He turned his talents on small town American life, suburbs, big business, medicine, and organized religion— to name but several of the targets of his novels of social commentary. In *Main Street* (1920) he blasted the complacency and anti-intellectualism of small town America. But Lewis's works were not mere cartoons. He also criticized those who adopt a patronizing air toward those less educated, less cultured, and more "provincial" than they. In *Arrowsmith* (1925) Lewis looked at the moral life of the medical profession. Organized religion would have to wait until his novel *Elmer Gantry* (1927). But the novel that either swayed the people most or allowed them to warm their own virtuous insides was *Babbitt* (1922). In *Babbitt* Lewis took on middle class American business puffery and boosterism. So effective was Lewis's novel that "babbittry," the smug acceptance of the social and ethical standards of business and middle class ideas of social respectability, has officially entered our dictionaries.

The second writer of the '20s to receive the Nobel Prize (1954) and whose career would evolve for three more decades was Ernest Hemingway. In *The Sun Also Rises* (1926) Hemingway showed Americans as the "lost generation" of young people both jaded and disillusioned by the war. They were fun-loving expatriates living without a code of behavior or purpose in life. *A*

Farewell to Arms (1929) was Hemingway's account of both love and war, and showed characters attempting to find meaning and order in a world which was war torn and inconsistent.

The 1920s also saw a major production by William Faulkner whose career, like Hemingway's, would stretch into the future years, culminating in the official recognition of the Nobel Prize in 1949. In 1929 *The Sound and the Fury* was published. Faulkner showed the disintegration of post-civil war Southern life through the technique of stream of consciousness narrative, retelling his story through the thoughts of his main characters and even utilizing the disjointed observations of a family's idiot child.

As rich as the '20s were in the expansion of previously "lost" minority literature and novelistic activity by major writers such as Dreiser, Lewis, Fitzgerald, Hemingway, and Faulkner, the activity in drama was perhaps even more impressive. The period from 1920-30 has been called the golden age of American drama. In every major city semi-professionals and amateurs formed "little theater" groups. These groups encouraged experimentation in acting, staging, production, and direction. They gave work to many actors and provided audiences for aspiring playwrights. The little theaters also served the purpose of introducing drama to the large audience of everyday Americans and made playgoing an accepted and common form of entertainment.

The period from 1920 to 1930 saw the activity of major American playwrights such as Eugene O'Neill, Elmer Rice, and Maxwell Anderson. O'Neill, whom the future may well judge as the best American playwright of the 20th century, produced works such as: *The Emperor Jones* (1920), *The Hairy Ape* (1922), and *Desire Under the Elms* (1925). *The Emperor Jones* detailed the tragedy of a Black porter-turned-island-emperor. It detailed the narrow line between civilization and primitivism. *The Hairy Ape* was a naturalistic tale of the sad fate of a man who attempted to rise above his station as a ship's engine stoker. He is destroyed because he does not know where in society he really belongs. *Desire Under the Elms* was O'Neill's reworking of Greek tragedy in the setting of a New England farm complete with adultery, oeidepal rivalry, greed, and infanticide. O'Neill was not only a productive and moving writer, he was also a pioneer in expressionist techniques. O'Neill deliberately violated the realm of possibility by personifying human emotions and depicting the physically impossible.

Elmer Rice, in his play *The Adding Machine* (1923), took a somewhat humorous and terrifying look at a future wherein the common man was literally "Mr. Zero" in an automated and "number only, please" world. Similarly in his play *Street Scene* (1929) Rice dealt with the problems of contemporary urban existence. Also in the '20s Rice's contemporary, Maxwell Anderson, deflated the thrill of warfare by depicting World War I in his *What Price Glory?* (1924).

The world of American poetry was no less active than that of the novel and the drama. *The Little Review*, which by its end in 1929 had published Yeats, Wallace Stevens, Carl Sandburg, William Carlos Williams, and others, continued to introduce struggling poets to an interested audience. *The Little Review* would be joined by other publications such as *Fugitive* and *Transition*, which were founded for similar purposes. In 1924 Robert Frost would be awarded the first of his string of Pullitzer Prizes. Carl Sandburg, whose "vulgarity" in his *Chicago Poems* (1916) had been a scandal to some, was hailed as the American National Poet as well as the poet laureate of industrial America. Sandburg was the official heir to Walt Whitman as the poet of the common man and was declared Phi Beta Kappa poet at Harvard. In the '20s he produced *Smoke and Steel* (1926) and *Good Morning America* (1928). He was to be a great influence on younger poets.

Other major poets of the period were Pound, Eliot, and Crane. The tradition of experimental and academic poetry that had begun before the war would continue with Ezra Pound and T.S. Eliot. Pound would continue to be both a poet himself and a promoter of other literary talents such as Eliot and James Joyce. In 1920 Pound published his poem "Hugh Selwyn Mauberly." This work considered the state of all poetry in English since the late 19th century. The first part of his world epic, *The Cantos I-XV*, was published in 1925. In 1929 *Personae* appeared and showed the transcultural range and variety of Pound's work.

Pound's colleague, T.S. Eliot, would publish *The Waste Land* in 1922, an analysis of the spiritual and cultural condition of 20th century man. In terms of craft and philosophic ideas it was the most influential poem of the 1920s. The poetic world of the 1920s would be brought to a close by Hart Crane's epic, *The Bridge* (1930), which had been in gestation since 1926. In the tradition of Whitman's longer poems, Crane would assess America's spiritual and historic development from colonial times to the problematic, technologized present of the 1920s. With a constellation of major and minor poets, magazines to publish and receive them, two epic attempts in *The Cantos* and *The Bridge*, and the continuation and strengthening of the Whitmanic and academic poetry traditions, America did not lack for poetic achievements in the '20s.

As for essayists and critics on the popular level there was H.L. Mencken (the Jack Anderson-Howard Cosell-Art Buchwald-William F. Buckley of his day) who, with pungent meat-axe prose, attacked censorship in the arts and the pious banalities of his day. Mencken held forth sequentially in the periodicals *The Smart Set* and *The American Mercury*. Essayists of a more academic type were typified by Joseph Wood Krutch. Krutch set, perhaps, the dominant tone of academics in his *The Modern Temper* (1929). A return to the old sureties of the pre-war period, the book declared, was impossible and man, his values, and his world ever more tenuous. "Today the gulf is broader," wrote Krutch, "The adjustment more difficult, than ever it was before, and even the possibility of an actual human maturity is problematic. There impends for the human spirit either extinction or a readjustment more stupendous than any made before."

In retrospect then, the 1920s was as brilliant a period in our literature as we have ever known. The voices of Harlem spoke to Black America and the world. American novelists both detailed and questioned American morals and social life. A creative record was kept of 20th century man's attempt to cope with a world where the old sureties were no longer so secure. Drama developed both as a major division in American poetry that endured to the present arose between the academic poets such as Pound and the followers of Whitman such as Sandburg. And both popular and scholarly critics freely debated the prospects of the arts and the country.

Mass Society Burgeoning

The chronological demarcations that historians make are often convenient and natural ones, but they are artificial too. The questions of political philosophy and foreign policy, the development and strains of our technological society, changes in lifestyle and work, and new trends in entertainment and literature—all these things obviously extended beyond December 31, 1929. The purpose of this chapter has been to inform, to sketch the general historical outline of the period. Particular people, movements, and events of the '20s will be dealt with in the other essays of this volume.

The 1920s has been shown to be very complex, yet there are some generalizations about the period that can be safely made. In the '20s America came to resemble the urban, industrial, mechanized, technological society we have today. America could no longer return to the pre-World War I period, no matter how nostalgic we might feel about it. Our politicians proved once again that, like the rest of us, they were subject to banal vices. While we had fought the war "to make the world safe for democracy," we had feared both foreigners and our neighbors. While America seemed to some to be isolationist in foreign policy, we attempted to preserve and expand the economic prerogatives of a world power and were active in the cause of world peace.

We had become a mass society in our habits of work, our patterns of consumption, our transportation, and our means of entertainment and information distribution. As a means of controlling and understanding the complexity of this mass society, America grasped the rhetoric and organization of business. Great prosperity occurred in the '20s, but not all shared in it. Business prosperity was neither self-regulated nor monitored by government, and it would not endure.

We invented and perfected new forms of mass entertainment that mirrored, safely questioned, and affirmed our national lifestyle. In literature the decade was one of the most productive in our history. Literature reflected world-wide artistic innovations and philosophical questions and reflected the search of modern man for new codes of value to replace those so badly disjointed by 1920. To sum up the period only in terms of images such as "roaring," "laughing," and "lost" is almost to deny the rich complexity of the decade and the cultural energy of the period that was manifested in so many forms.

Why Modernism?

Alfred Kazin

Alfred Kazin was born in Brooklyn of Russian immigrant parents who through their son sought to keep alive their intellectual and cultural aspirations. The first book of his autobiogrpahy, A Walker in the City, *deals with his early life and his effort to understand the world around him. Perhaps it was this drive that led to his preoccupation with history, literature, and society, for Alfred Kazin's famous study of American prose,* On Native Grounds, *illustrates not only his prowess as a critic of American literature, but of American life and social trends.*

Working from a social, historical, and biographical perspective, Mr. Kazin is usually called a "traditional" critic. This suggests that he is less likely to analyze a work on the basis of textual analysis or from the post-structuralist perspective of recent criticism. Mr. Kazin sees literature as "a deed in human history," and his specialty is the American writer. With books on Fitzgerald, (F. Scott Fitzgerald: The Man and His Work, 1951), Drieser, (The Stature of Theodore Drieser, 1955), Melville, (Moby Dick, 1956), Emerson, Hawthorne, as well as a series of historical-literary essays, and the classic On Native Grounds, *he is an ideal critic to examine the writing of the '20s.*

Beginning with a definition of modernism as the synthesis of the individuality of earlier cultures he goes on to examine the unique individualism of the writers of the '20s. These writers, he tells, us, the Hemingways, Faulkners, Fitzgeralds, Eliots Joyces, saw themselves as the hub of a self-centered culture of elitists and individualists. The world around them was disintegrating from lack of tradition, ritual and religion, but they were not content to merely catalogue that disintegration. Instead they felt spiritually compelled to describe in innovative language that decline and by comparison to set in its place a more ideal world where truth and courage and honor are paramount. The modernist, he tells us, struggles to order things through a coherent structure, to give shape and significance to the fragmentation by using myth as a recurrent and universal way of shaping lives.

In the '60s and '70s Kazin claims that we have the new lords of technology and science and that the art educated intellectuals have been dethroned. We look at them as curiosities not easily understood from our "Big State-mindless mass culture." We have become a more egalitarian culture leading to the belief that everyone is worthy of attention. What this had led to in art is the novelist who plugs in his emotions to "tune into oneself," and works that are little more than personality tracts, emotional release, and at best a window from which to view contemporary disintegration. There is no mirror that might reflect back some way of organizing the chaos, and the present age seems content to produce documentaries of disintegration.

It is precisely for this reason that we look back at the '20s with such nostalgia. In a time when we can only see chaos we look back to a time when the chaos was at least being made comprehensible by its artists and we gaze back to find what was lost in an "effort to rejoin ourselves to ourselves."

* * *

These essays are collected here because of a certain nostalgia. Oddly enough, the nostalgia is for novels, poems, plays, satires, movies, fashions, jazz, old musical comedies that are part of our lives, that have been part of the national style since they became popular in the 1920s. Modernism, as we still call it to distinguish it from the old-fashioned nineteenth century, has been *our* tradition since the early twentieth century. The whole century has been "modernist." Modernism has absorbed so many earlier cultures that many people know Dante only through Eliot, African sculpture through Picasso, Oriental painting through the post-impressionists, Chinese ideograms through Ezra Pound.

Modernism is ours and we are—we still hope to be—"modernists." It is the only culture on which our students feed. Yet there is this nostalgia, in movies about the twenties, in time-conscious dresses and hats, in the perpendicular figure, in the equally perpendicular lines of Art Deco, in the sudden revival of Scott Joplin and ragtime. These things have never really disappeared from our culture. They are fashions just a little less fixed in our minds by now than *The Waste Land, Rhapsody In Blue, Le Sacre du Printemps,* cubism, functionalism, free verse, Gertrude Stein, *The Great Gatsby,* Jimmy Walker, the corruptibility of American politicians, the unpredictability of the stock market.

What are we nostalgic for? Why so many commemorations, appeals to the past, imitations of what has never really disappeared from our lives? Nostalgia is never for what we have lost, but for that part of ourselves, like childhood, that is the part we no longer understand. Nostalgia is the claim of the past upon the present, the effort of the too-conscious present to understand itself in the light of the unconscious past. Nostalgia is the effort to rejoin ourselves to ourselves—when the effort is in one sense too late.

Still, the nostalgia is urgent, even obsessive. In the ebbing of the twentieth century it is clear that we are drifting further and further away from the context in which modernism arose more than seventy-five years ago. We are in the era of the Big State, the organized military-technological state. The imperialism of the West is being replaced by primitive authoritarian socialism. Ours is a world of incessant nationalistic, tribal wars and revolutionary disruptions, of a slavish culture organized not only through the "media" but somehow *for* them. We are getting farther and farther away from the early twentieth century world in which a self-centered, white, individualist, still "elitist" culture thought of itself as the center of existence.

The revolutions of the twentieth century—in literature, painting, music, architecture, photography, movies—represent the *technical* breakthrough in language, style, form, of an elite essentially conservative and even traditionalist culture. It was often profoundly anti-democratic in its politics, contemptuous of the as-yet *unformed* mass taste. As the modernist revolution became popularized and academicized, became what e.e. Cummings mocked as the sophisticated *"att-i-tude,"* it in fact became (like gourmet cooking, Picasso prints, professionalism in the seeking of sexual pleasure) part of middle-class professional society. The intellectuals became not the creators of culture—that was reserved for a few poets, composers, "inventors" in every sphere—but the indispensable professional middlemen and the most eager consumers of modernist culture. Unlike Eliot, Pound, Stravinsky, Joyce, who were conservative in everything except their talents, the intellectuals as a class *and* mass believed that modernism applied to everything in their lives and to the re-ordering of society. What an illusion!

But this is to get ahead of our story. Modernism, now our only real tradition in the arts, is the poetry of Eliot, Pound, Frost, Stevens, Cummings, the novels of Hemingway and Fitzgerald and Faulkner, the plays of O'Neill, the architecture of Frank Lloyd Wright, the movies as a major narrative form, the modern dance, ballet, the comic strip, the musical comedy. But though all this is ours and many of its forms became national only in the twenties, it is chilling to see how little the increasingly despotic, over-organized society of the 1980's resembles the "careless" society of the 1920s.

This is where nostalgia comes in. We are not looking for the *language* of freedom and experimentation, in which the culture of rock, the post-Hollywood films, open poetry, abstract expressionism, action art, pop art, psychedelic art, women's literature, sexual revolution, are all rich. We are looking for the substance. We are looking for the spirit of the founders, the reasoning behind certain fundamental achievements that we have incorporated in our own minds so firmly that we are now suspicious of the contemporary. Like Hugh Kenner in his brilliantly arbitrary book on modernism, *A Homemade World*, we say that Faulkner is the "last" novelist. The modernism that fought so hard to be heard—but that was long ago—is often our last word, our only word. Pierre Monteux could not conduct *Le Sacre du Printemps* in 1913 without umbrellas flying at his head, hisses and curses. Stravinsky is for many people now so much highbrow muzak, muzak to make love by, that they groan when a concert program announces any composer born as long ago as 1925. The Bauhaus, the great pre-Hitler German modernist academy of architecture, painting, city planning that brought out Walter Gropius, Marcel Breuer, Josef Albers, has so thoroughly stamped the style of the 1920s on certain chairs, the Whitney Museum, the multi-color wall, the Art Deco poster, that you cannot go into any new museum in the country without seeing in the glass wall, the unframed photographs, the ramps, the atmosphere of modish purity and spartan simplicity that so many distinguished German refugees have imparted to their American students. Any college teacher of English—which now so often means 20th century writing as the code by which to understand everything else—must have this same writing analyzed, word for word, in this pathetic travesty of the New Criticism for an audience of non-readers. We have guided, led, driven, cajoled, hypnotized so many obedient sheep over so many "difficult" passages in Eliot, Pound, Joyce, Hemingway, Faulkner, Cummings, Yeats that it is no wonder the sophisticates have as much trouble understanding *Gravity's Rainbow* in 1974 as they did *Ulysses* in 1924—before all the commentaries came out.

The 1920s were so powerful in establishing the new taste that even our favorite nineteenth-century American writers—Melville, Dickinson, Henry Adams, Whitman—did not become popular until then. The Russians have had practically no one to read since Babel, Biely, Mandeltam, Maykovsky, Nabokov—the typical Russian experimental writers of the 1920s—no paintings worth looking at but those by Russian cubists and abstractionists— Malevitch, Kandinsky—whom Russians can see only when *they* go into exile. Kafka died in 1924, Proust in 1922, Virginia Woolf and Joyce early in the Second World War—but they are still our saints and heroes of modernism. Even our more "original" magazines, like *Time* and *The New Yorker*, founded by literary intellectuals of the 1920s, still show as their main qualities a feeling for "style," for wit, for sharpness and effectiveness of narrative, that makes their writers regard themselves as "artists" of journalism.

Whenever one looks, our "advanced," highbrow culture is modernism, while our modernist idea of culture is that formed by the insurgent, emancipated, rebellious, anti-institutional spirits of the 1920s. Yet these founding fathers of the modern style, of our modern dash and verve, were as a group profoundly conservative, traditionalist, often offensively reactionary to our liberal way of thinking. Their pioneer audacities and experiments, from William James's "stream of consciousness" and Freud's interpretation of the stories-we-tell-ourselves-in-our-dreams to Gertrude Stein's practice in writing of a repetition essentially oral and Eliot's experiments with a schizophrenic persona in *Prufrock*, were significantly technical innovations and discoveries—extensions and modifications of an already established line of technical workmanship and interest. But they were based on the supremacy of the upper-class individual whose consciousness was sacred to himself.

We no longer really understand the modernism that makes us up, for we—at the end of the twentieth-century—are more and more egalitarian in a primitive sense. We believe that all cultures are inherently equal, all persons inherently worthy of recognition and attention. From this has followed the belief that "feelings" so-called, the thrust of personality, are enough to make a work of art. Art has become a matter of releasing oneself, tuning into oneself, a matter of sincerity, frankness and openness. In short, art is a "communication" of love, just as "love" long ago became super-conscious and all-articulate, a form of expression.

The founders of modernism thought differently about the virtue of the individual and the necessity of art. What bothered them about society was not that it was unjust to the many, but that it was disorganized, messy, fragmentized, without respect for authority and tradition and ritual. It was alleged that these essential supports had disappeared with the emergence of modern mass society and the decay of religion. The modernists were most against the modern age, which they identified with the secular passions of the French Revolution, the power of the organized nation-state, popular education, the domination of classical learning by science. Kafka, whom Auden called *the* representative writer of the twentieth-century because of his (and our) obsession with anxiety, was profoundly shocked by all forms of swearing and profanity. He considered them desecrations of language. He said to a young admirer in Prague—"Swearing is something horrible...destroys man's greatest invention—language. It is an insult to the soul and a murderous offense against grace...But so is any use of words without proper consideration. For to speak implies to consider and define. Words involve a decision between life and death."

Kafka said of an anthology of young poets—"a frighteningly authentic proof of disintegration. Each of its authors only speaks for himself. They write as if language were their personal property. But language is only lent to the living, for an undefined period. All we have is the use of it. In reality, it belongs to the dead and to those who are still unborn. One must be careful in one's possession of it. The writers in this book are...language destroyers. An offense against language is always an offense against feeling and against the mind, a darkening of the world, a breath of the ice age.

"One ought not to provoke people. We live in an age which is so possessed by demons, that soon we shall only be able to do goodness and justice in the deepest secrecy, as if it were a crime. War and revolution haven't ceased to rage. On the contrary. The freezing of our feelings stokes their fires."

I have often thought that pornography today and all its more pretentious equivalents exist in order to satirize passion. Perhaps sexism in literature and art and films exists in order to make passion immoral. That is what Eliot meant when he said that poetry is not an expression of emotion but an escape from emotion, but that only those who have emotion know what it is to need to escape from it. Eliot seems to have thought of society as an ideal work of art in the medieval Christian style, an imaginary country that can only exist, like More's *Utopia*, through the written word. That is not our idea of society—if it is still a single *idea*, in Marx's sense, that we can be said to have. Society has simply become humankind at the end of the 20th century, in all shapes and conditions and colors and manners of servitude, humankind that has doubled itself in our century, that has become so numerous and innumerable and voracious that it can no more account for its acts, or be held accountable, than can the animal kingdom. Humankind has returned, morally, to a state of nature.

But contrary to this statistical and more and more unveiling reality, here is Eliot in the 1920s, hailing Joyce's *Ulysses*: "It is simply a way of controlling, of ordering, of giving shape and significance to the immense panorama of futility and anarchy which is contemporary history." Eliot, no great fan of the traditional English novel of middle-class lives, was excited in *Ulysses* by the power of myth. The significance of myth is that it is recurrent and universal. All mythologies are profoundly conservative readings of man repeating the same story.

The predominant religion of the Orient today is Leninism. Against the background of this authoritarian reordering of the masses, it is fascinating to recall the conservatism in art matters of Lenin and Mao—those great modernists of *political* revolution. Lenin had no patience with music later than Beethoven, but distrusted even Beethoven because he was "too moving," leaving him unfit for stark strict revolutionary action. Lenin detested Mayakovsky and other avant-garde Russian poets. Mao, as visitors who have studied him have noticed, kept scrolls of classical Chinese poetry, and seemed to be the one poet in China who was allowed to practice this officially forbidden ritualistic art. Hitler screamed that all modern art was "degenerate," but proved himself the most terrible destroyer of the established order. So Lenin and Mao have alone succeeded in what Eliot called "controlling, ordering, giving shape and significance to the immense panorama of futility and anarchy which is contemporary history." Totalitarian socialisms takes on the same external look of order and control that Eliot thought he saw in the middle ages, that Ezra Pound attributed to American history before the Civil War. The lack of this in Ireland led Yeats to call for an Irish Fascism:

Politics are growing heroic...A Fascist opposition is forming behind the scenes to be ready should some tragic situation develop. I find myself constantly urging the despotic rule of the educated classes...I know half a dozen men any one of whom may be Caesar or Cataline. It is amusing to live in a country where men will always act. Where nobody is satisfied with thought. There is so little in our stocking that we are ready at any moment to turn it inside out, and can we not feel emulous when we see Hitler juggling with his saisage of stocking...The chance of being shot is raising everybody's spirits enormously.

The continuing blood bath in Northern Ireland is not what Yeats had in mind. Lawrence's vision of the superman, the writer as cultural despot, has not been taken up satisfactorily by Norman Mailer. The "usury" hatred by Pound was not eliminated by Hitler's elimination of six million Jews. Joyce's conception of a single day, a single moment in historic time as the perfect classical subject for a great modern novel has not eliminated the urgency of Stephen Dedalus's outcry: *History is the nightmare from which I am trying to awaken.* Modernish art, the revolution of the word, the fabulous rise in our technical consciousness of objects and materials, all the new ways of seeing that we associate with modern painting and movies, of rhythm that we associate with jazz and atonalism, the growth of a poetry of the vernacular, of a novel-telling technique that is as agile as the polymorphic sense of time that came in with the enthronement of personal consciousness as our greatest subject—all this has been a revolution in itself. And meanwhile another has been going on all the time—the most concentrated systematic effort of mind in recorded history—the technical revolution in all possible ways of encoding knowledge and distributing it. Everywhere before our eyes the human mind is learning new skills as if there were a new babyhood to the race. H.G. Wells said that science is the "mind of the race." By now the post-industrial society, the society of technical expertise, has become the custom of the race. And custom, as Pascal said, is second nature.

Technology lords it everywhere over the old-fashioned, art-educated intellectuals brought up on modernism. Technology and bureaucracy, aided by all the sciences of manipulation and propaganda, mass culture and mass emotion, make up our public drama. Billions of people are being whipped into shape at any cost to the so-called individual, as in China; or are being left to die in the class wars, civil wars, merciless political wars, of Southeast Asia; or are left to starve and die on the pavements of Calcutta and Bombay. Everywhere in the West there is panic, the most obvious slackening of will and hope and faith in anything more than the ever-more urgent whiplash of the money motive. We are under the gun. As the century drives to a close in a frenzy of race wars, nuclear threat, mass starvation, the daemonic threat that there are just too many people on earth, along with mankind's first views of earth itself from outer space, we have a sense of unlimited creativeness and destructiveness that makes the arch-individualists and culture-snobs of the 1920's seem archaic.

They are our founders, our master guides still—in retrospect, the 1920s make up the most concentrated single advance in physics as well as in painting and poetry, architecture and physical exploration. But ours is hardly a period of arch-individualism, of lonely patricians. Modernism was and remains an upper-class revolution, a necessary perception of the radical forms necessary to guarantee the continuity of our traditional culture. That culture is no longer believed in by those who still live in it. The masses still have no access to it and can hardly have a reason for finding one now. The present age has shown itself all too revolutionary, disruptive and uncontainable to be a "modernist." That is what Eliot meant when he, the incarnation of difficult modernist poetry, said in 1928—

Modernism is a mental blight which can affect the whole of the intelligence of our time...Where you find clear thinking, you usually find that the thinker is either a Christian (if he is a European) or an atheist; where you find muddy thinking you usually find that the thinker is something between the two, and such a person is in essentials a Modernist.

Taps for the Lost Generation

Malcolm Cowley

Born August 24, 1898, in Belsano, Pennsylvania—roughly concurrent with the advent of the Twentieth Century—Malcolm Cowley before his death in 1989, had earned the distinction of becoming part of the literary, cultural, and historical legend he recorded. In the present era of second-hand scholarship and thrice-told-tales, the venerable Mr. Cowley seems especially refreshing because he recounts the seasonal changes of passing generations with all the vitality of this year's spring.

More specifically, in terms of the decade under consideration in this anthology, Cowley's graduation from Harvard University, B.A. (cum laude), 1920 happily coincided with what he himself termed "A Second Flowering" in American literature—those "Works and Days of the Lost Generation" that Cowley himself helped to nourish in a lifetime of active participation near the core of panoramic events and in a plethora of subsequent contributions to literary history, critical evaluation, and personal reminiscence. Whatever his medium, Cowley seems especially convincing because he was there.

He was there when he interrupted his undergraduate studies in 1917 to join Hemingway, Dos Passos, e. e. Cummings and other talented American expatriates to drive ambulances or camions in Europe during the First World War. After six "spectatorial" months as a camion driver for the French army and a timely (as it turned out) rejection by American aviation, Cowley returned to Harvard where he was elected president of The Harvard Advocate *in April, 1918. Following in the "modernist" tradition of young Tom Eliot, Cowley found himself in a position to form literary acquaintances and lasting friendships with a nucleus of influential poets, including S. Foster Damon, who introduced the young editor and aspiring poet to the stylistic devices of Jules LaForgue. Other literary friends of the time: Amy Lowell (wreathed in cigar smoke) and reclusive though prolific Conrad Aiken, who learned to feel at ease with Cowley.*

By the spring of 1919 Cowley literally experienced Bohemian life in Greenwich Village, where he found himself "living in sin," as he puts it— though he married within the year—with his first wife, Peggy (Marguerite Frances Baird) while he tried to pay rent, purchase food and tobacco by reviewing a handful of books for The Dial *at the going rate of $1.00 per published review. After grubbing for work at other editorial offices, Cowley served out his apprenticeship by writing reviews for* The New Republic *at two cents a word—still not enough to keep a young free-lance reviewer from fainting on the sidewalks of New York.*

After completing his degree at Harvard, Cowley once more returned to New York where he managed a precarious though relatively adequate living by expanding his commissioned prose writing to The Literary Review of the New York Evening Post *and accepting a year of regular employment with* Sweet's Architectural Catalogue. *In 1921, however, he accepted a modest Fellowship from the American Field Service at the* Universite de Montpellier *and joined the exodus of young writers to France. Before returning to New York with his diploma in 1923, he took the opportunity to broaden his literary reputation by publishing portraits of well-known French authors in American and European periodicals. He continued working as a free-lance writer until 1929 when ironically his professional stock soared almost simultaneously with the crash on Wall Street. With some prodding from Hart Crane, Cowley's first book of collected poems,* Blue Juniata, *appeared in 1929. Almost simultaneously he began an important association as associate editor of* The New Republic *that lasted until 1944. During this period Cowley became identified with "Liberal" causes. However, as the Stalinist purges increased in the mid-thirties, and particularly after the Russian-German Pact of 1939, the aspiring visionary and literary advocate for "Men of Good Will" felt his efforts on behalf of "universal brotherhood" increasingly betrayed. Nevertheless, Cowley remained in his position at* The New Republic *primarily because he felt (as did Churchill and many American intellectuals) that one had to choose between Stalin and Hitler in order to advance the Allied Cause and ultimately to win The Second World War.*

Despite the complexities of political events, Cowley became an important autobiographical literary historian in 1934, with the publication of Exile's Return: A Literary Odyssey of the 1920s *(revised in 1951). Despite some understandable subjectivism, Cowley became for many "the acknowledged historian of his literary generation." Notwithstanding his talent for remaining on speaking terms with literary acquaintances to the right and left, he became a prime target of the MacCarthey era, not surprisingly losing his job as a member of the wartime Office of Facts and Figures (1942).*

But Cowley's humane and meditative literary acumen proved to be a much more durable national asset—and his literary histories and judicious critical evaluations have transcended polemics and politics. Even a selective listing of his contributions culled from half a century of "being there" can only suggest his profound dedication to Twentieth Century literature: Blue Juniata *(1929);* Exile's Return *(1934; rev. 1951);* The Literary Situation *(1954);*

Black Cargoes *(1962: With D. P. Mannix)*; The Faulkner-Cowley File *(1966)*; Think Back on Us *(1967)*; Blue Juniata Collected Poems *(1968)*; A Many Windowed House *(1970)*; The Lesson of the Masters *(1971-with Howard F. Hugo)*; A Second Flowering: Works and Days of the Lost Generation *(1973)*; -And I Worked at the Writer's Trade: Chapters of Literary History, 1918-1978 *(1978)*.

In addition, Cowley served as an editor of the following influential books: After the Genteel Tradition *(1937, rev. 1964)*; Books that Changed Our Minds *(1939: with Bernard Smith)*; Great Tales of the Deep South *(1955)*; Writers at Work: The "Paris Review" Interviews *(first series, 1958)*; Fitzgerald and the Jazz Age *(1966)*.

Many critics feel that one of Cowley's most important contributions as a critic has been his timely introductions or "discoveries" of works by others (especially as in the case of William Faulkner). Such editions (all with introductions) include: Adventures of an African Slaver *(autobiography of Theodore Canot, as told to Brantz Mayer, 1928)*; The Portable Hemingway *(1944)*; Poet of the French Resistance *(1945, with Hannah Josephson)*; The Portable Faulkner *(1946)*; The Portable Hawthorne *(1948)*; Stories by F. Scott Fitzgerald *(1951)*; Fitzgerald, Tender Is The Night *(1951)*; Three Novels by F. Scott Fitzgerald *(1953)*; Whitman's Leaves of Grass—the first edition, 1855 *(1959)*; Sherwood Anderson, Winesburg, Ohio *(1960)*. *Not included are a number of translations of important French authors.*

In addition to this impressive list of literary credentials, Malcolm Cowley managed an active membership in The National Institute of Arts and Letters (serving as its President from 1956-1959, and from 1962-1965). He also served as Chancellor of the more selective American Academy of Arts and Letters. Truly Cowley was one of America's authentic men of letters. But despite this plethora of credentials and honors, the attributes that set him apart from the typical academic resume collector involve certain conditions that Cowley himself demands of those who would hope to create or record "real literary generations": First, the generation must possess its own "sense of life...an intricate web of perceptions, judgments, feelings, and aspirations shared by its members." Second, it must cast aside "parental or merely prevailing notions." Third, the generation has to have precursors in literature and the arts whose "bold ideas...give an intellectual structure to their own rebellion." Fourth, a literary generation "must participate in, or at least be witness to, historic events that will furnish its members with a common fund of experience." Fifth, "the generation must have what Fitzgerald called 'its own leaders and spokesmen'." By way of illustration, Cowley invites his readers to consider Fitzgerald and Hemingway as spokesmen for World War I and the Twenties. Fair enough—though when one considers that Malcolm Cowley himself fulfills every one of these conditions, and from his vantage point of decades "knew them all," it is difficult to imagine anyone better qualified to intone the requiem for the Lost Generation.

* * *

There are no happy endings, but still, everything considered, it was more a lucky than a lost generation. Fitzgerald and his contemporaries were lucky, first of all, in the time they chose for being born, when the country was emerging from the long depression of the 1890s and when almost everyone looked forward to the miracles that were certain to be wrought by a new century. As little boys they witnessed the early miracles: self-propelled vehicles among the carts and carriages (drawn up at the curb for repairs) and the first movie houses, admission five cents, where they could pass an enchanted hour. Cities were growing as everything grew, but still the countryside began at the end of a five-cent streetcar ride, and it would always be there, always with fields to race across and woods to gather chestnuts in. So at least they felt as boys, and they were to be the last generation—except in the South— that could not help feeling close to the land.

They were lucky to grow up in a period that Van Wyck Brooks found the right name for: "The Confident Years." Under a rumbustious President, the country was flexing its muscles and sending its fleet around the world. Oh, there were lots of things wrong with the country, including trusts, political bosses, and slums (what were they?) in the back streets, but there was nothing in its future that middle-class boys had to worry about; nothing that wouldn't mend itself automatically if the boys grew up to be honest and if each of them worked hard for personal success. They all had a Protestant ethic drilled into them, even if they were Catholics like Fitzgerald. Later, after he lost his faith, the Protestant ethic remained with him. "All I believe in in life," he was to say in a letter to his daughter, "is the rewards for virtue (according to your talents) and the punishments for not doing your duty, which are doubly costly." It is an old-fashioned belief, but he was lucky to have it, and the stamp of it went into his stories, as into the work of his contemporaries.

They were most of them lucky in their early education, as compared with the boys and girls who followed them into high school fifty or sixty years later: that is, they weren't "exposed to a learning experience." Instead they were taught, and abhorred the teaching, and still were left with a residue of skills. They were taught such irrelevant subjects as ancient history (not social studies), English literature (with poems to be memorized), syntax, composition, and Latin grammar. They confronted English grammar, too, and rebelled against it, but at least they knew when they were breaking the rules. At some point in their high-school or college years, they were introduced to recent European literature.

Perhaps the introduction was made by a gifted teacher such as Dean Gauss at Princeton or John Crowe Ransom at Vanderbilt; perhaps by an older friend such as S. Foster Damon at Harvard or Phil Stone in Oxford, Mississippi, who lent young Faulkner the books he carried off to read. That reading was a crucial event in the lives of Faulkner and others. It led to a series of discoveries: first that there were subtler methods and more difficult standards in literature than those of *The Saturday Evening Post*; then that there was something later to be called the modern sensibility, which was ironical, introspective, and self-questioning; then finally that the production of great works expressing that sensibility was an aim to which one's life might be devoted. The aim might even become—and did become for many of the future writers—a sort of religion with its own moral precepts. These included the Protestant or middle-class ideal of earning success by hard work done honestly—as regards the work itself—but they bore no other resemblance to the morality of churchgoing citizens. "An artist," Faulkner was to say late in his career,". . . is completely amoral in that he will rob, borrow, beg, or steal from anybody and everybody to get the work done." He might have been repeating a lesson implied by books he had read before going off to the Great War.

It was a nice war, so Gertrude Stein used to insist to those who sat at her feet. In a longer perspective than hers, it was a disaster that ended the most hopeful era in Western history, but still it was a lucky war for the young American writers who served in it briefly. It immensely widened their horizons, it sharpened their enjoyment of life by the real or imagined nearness of death; then unexpectedly it was over before they had time to become truly disheartened. They went home, as Fitzgerald said, with an unexpended store of nervous energy, enough to carry them through the next ten frantic years.

But my theme here is the luck of the generation, not its familiar adventures in New York and Paris. It continued to be lucky in the decade after the war, when most of its writers published their first books. The new age proved to be one of success for beginners in all fields. An older generation feeling unsure of itself, perhaps a little guilty, was eager to learn what the youngsters were thinking and doing. Fitzgerald spoke up for the youngsters, and his first novel, published when he was twenty-four, made him an instant celebrity. Thereafter he would help to hold the generation together by his feeling, expressed time and again, that all his contemporaries were friendly rivals playing on the same bound-to-be-winning team.

The generation was lucky again in having Edmund Wilson as its young Sainte-Beuve. From his editorial desk first at *Vanity Fair*—where he shared it with John Peale Bishop, a gifted friend from Princeton—then after 1926 at *The New Republic*, he scanned the horizon for new talents and wrote perceptive comments on each of them. Sometimes his comments were the first, as those he made on Hemingway. He took almost as much interest as Fitzgerald in writers of his own generation, and he did a great deal to shape the critical image of Fitzgerald, Dos Passos, Wilder, Cummings, and others including the Nashville poets of the *Fugitive* group.

Curiously he hadn't planned to be a critic primarily; he had dreamed of having all literature as his imperium. Perhaps he wanted most to be a dramatist, but he also hoped to distinguish himself as a novelist, a poet, a publicist, a historian, and, in general, a man of letters. That he became a critic was largely by popular demand. His contemporaries realized quite early that he read more books more attentively and had more opinions about them than anyone else in the country. Writers listened to him as they did not often listen to other critics, and many of them tried to meet his difficult standards. At Princeton (class of '16) Dean Gauss had inspired him with the ambition to create "something in which," as he says in his tribute to Gauss, "every word, every cadence, every detail, should perform a definite function in producing an intense effect." That effect was what he hoped to find in new writers, and he scolded them, if in reasonable terms, when they fell short of producing it. He helped to keep Fitzgerald and his other brilliant contemporaries up to scratch.

By the late 1920s men of the generation were being published in Europe, and there again they profited from special circumstances. The new European writers who might have overshadowed them had died by age groups at Verdun and on the Somme. The new Americans had something of their own to say and part of it was a message that pleased the European public. That public resented the wealth and complacency of the empire across the Atlantic, but was impressed by it, too, and was waiting to learn whether its new literature would be as rugged and efficient as its motor cars. When some of the literature appeared in translation and when Europeans found that it was largely, so it seemed to them, a protest against wealth and complacency, presented in scenes of violence and abject suffering, they were rather quick to accept the new authors. Dos Passos, Hemingway, Wilder (who appealed to a different audience), and Wolfe were all international figures at thirty. Even Faulkner—though Europeans felt that he was more foreign than the others—was enthusiastically read in France during the Depression years, when his work was being disparaged at home.

Most of these writers suffered less from the Depression itself than did the younger men who followed them after 1930. Established in their profession, they didn't have to waste time in employment agencies or sit moldering in lunch wagons, and not many of them marched in those United Front parades that furnished a collection of names to the FBI. Hollywood was a source of income for some, including Faulkner and Fitzgerald, whose books then had a disappointing sale. Still, these and others continued writing the books, and they were becoming the dominant age group in American letters before this country entered World War II.

That was not a lucky war for the younger writers who came after them. The younger men suffered more casualties, they served in uniform for as much as five years, during which they had little time for writing, and they returned to civilian life without any great residue of stored-up energy. (All the more credit, one must add, to Bellow, Mailer, Styron, Jarrell, and others who did admirable things after World War II without any special favors from fortune.) Writers of the World War I generation were luckier once again, but still this wasn't their war. Crane, Wolfe, and Fitzgerald were dead before we entered it. Most of the others had done their best work, as would later be discovered, but they continued to rise in public estimation. One after another was invited, as it were, to sit in the high-backed chair at the head of the table, where Hemingway had already sat after *A Farewell* to *Arms* and Dos Passos had sat in the middle 1930s. Wolfe enjoyed an extraordinary posthumous reputation during the war, when it seemed that every literate young man in the army camps was reading his novels. Then it was Hemingway's turn again; then Faulkner's after his Nobel Prize in 1950—critics paid him triple honors in recompense for the years of neglect; and Wilson's turn came round in his later years. After 1950 a special chair had been installed for the glittering shade of Fitzgerald.

All these presided in turn or jointly over the long table without having their places seriously threatened by younger writers. It is not at all that talent was lacking among those who came shortly after them. To mention names, if only a few, Steinbeck, Cozzens, Farrell, West, Warren, O'Hara, Roethke, and Welty were all born between 1902 and 1909 and all produced good work from the start, but they did not form a cohesive age group. Some were drawn into the orbit of the Lost Generation—as notably Nathanael West and, in his early books, O'Hara—while the others did not rebel against it. With some exceptions the same statement holds true for writers of talent born between 1910 and 1925. All this might suggest that a generation, in historical terms, is no more a matter of dates than it is one of ideology. A new generation does not appear every thirty years, as Pio Baroja and other theorists have maintained, or "about three times in a century," to quote Fitzgerald; it appears when writers of the same age join in a common revolt against the fathers and when, in the process of adopting a new life style, they find their own models and spokesmen.

According to Baroja's scheme—and Fitzgerald's too—a new literary generation should have appeared in the 1950s, but the young writers who came forward then had no apparent sense of group identity.[1] Frank Conroy, one of the more talented, was asked to describe his contemporaries in the same issue of *Esquire*—October 1968—that first printed Fitzgerald's article "My Generation." "It is clear that most of us now in our early thirties," Conroy says, "were not a generation in any self-conscious sense. We had no leaders, no program, no sense of our own power, and no culture exclusively our own." He says of his high-school classmates, "Our clothing, manners and life styles were unoriginal—scaled-down versions of what we saw in the adults"; this time there would be no instinctive revolt against the fathers. In college his contemporaries were called the Silent, the Cautious, or the Apathetic Generation, another way of implying that they were not a generation at all, in Fitzgerald's sense of the word.

Conroy says of their college reading, "The New Critics had filled us with an almost religious awe of language. We read Leavis, Edmund Wilson and Eliot as well, taking it all very seriously, worrying over every little point as if Truth and Beauty hung in the balance." Those last remarks bring to mind an important feature of the 1950s: that the New Critics— and some fewer older ones—were doing more original work at the time and exerted more influence over bright young people than did new writers of fiction and poetry. The critics paid little attention to new work in any field except their own. They practiced their art of exegesis on the masterpieces of older writers, including several of the World War I generation: Faulkner especially, but also Fitzgerald, Hemingway, Cummings, and Hart Crane. Students admired the masterpieces and dreamed of the age in which they were written, a time when nobody, so it seemed, was silent or cautious or apathetic and nobody was tempted to ask the anguished question "Who am I?" The result was that members of the Lost Generation were lucky once again, basking, as it were, in a late afternoon of adulation and nostalgia.

Hemingway and James Thurber died in 1961, Faulkner and Cummings in 1962. Those four deaths in a little more than a year changed the whole order of precedence in the literary world. *The New York Times Book Review* printed the results of an inquiry—one can hardly say "inquest" in this connection—into opinions about who would take their places at the long table. The six critics queried by *The Times* had dozens of authors to mention, but reached no agreement as to which of them ranked highest. There was in fact a three-year interregnum in the kingdom of letters. Then suddenly in 1965 a new generation came to public notice, ten or fifteen years behind schedule, but complete by then with its leaders and spokesmen, its costumes, its music, its new style of life, and moving with disciplined indiscipline toward a general assault on the fathers. It had political opinions, too, and poured them forth in something that was close to being a new language, a free-swinging mixture of jive and pedantry. The new men had no patience at all with the religion of art or with lives sacrificed to the dream of ultimately producing masterpieces: "Now! Now!" they kept demanding. If more of its members had survived, the Lost Generation might have felt lonely and puzzled in the new atmosphere. One might say that its luck had continued to the end, with many of its members choosing the right time to die.

I knew them all and some have been my friends over the years, but I saw less of them after 1942 or thereabouts. By that time a few of them were dead and the Second War was scattering the others. I was a deaf man living in the country, hoeing my garden. Some of them I saw on weekly visits to New York, which was still the center of literary life—but it was rather less of a center than before and chiefly one, it seemed to me, for younger age groups. Among middle-aged writers the political arguments of the 1930s—over the New Deal, Trotsky, the Spanish Civil War, and the Russian purges—had left fissures some of which were never to be closed (as for instance the one between Hemingway and Dos Passos). That may be part of a pattern in writers' lives: at first they are happy to roam in bands, then year by year they retire from the herd like old bull elephants. Still, the famous writers of my own age and others who deserved to be famous were reassuring though invisible presences. Pleased by each public sign of recognition, I did what I could to explain features of their work that I thought had been missed. They were our spokesmen, after all, and every glittering success they made reflected on the rest of us. Fitzgerald was not the only one to feel that we were all playing on the same team.

Now most of the team is gone and the survivors are left with the sense of having plodded with others to the tip of a long sandspit where they stand exposed, surrounded by water, waiting for the tide to come in.

In later years I have wondered whether certain types of criticism are possible except in relation to authors of one's own age group. Those types are not the highest ones, I suspect; they do not often lead to universal principles and they are not as persuasive in the classroom as the reinterpretation of an older work for a new age. The text of the older work remains and every critic has the privilege of reading it attentively. But there are values in the text, there are images and associations, that can be grasped intuitively by those who grew up at the same time as the author; "empathy" is the abused word. In reading Hemingway's Michigan stories I remember—as he obviously did—walking through first-growth hemlock timber and feeling the short, warm, dry, a little prickly needles under bare feet. "One year," he was to write, "they had cut the hemlock woods and there were only stumps, dried treetops, branches and fireweed where the woods had been." I remember that too, if not from Michigan. In reading some of Faulkner's novels I remember the first automobile that chugged through the village in a cloud of dust and running boys, while men in overalls craned forward from the bench in front of the general store; that was in Belsano, where I was born, but it might have been in Frenchman's Bend. Such memories enforced the feeling of both novelists that they had lived in two worlds and that the earlier one was better in many ways, perhaps in most, but "You could not go back." Critics who did not know the earlier world sometimes offer reinterpretations—I have read them by the dozen—that are inspired, compelling, and completely wrong in their sense of values.

I confess to sharing the weakness I imputed to members of the generation, Dos Passos and Hemingway in particular, that of living too much in the past. "But we had such good times then," I find myself saying with others. We thought of ourselves as being wise, disillusioned, cynical, but we were wide-eyed children with a child's capacity for enjoyment. Did other generations ever laugh so hard together, drink and dance so hard, or do crazier things just for the hell of it? Perhaps some did—most certainly they did—but they did not leave behind such vivid records of their crazy parties and their mornings after. Those records testified to a bargain struck with themselves by writers of the generation. They had taken more liberties than other people, and in return they had accepted the duty of portraying their new world honestly, in all its exultation and heartbreak.

The good writers regarded themselves as an elite, a word that later came to be a sneer. They were an elite not by birth or money or education, not even by acclaim—though they would have it later—but rather by such inner qualities as energy, independence, vision, rigor, an original way of combining words (a style, a "voice"), and utter commitment to a dream. Those qualities they grouped together as their "talent," about which they spoke as if it were something precariously in their possession, a blooded animal, perhaps, to be fed, trained, guarded carefully, and worked to the limit of its power, but not beyond. At a time when Faulkner needed money, he refused a tempting commission to write a nonfiction book. "I'm like the old mare," he wrote me, "who has been bred and dropped foal 15-16 times, and she has a feeling that she has only 3 or 4 more in her and can't afford to spend one on something outside." I have quoted elsewhere a remark made by Wolfe to his editor Max Perkins: "As for that powerful and magnificent talent I had two years ago," he said, "—in the name of God is that to be lost entirely...?" He seemed to regard his talent as a proud stallion that could be stolen or crippled by his enemies. Hemingway had a different comparison: he said that his talent was like a gas flame that he kept turning lower and lower until there was an explosion. Fitzgerald wrote to his daughter the spring before he died, "I am not a great man but sometimes I think the impersonal and objective quality of my talent and the sacrifice of it, in pieces, to preserve its essential value has some sort of epic grandeur."

That last was too big a phrase and Fitzgerald apologized. "Anyhow," he concluded, "after hours I console myself with delusions of that sort." But the earlier phrase "impersonal and objective" was not delusive when applied to the talent of all those writers. For one thing, they tried to be accurate observers of their age; for another, they regarded their talent as something apart from their ordinary selves. Hence, their efforts to preserve the talent were selfless, after a fashion, or at least ran counter in many cases to their material interests. A question they asked themselves was "How can I best live in order to produce the books that are in me?" It was a *professional* question, and the adjective reminds me of a brief scene in *Tender Is the Night*. The scene is from the section of the novel that presents Dr. Richard Diver as a brilliant young psychiatrist. While studying in Zurich he has met Nicole Warren, beautiful, rich, and a patient, at the time, in Professor Dohmler's psychiatric clinic. Nicole falls in love with Dick, and the experience leads to a partial cure of her psychosis. The Swiss doctors are afraid that Dick will either jilt her and cause a relapse or else marry her and ruin his career.

"I have nothing to do with your personal reactions," Professor Dohmler says. "But I have much to do with the fact that this so-called 'transference' must be terminated."

"It's certainly a situation," Dick says.

The eminent professor raises himself, Fitzgerald tells us, "like a legless man mounting a pair of crutches." "But it is a professional situation," he thunders quietly.

And so it is with many of the situations recorded in this book (or not recorded and left to the biographers). Marriages, divorces, friendships made and broken, bouts of drinking, follies of various sorts—not to mention "strategies," as Kenneth Burke would call them, such as creating a persona to serve as the imaginary author of one's books—even fits of madness in one case and suicides in two others—were they not largely the result of professional decisions made in the hope or despair of producing masterpieces?

Writers of the generation were intensely ambitious, but only in the professional field. Hemingway was an exception here: he was cursed with that passion to excel in every field, but writing came first for him, in the beginning as in the end. The others—not counting Fitzgerald in the time of his early success—were rather modest in their demands on life. No, they didn't in the least object to earning money, but they devoutly planned to earn it in such a way as not to forfeit their independence or diminish the future value of their talent. They also didn't object, as a general rule, to living in comfort, to having rich or prominent friends, and to being looked at admiringly by beddable young women (a prerogative of success to be observed in many fields, but perhaps in the literary field more than in others outside the performing arts). Sometimes they pretended to be indifferent to such things, and money too, and the pretense led to a number of farcical situations. But their taste, such as it might be, for worldly rewards was never a "dirty little secret," as Norman Podhoretz was to call it in speaking of his own contemporaries. I am trying not to idealize the picture. There were acts of generosity toward rivals, and there were also jealousies galore, backbitings and scratchings, and jabs to the kidney in a clinch. It has to be said with emphasis, however, that the good writers of the generation were not bent on "making it" in the later sense of the phrase: that is, they didn't want to acquire power over others in the contemporary world or to be the boss man of an organization. Those ambitions would have seemed to them cheap and conventional, like the dream of owning a chauffeur-driven Cadillac. Their dream was of having place and power in a more lasting world; of being the lords of language and the captains general of plots and characters.

"I want to be one of the greatest writers who have ever lived, don't you?"

That remark of Fitzgerald's to Edmund Wilson, made shortly after they both got out of Princeton, has been quoted many times and by Wilson first of all, in his "Thoughts on Being Bibliographed." Wilson's comment on the remark has also been quoted, but it will bear repeating once again. "Scott," he says, "had been reading Booth Tarkington, Compton Mackenzie, H. G. Wells and Swinburne; but when he later got to better writers, his standards and his achievement went sharply up, and he would always have pitted himself against the best in his own line that he knew. I thought his remark rather foolish at the time, yet it was one of the things that made me respect him, and I am sure that this intoxicated ardor represented a healthy way for a young man of talent to feel." Other young men of talent felt the same desire, at the time, to pit themselves against the best they knew. It is a feeling that casts light, for example, on Hemingway's later brag to Lillian Ross of *The New Yorker*. "I started out very quiet and I beat Mr. Turgenev," he said. "Then I trained hard and I beat Mr. de Maupassant. I've fought two draws with Mr. Stendhal, and I think I had an edge in the last one." Apparently "the last one" was not *For Whom the Bell Tolls*, in which it is hard to find a suggestion of Stendhal. My notion about *The*

Bell is that he wrote it with at least a vague image in mind of *War and Peace* and that the image spurred him on to produce what is truly the best and richest of his novels. One can say that its low standing with the critical profession is a scandal, but to compare the finished book with *War and Peace* is more than Hemingway himself would dare. "Nobody," he told Miss Ross long after *The Bell* was published, "is going to get me in any ring with Mr. Tolstoy."

Now that time and men have passed, comparisons—not that one—have to be drawn and general statements, some of them negative, have to be made. Not one member of the generation carried out Fitzgerald's ambition of winning a place among "the greatest writers who have ever lived." Not one of its novelists, even Faulkner, can be set rightly beside Dostoevsky or Dickens, let alone Tolstoy, and not one of its poets ranks with Browning or Whitman, let alone with the giants of earlier times. Faulkner was its greatest man, the one most likely to remain a world figure by virtue of an imaginative power that has seldom been equaled. His place would be still more secure if *A Fable,* to which he devoted most of his energy for twelve years, had become the great novel he intended it to be; but that project of retelling the Gospels in terms of the Great War was not the one he should have undertaken. The Yoknapatawpha books are his achievement, and this in retrospect seems very deep and not so broad as we had hoped, a Grand Canyon rather than a continent.

Hemingway is out of favor, partly because of his public image and partly because his work is seldom considered as a whole. There are interconnections that make the books more impressive when taken together: for example, Robert Jordan's death at a bridge in Spain is a sequel to Frederic Henry's escape from death—and from the Italian Army—at a bridge over the Isonzo. Also it must not be forgotten that Hemingway effected a change in the style and vision of writers all over the world, including many who never acknowledged the debt. Fitzgerald seems a great man in retrospect, but his greatness has to be pieced together—from *Gatsby,* from the Rosemary section of *Tender Is the Night* (yes, and from the final chapters too)—then has to be cemented with the legend of his life. The figure he presents is that of a broken Apollo, salvaged by divers from the wreck of an Athenian galley, powerful in conception, but with fragments missing.

Those three men and several of their contemporaries were extraordinary persons, but they lacked the capacity for renewed growth after middle age that has marked some of the truly great writers. After all, that is a rare capacity: one thinks of Goethe first, then of Tolstoy (but with questions about his later work), then of Hardy, Shaw, Thomas Mann, André Gide, but not of many others. In American literature there is only Henry James, who set out in a new direction at fifty-two after his venture into the theater had ended with a disaster. The writers of the Lost Generation, as a rule, had done their best work before they were forty-five and they had no second careers. Wilson might be an exception here, with his intellectual stamina and his lifelong rage for exploring new subjects, but even in his lonely case one feels more vigor of conception in the earlier work. Of the others who lived beyond sixty, the most one can say in this connection is that they held out, guarded their talent as best they could, and remained in a true sense incorruptible.

And what of the dream that seems to have been rejected by a new generation, to judge by its literary manifestos; I mean the dream all these writers had of bringing new masterpieces to birth? Some of these they left behind, but fewer than they had hoped. Of course the word "masterpiece" has two different and rather special connotations: it is applied either to works that are impressive in scope (without being overblown) or else to more limited works that are relatively faultless in execution. Only two works of the first type were produced by the generation: they are *U.S.A.* which is grand in conception but often tedious in the writing, and *For Whom the Bell Tolls*, which, for all the faults that have been urged against it, is on the scale of the great nineteenth-century novels. Works of the second type are more numerous, as one might expect of a generation preoccupied with form: there are *Gatsby, A Farewell to Arms, Our Town, The Old Man and the Sea*...not to mention half a dozen books by other writers. There are also the works that are unforgettable in spite of some obvious weakness in design: *The Sound and the Fury, Tender Is the Night, The Hamlet* (my favorite among Faulkner's novels, though I wouldn't ask others to agree), and Hart Crane's cycle of poems, *The Bridge*. It may be that such works, flawed but not by any means failed, represent the generation in its essence. What I said of Fitzgerald might be true of his contemporaries as a group: that their greatness has to be pieced together.

And how do their productions compare with those of earlier times in American literature, especially with those of the 1840s and 1850s, the period that F. O. Matthiessen and others have called "the American Renaissance"? Are any of their works on the same level as *Walden, Moby-Dick, The Scarlet Letter*, or "Song of Myself"? Instinctively I distrust the question. The game of choosing Books That Will Live or Ten Books to Take to a Desert Island is one for innocents or retired professors with time on their hands. Every work has an absolute, not a comparative, value. Still, I should say that Faulkner's story "The Bear" is as grand in its briefer fashion as *Moby-Dick*, that it may be read for as long, and that other works by members of the generation will have their place among the American classics. Beyond that I am unwilling to depose.

A more fruitful comparison might be one between the two eras, just eighty years apart, as periods of literary activity. Before the first era Emerson had prophesied, in his bold address "The American Scholar," that a new literature would soon appear on this continent. "Our day of dependence, our long apprenticeship to the learning of foreign lands, draws to a close," he said. "...Events, actions arise, that must be sung, that will sing themselves." Dozens of more or less talented young writers, surrounded by hundreds of cranks and come-outers, rushed to answer his call, each with the feeling that anything was possible in the new day. That same feeling of unlimited possibility prevailed in literature after the First World War. Young writers then were answering a call not from Emerson, whom they did not read, but from Joyce and Eliot (with Ezra Pound as prompter of one and promoter of both). *Ulysses* and *The Waste Land* had appeared in the same year, 1922. It seemed at the time that their authors had pushed beyond the mountains and opened territories for men of the new generation to explore. Those younger men were also heartened by the example of older American writers—Dreiser, Anderson, Cather, Mencken—who were doing some of their best work in the postwar years; and before the Second War they were being jostled ahead by still younger writers of talent. With all this growth and bustle, as in a midsummer garden, the period in American literature was clearly a second flowering.

Even after frost, the period retains an afterglow. One reason for its appeal to younger people, including those who reject most of its aims, is a gift that many of its writers possessed in common: they were almost all great spinners and weavers of legend. Most obviously the gift was shown in the legendary heroes they presented as models that would be followed, in each case, by thousands of their readers; here one thinks of the Hemingway young man like an Indian brave, the Fitzgerald young man who believed in the green light, and the Thomas Wolfe young man bent on devouring the world. Behind such heroes are larger patterns of myth,... Hemingway and Faulkner most of all, but other writers as well, seemed to plunge deep into the past, or into themselves, to recover a prehistoric and prelogical fashion of looking at the world; then they looked in the same fashion at events of their own time and thereby surrounded them with a feeling of primitive magic (as Faulkner did in "The Bear" and Hemingway in "Big Two-Hearted River"). Perhaps that feeling explains the legendary quality of other stories, by these and other writers. In a sense the men of the generation were all working together to produce a cycle of myths for a new century which—so they had felt from the beginning—was to be partly a creation of their own.

Note

[1]And what about the so-called Beat Generation? That was in fact a small rebel band, one that hoped to speak for the new writers of its time, but found that most of these were a different breed of duck with a different sort of quack. Some of the Beats, however—notably Jack Kerouac (b. 1922) and Allen Ginsberg (b. 1926)—were among the "madmen and outlaws" who served as models for the real generation that was later to appear.

Afterthoughts on the Twenties

John W. Aldridge

Born September 22, 1922 in the bland and secure community of Sioux City, Iowa, John W. Aldridge suffered a stimulating jolt to his boyhood sensibilities when his father's business collapsed during the Depression. The eleven-year old boy soon found his sense of dislocation compounded when his father resettled his family on a small farm near Chattanooga, Tennessee. Notwithstanding the rough-hewn nature of this search for a lost Eden, young Aldridge survived both his hard farmwork and hill country initiations to win a scholarship at the University of Chattanooga. Thus began a brilliant, controversial, sometimes stormy Odyssey into the academic and literary world.

After acquiring his B.A. and a local reputation as a creative writer and newspaper editor at the University of Chattanooga, his considerable promise was rewarded with a fellowship to Breadloaf School of English in Vermont. That was the summer of 1942. He spent the following three years fighting in France and Germany.

In 1946, Aldridge entered the University of California at Berkeley. His subsequent accomplishments appear both meteoric and prolific. With the 1947 publication of an article in Harpers *defining the new postwar generation of writers, the returned veteran shifted his theatre of operations to the literary homefront. His considerable intellect attracted a good deal of critical attention and stirred up more than a little controversy. Subsequent publications, including his first book,* After the Lost Generation *(1951) tended increasingly to attack established critical clichés and cherished shibboleths regarding the sanctity of certain well-known American writers and their literary legendry. It is fair to suggest that Aldridge was among the first to define a new generation of post-World War II writers before most people were aware that such a generation existed.*

This kind of critical attention led to teaching positions at a number of colleges and universities, including seven years at the University of Vermont (1948-55), an interim year at Princeton (1953-54) as a lecturer in the Christian Gauss Seminars in criticism, member of the literary faculty at Sarah Lawrence College, and the New School of Social Research (1957), professorships at Queens College (1957), and New York University (1958); Fulbright Lecturer at the University of Munich, Germany (1958-59); Writer in Residence at Hollins College (1960-62); Fulbright Lecturer at the University of Copenhagen (1962-64) and finally a post as Professor of English at the University of Michigan (1964 to date). Meanwhile Aldridge managed to serve in various critical or advisory capacities with the New York Herald Tribune *(1965-66),* The Saturday Review *(1970-79), the Bread Loaf Writers' Conference (1966-69), and as Special Advisor for American Studies U. S. Embassy, Germany (1972-73). His writings include* After the Lost Generation, *1951:* Critiques and Essays on Modern Fiction, *1952:* In Search of Heresy, *1956:* The Party at Cranton, *(1960—a novel):* Time to Murder and Create, *1966:* In the Country of the Young *(1970):* The Devil in the Fire, *(1972) and* The American Novel and the Way We Live Now *(1983).*

Many of these works invited controversial reactions from established and self-effacing critics who often found Aldridge contentious and dogmatic as a literary theorist. But his talent lay precisely in his willingness to take critical leaps—even at the risk of personal castigation. Indeed Aldridge seems to take considerable pride in what he himself terms his "controversial career." As he puts it, "All my books have provoked argument and discussion. And I am pleased that this should be so, for I function best in an atmosphere of controversy and would very probably die if I were read with indifference."

If the present essay is a case in point, Aldridge will be pleased, for herein he takes on no less a target than such purveyors of literary opinions as Malcolm Cowley who persist in defending a select group of Twenties' writers—Hemingway, Fitzgerald, Dos Passos, Cummings, Wilder, Faulkner, Wolfe, Hart, Crane—as something of "A Second Flowering." Aldridge's provocation is, of course, engendered by the title of Cowley's book, which (on the whole) celebrates the aforemention writers and "the works they produced during a period that now seems to have been a second flowering of American literature."

Aldridge's attitude toward this "aristocratic fraternity of talent," though not devoid of concessions to what he considers genuine artistry, appears iconoclastic when set beside Cowley's general bias toward the "Lost Generation" writers. In Aldridge's view their novels and poems suffered all too frequently from a variety of youth-centered narcissism, resulting in a pseudo-elitist incapacity to see themselves, their traditions, their world in a coherent, synthesizing, emotional maturity and sustaining cultural or moral perspective. Aldridge builds his premise from a traditional point of view, insisting that the artist should assume at least as much responsibility for the universality of experience as for his own dislocated sensibilities. Thus solipsism is put down as an artistic lapse. Excessive preoccupation with one's own experience is suspect. He reminds us that "The act of moral reclamation may be a necessity for every literary generation." And in one of his strongest indictments regarding the Twenties' writers he charges that they were misled or self-deluded into thinking that "their own experience was indeed unprecedented, and that the older modes of literary statement were inadequate to describe it. They, therefore, became excessively preoccupied with experience and, in both their writing and their lives, with the innovative and the defiant. For reasons of temperament and historical position they were fixated permanently at the level of rite de passage, where they were condemned forever to play the roles of rebellious sons and wayward daughters, able to find their identity only in the degree of their opposition *to the literary and social conventions of the past." In the context of this anthology, however, his wish to become the center of controversy is destined to be fulfilled.*

* * *

The publication in 1973 of Cowley's *A Second Flowering* reopened a question most of us might prefer to leave closed. Yet it continues to obsess us like the puzzle of some ancient unsolved crime. Just how important, really, were the generation of writers who are commonly assumed to have produced a renaissance of American literature in the 1920s; what is the meaning and value of their contribution in the perspective of all that we know about them and all that has happened in our literature since their time?

Mr. Cowley, having spent fifty years studying these writers, may be forgiven if, at seventy-five, he was unable or unwilling to offer much more than a reiteration of opinions that over the years have grown habitual with him, and that have come to represent the official Establishment answer to this question. His understandably strong feelings of proprietorship toward the Twenties writers have caused him to take it for granted that, in spite of individual shortcomings of which he is well aware, they were, on the whole, the most distinguished literary generation the century has so far produced—the most distinguished, in fact, since the great first flowering of American literary talent in the generation of Emerson and Thoreau. Cowley has written eloquently in support of his position, and one can scarcely fault him for taking it. He has had a long career as a highly influential critical spokesman for these writers, most of whom were his personal friends. He was on the scene in Paris during the time when they were doing some of their best work, and he was one of the first critics to understand the significance of the whole artistic phenomenon which so profoundly affected the character of our literature after World War I. Today he is conscious of being a last survivor of the '20s generation—left, as he has said, "with the sense of having plodded with others to the tip of a long sandspit where they stand exposed, surrounded by water, waiting for the tide to come in." If anyone has earned the right to his biases, Cowley surely has.

For the rest of us the problem of coming to terms with the Twenties writers is considerably more complex. We have existed for years in a state of gross informational surfeit, in which we have become so drugged and bored with knowledge concerning every aspect of their lives and works that the possibility of making new and original assessments of them must strike us as being very remote indeed. Furthermore, their achievement as artists is now effectively inseparable in our minds from the legendry of their lives, while their works are so commonly seen as source-books of gossip and invitations to nostalgia, that no balanced view of their literary merits can be maintained for long.

Many of us have to contend with our own emotional relation to these writers, a relation which cannot be as intimate and avuncular as Cowley's, but is no less affected by sentiment or what, in the case of literary people younger than he, has so often been the most abject kind of filial admiration. After all, the Twenties generation were once our very special and personal property. We came to love them long before it became official wisdom to do so, and there are complex loyalties that bind us equally to them and to that part of ourselves which was formed by their influence. For many of us who discovered them at the right (or the wrong) age, they seemed quite simply the only real writers there were, and so they became our proxy writers. They had all the experiences we would have liked to have, and they wrote exactly the books we wished we might have written. It could be fairly said that they were the first and perhaps the only generation of writers to capture our imaginations and to dramatize an image of the literary life with which we could identify because it combined creative achievement with the freedom to explore the fullest possibilities of feeling and being. We may have had the greatest respect for the work of such older men as Dreiser, Mencken, Anderson, and Lewis, but we did not envy them their lives. Their generation seemed grey, remote, and eternally middle-aged. There was something about them that smelled of beer, cigars, pool halls, and the heavy sweat of craft and naturalism. One imagined them going off to the office every morning—pot-bellied businessmen of letters—carrying their inspiration in a lunch pail. But the Twenties writers were a very different breed—elegant, esthetic, temperamentally gifted rather than soberly skilled, as extravagant and wasteful as young British lords, yet profoundly self-serving in their function as writers. They were distinguished from their elders, above all, by their dedication to the Flaubertian ideal of the artist, their sense of belonging to an aristocratic fraternity of talent. But they also believed in the interdependence of art and experience, the necessity that literature partake of, even as it transformed to suit its own purposes, the felt realities and passions of the individual life.

They thus embodied for us an adolescent ideal which is deeply rooted in our native mythos but which, in recent years, only Norman Mailer has been able to emulate with any conviction, the ideal of the writer as poet-profligate, our fantasy inheritance from the English Romantics and the disciples of Walter Pater which for the first time among the Twenties writers became a practical model of conduct for Americans. Hence, they found it possible to live the life of sensation with great vigor and still live the life of literature with great dedication and success. They were able to have it both ways so splendidly, and they made such excellent use of the opportunity, that some of us will probably never manage to see them except against the high colorations of jealousy or adoration.

Another factor obscuring our view of these writers is that they were largely responsible for developing in us the standards by which we might have been able to judge them. For it was on the evidence of their work and that of their European contemporaries that we formed our first impressions of what literary effects were possible to the modern sensibility. No other standards derived from other historical periods seemed quite applicable to them, if only because so much of their significance resulted from their collective belief that they had outmoded the past by confronting a new reality in ways wholly unique to it and to them. Also, in a very real sense, the Twenties writers provided the basic assumptions through which we came to perceive, and some of us to express, the experience of the modern world. Their works for a very long time seemed to have done all our essential imagining for us, just as they themselves seemed to have done our essential living, so that we had very little sense of being engaged with life that was not in some way connected with the profoundly seductive images of life with which they first came to dominate our imaginations.

By the same token, our view of the literary life of the Twenties is a complex mixture of myth and reality, of reality fantasized into myth and myth personalized to the point where it seems like something we ourselves experienced. One does not know, for example, whether the literature created the fantasy or the fantasy found its embodiment in the literary life. But surely a strong attraction of the period for young people was, and may still be, the fact that it represents their vision of the perfect college literary apprenticeship exported to Paris and prolonged for a decade. The intense, free life of Montparnasse was the idealized equivalent of the intense, free life of the campus literati. There, happily far away from parents and hometown, it was possible to get drunk as often as one pleased, to stay up all night making love, wander the streets howling into the dawn, be eternally young, sensitive, and promising, do all kinds of experimental work and publish it in the little magazines, be read by an audience of friends who were the perfect classmates, all people of brilliant talent and wit and yet, except for a few, remarkably kind and helpful about one's own work. There too one could enjoy the presence of older teachers and mentors like Pound, Anderson, and Stein, the quintessential writing instructors who were the first to recognize one's gifts and who gave so generously of their advice and encouragement. But perhaps even more important were certain other perquisites of these literary junior years abroad: the advantages of not having to hold down a job because checks were coming regularly from home or one was on a fellowship, not having to be compromised by the bourgeois values of one's parents, not having to worry about marriage and a family, not having responsibilities of any kind except to Art, Truth, and one's friends.

It is not surprising that this image of the Paris literary life should be embellished in our minds by a cast of personages, both fictional and actual, who have the clarity of outline, the individuality, and the emotional openness which, as a rule, only young people of college age seem to possess. Their appearance and behavior remain with us almost as if recollected from life or recorded in a class yearbook in which we seem to find versions of our own former selves. Nobody will ever be like them again, and nobody will need to be. For these people exist eternally in the roles fixed for them by memory and sentiment—larger than life because they belong to a generation which managed to mythologize its experience while still in the act of having it.

There is young Jay Gatsby, helplessly in love with the rich and sophisticated sorority girl, holding out his arms to the green light at the end of her boat dock; Amory Blaine proclaiming his valedictory "I know myself but that is all"; Eugene Gant forever seeking "the lost land-end into heaven...a stone, a leaf, an unfound door..."; Jake Barnes muttering through those bitter, bitter teeth the best line in the senior play, "Yes, isn't it pretty to think so."; Scott and Zelda, the most popular and beautiful couple on the campus, behaving insufferably at parties, jumping fully clothed into the Plaza fountain; Hemingway, the most talented boy in the class, writing his first stories at a table in the Closerie des Lilas; good old Tom Wolfe, a boy who never seemed to stop growing, getting very drunk, waving his arms, and knocking out the electrical system of an entire town. And remember the others, the people like Harry Crosby, Slater Brown, William Bird, Robert McAlmon, and the Gerald Murphys, who matter only because they were friends of the famous and now belong to history simply because everyone connected, however remotely, with the Paris literary life in the Twenties now belongs to history.

The writers whom Leslie Fiedler once called "great stereotype-mongers" have bequeathed us themselves and their characters as clichés, and criticism has made more clichés out of the essential arguments that can be brought against them. Yet the most familiar argument is also the least avoidable. They were a group of highly talented but narrow writers, and their narrowness was most dramatically revealed in the fact that they had one abiding interest, themselves when young, an interest which, in the case of some of them, became the literary preoccupation of a lifetime. Their books had all the attributes of young consciousness. They were lyrical, nostalgic, sentimental, stylish, experimental, and iconoclastic, and they told over and over again the story of self-discovery through the first conquest of experience. We learned from them what it is like to grow up in the small towns of America, how it feels to fall in love, have sex, get drunk, go to war, to be an American in Europe, all for the first time, to be so hungry for life that you want to consume all the food, liquor, and women in the world, or to discover that the system created by adults is capitalistic and corrupt or hypocritical and dull.

Fitzgerald wrote the story of young romance and riotous youth and, remarkably enough, became famous at twenty-four largely on the strength of the fact that he informed the older generation about just how badly the young really behaved. Hemingway's first and best materials were an adolescent's adventures in Europe, his initiation into the mystery cult of foreign sports, bullfighting and big-game hunting, the loss of his innocence through the death of his ideals and his love in European war. Dos Passos found his most dependable subject in the totalitarianism of social hierarchies, whether political, economic, or military, in which the integrity of the young was destroyed or severely compromised and the artistic spirit broken under the grinding pressures of the machine. There are very few people over forty in this literature, and when they do appear, we can usually recognize them by their stigmata of physical ugliness, venality, and hypocrisy. Only the young are truly human, but then the young are doomed to be the victims of the old, to die in their wars, to be tricked by their deceits, ruined through seduction by their false gods.

It is logical that the qualities we remember most clearly in this literature are those that impressed us when we ourselves were young—the marvelous intensity about people and raw experience, the preoccupation with the self, with love, sex, freedom, time, adventure, the irreverence toward the world of the fathers, the disdain for the adult religion of work, self-sacrifice, expediency, competition, and conformity. It is also logical that so many of these writers were able to function effectively only so long as they could keep alive their youthful responses. A number did not live into middle age. Some died romantically young, others like Fitzgerald died old while still chronologically young. Of those who survived beyond fifty, almost all were engaged in reiterating the experiences of their youth or continued, as did Hemingway, to write out of a fading memory of emotional and intellectual premises established during the time of their first intense engagement of life.

They were, in fact, the first American literary generation to make being young into both a style of life and a state of grace. It is largely because of their influence that so many Americans are unable to perceive experience except as something that happens to one up to the age of thirty, or to understand that life can on occasion be other than a process of losing the intensities one was once able to feel. At the end of that fateful confrontation between Gatsby and Tom Buchanan in the Plaza Hotel, Nick Carraway suddenly remembers that it is his thirtieth birthday—"Thirty—the promise of a decade of loneliness, a thinning list of single men to know, a thinning brief-case of enthusiasm, thinning hair." Read for the first time at eighteen, the passage seems one of the most poignant in the novel. But then, perhaps years later, we come to recognize that our sympathies should go not to Nick but to Fitzgerald. It is his limited vision of the possibilities of life which is exposed here, even as it is this same limitation which makes Gatsby a convincing and pathetic character.

One reason for this preoccupation with youth is that the first world war had the effect of seeming to annihilate past history and the old styles of history. Hence, the generation which had fought in the war felt urgently the need to establish new premises, to redefine the terms of existence. Not only was this necessarily a task for youth, but it placed unique and dramatic emphasis on the responses of youth. Only the young were sensitive and adjustable enough to be able to determine whether a given emotion or experience conformed to the new standards of authenticity produced by the war. Besides, they were the ones who had "been there," been initiated, either directly or vicariously, had heard all the big words and learned that those words did not describe how they felt or what they had been through. Thus, the literature of the Twenties is not merely a narcissistic but a testing literature, one in which writers were trying to create an accurate new idiom and at the same time determine the truth or falsity of a radically new experience— most often according to the responses of a provisional and existential, inevitably youthful self.

Fortunately, there were elements that worked powerfully to their advantage. First, there was the fact that their consciousness of being unique, and their experience unprecedented, was validated by social and moral changes so profound that a literary career might be constructed around the process simply of recording them. These writers were in a position to be among the first to witness such changes, and they were aided greatly by what Frederick J. Hoffman once called their creatively "useful innocence," their small-town sensitivity to forms of conduct which, in spite of their surface sophistication, they could not help judging by the provincial standards they had been brought up on. It is not surprising that some of their best work has the incandescent quality of the astonished spectator, privileged to be on the scene of first encounters involving people who suddenly seem no longer to know by what assumptions they should behave.

Secondly, their prolonged apprenticeship in Europe enabled them to view American life from the perspective not only of distance but of adversary cultural values. They had inherited from their predecessors—most notably Lewis, Mencken, and Van Wyck Brooks—an intellectual arrogance, a disdain for bourgeois society, and a belief in the absolute supremacy of art and the artist, which were formed into a metaphysics under the, tutelage of Stein and Pound. They became cosmopolitan provincials abroad; they learned to judge America by essentially élitist European standards; and of course they found America provincial. But since they were themselves provincial, their attitudes retained a dimension of ambivalence that helped to humanize their satire and finally made it seem an expression more of regret than contempt.

They had, in short, a strong sense of belonging to, or being able to identify imaginatively with, place, perhaps just because they were physically so displaced—not only from home but from the past represented by home. They may have been creatively stimulated by the experience of living in a dramatic, changing present, but they could also feel anxious and uncertain and in need of the structures of coherence and identity they had left behind in the Midwest and South. This undoubtedly accounts for the fact that Hemingway and Fitzgerald were so continuously preoccupied with *procedural* questions, with the effort to formulate dependable rules of feeling and conduct. Hemingway's works can be read as a series of instruction manuals on how to respond to and behave in the testing situations of life now that the rules have changed. It might also be argued that some of his most dependable instructions are those he was able to reclaim from the past, in particular the American frontier past, the lessons of courage, fidelity, and honor which might still have the power to influence human conduct when all other values were being called into question. Fitzgerald's best novels are restatements of Henry James's great theme: the implications of the misuse of power over those who are innocent and helpless by those who are strong and unscrupulous.

In short, one finds in these writers and in some of their contemporaries a concern with the moral authenticity of certain traditions they might have presumed to be outmoded. It may be expressed only in a nostalgic recurrence to the locales that provided security in childhood—Hemingway's Big Two-Hearted River or Wolfe's Old Catawba. But it may also involve complex loyalties and codes of honor that once gave a human dimension to life—as Nick Carraway discovers through the experience of Gatsby, and Dick Diver through his marriage to Nicole. Both characters derived a "sense of the fundamental decencies" from their fathers, and so can evaluate and ultimately condemn a society in which such decencies no longer have meaning.

One of the very best of Fitzgerald's stories, "Babylon Revisited," is yet another expression of the desire to reconstitute certain values of moral discipline and self-control after the violent dissipations of the decade that ended in bankruptcy in 1929. Charlie Wales, a battered survivor of his time, returns to Paris in the hope of regaining custody of his daughter. To do this; he must prove to his sister-in-law that he has become a fit and responsible person. He very nearly succeeds in convincing her, but fails at the last moment when two of his old drinking friends reappear and destroy his chances of making a new life. Just as Nick after Gatsby's death wanted "the world to be in uniform and at a sort of moral attention forever," so Charlie felt the need "to jump back a whole generation and trust in character again as the eternally valuable element." But there is no escape from the consequences of his wasted past: "Again the memory of those days swept over him like a nightmare—the people they had met traveling; then people who couldn't add a row of figures or speak a coherent sentence...the women and girls carried screaming with drink or drugs out of public places--

--The men who locked their wives out in the snow, because the snow of twenty-nine wasn't real snow. If you didn't want it to be snow, you just paid some money."

The act of moral reclamation may be a necessity for every literary generation. In America we do not so much build on tradition as steal from it those elements we think may help us to understand the always unprecedented experience of our own time. The Twenties writers had a singular relation to the problem. They had the strongest sense that their experience was indeed unprecedented, and that the older modes of literary statement were inadequate to describe it. They, therefore, became excessively preoccupied *with* experience and, in both their writing and their lives, with the innovative and defiant. For reasons of temperament and historical position they were fixated permanently at the level of *rite de passage*, where they were condemned forever to play the roles of rebellious sons and wayward daughters, able to find their identity only in the degree of their *opposition* to the literary and social conventions of the past.

Yet in reviewing their achievement one is struck by how often their most admirable qualities seem to have been achieved at those rare moments when the writer was able, perhaps by accident, perhaps out of desperation, to transcend the limits of the adversary stance and define his materials in some clear relation to the sustaining values of an older tradition. If Fitzgerald and Hemingway experienced such moments, as some of their best work would seem to indicate, they did so only occasionally; because the life of their own time absorbed them much too completely, and they were never able to see that life in a consistently maintained moral perspective.

All that Dos Passos essentially had to support his intricately panoramic vision of American society were the values of an adversary politics, and it is significant that as he grew older, his vision did not deepen: only his *politics* aged. E.E. Cummings and Hart Crane were, in their very different ways, poetically adversary. Cummings made a limited kind of artistic convention out of wit and irreverence, while Crane, like Wolfe, sought all his life for a convention that would give shape and significance to the chaotic responses of his personality. Both poets had the defect of being confined by personality, and Crane in particular existed in that state of psychic nihilism in which, as one critic has observed, "any move is possible because none is necessary."

The examples of Faulkner and, on a much lower level, Thornton Wilder should serve to remind us that there were alternatives to the more fashionable positions taken by so many of the Twenties generation. There were alternatives *if* one possessed, as Wilder did, an intellectual culture broad enough to enable one to draw creatively on the whole of Western literary tradition, or *if* one had Faulkner's access to the abundant resources of the Southern tradition. But without these advantages, supplemented by talent of very large size, too many of the Twenties writers remained locked into their first youthful responses to an experience that was too overwhelmingly intense to serve as very much more than the material of an often brilliant, but very personal and limited literature. They may be forever established in our minds as the immensely charismatic personages of one of the most dramatic decades in our literary history. But it is significant that we can never separate them from the image we retain of the life of their time, just as they could never separate themselves and, in so doing, become larger than their experience, its imaginative possessors, the shapers of those truths it contained which might have made timeless in art what is otherwise lost to history.

Most of the attitudes of the Twenties may seem frivolous or downright subversive in the context of our present urgencies. The dedication to the Flaubertian ideal of the artist, the elitist contempt for the bourgeois and egalitarian, the belief in individual experience as a dependable source of general truth, the belief in the *individual*—all these were heavily damaged in the ideological wars of the Thirties, and the intervening decades have done nothing to restore them except as the chic postures of museum romance. It is true that the treatment given certain aspects of American life by the

Twenties writers has rendered them unavailable to us, but the small town and Midwest, the sensitive young man fighting to survive in a world of giant Babbitts, the discovery of sex, liquor, war, and Europe are simply no longer representative of experience most of us think important. The social novel based on the possibility of connection and communication among social groups, the abrasive reality of social class, has ceased to be a form in which American writers can effectively work, and the old-style picaresque novel died with Jack Kerouac. The minority literature of the last twenty years has little in common with the Twenties tradition, while the retreat from realistic social documentation in the so-called fabulist writers has made that tradition seem even more obsolete. The use of internal metaphors and pseudo-myths that are validated *not* by objective reality, but only by the action of the work in which they are used—such an effect may owe something to the experimentation of the Twenties, but the metaphysics behind it is very different. Vonnegut's preoccupation with a vast society of cartoon figures bedeviled by cosmic conspiracies, in which the individual is helpless or ridiculous or so emotionally trivialized that he feels nothing—these too clearly belong to another era, a new configuration of reality and time. Apparently, the novel has once again made its adjustment to the shifts of history. Yet there is a significance to be noted if one juxtaposes two of the best-known lines in the literature of the two periods: "So we beat on," says Fitzgerald's Nick Carraway; "So it goes," says Vonnegut's Billy Pilgrim. The difference between the statements is metaphorical and perhaps historically inevitable. But the first tells us something important about why it is that the Twenties continue to possess our imaginations and command our respect. The second tells us something important about the ground we have covered from the excitement and idealism of being young *then* to the dread of being old in the Seventies.

It may be that we have grown in wisdom, if wisdom is the capacity to be cutely cynical about what is happening to the world. But what we have lost is more than romantic sentiment. It is some luxury of feeling and caring, and it is a sense of the possibilities of a life, which over the years and after all that has happened, we have evidently ceased to love.

The Lost Generation:
War, Home, and Exile

Philip Young

*Philip Young came to Penn State in 1959 as Professor of American
Literature; in 1966 he was made Research Professor of English and Fellow
of the Institute for the Arts and Humanistic Studies. He was named Evan
Pugh Professor of English in 1980. Born in Boston, he received his B. A.
from Amherst College, served four years in World War II as an artillery
officer, European Theater, then took his doctorate at the University of Iowa
in 1948. He taught there, next at New York University, Kansas State
University, and the University of Minnesota. He received an honorary
doctorate from Westminster College in 1970.*

*In 1957 as a State Department Specialist in India he gave a series of
lectures on American literature at a dozen universities; on a "Roving
Fulbright" in 1962-63 he visited a number of French and Italian universities
for the same purpose. In the United States he has lectured coast to coast,
border to border.*

*Best known for his work on Hemingway, his first book on the subject
appeared in 1952, and was subsequently published in England, German,
Spanish, and Japanese. A 1959 pamphlet on Hemingway has been translated
into Pushtu, Polish, Urdu, Greek, Arabic, Marathi, and many other
languages. His book* Ernest Hemingway: a Reconsideration, *1966, is still
in print. Young has edited or co-edited two of Hemingway's posthumous
works, and several other books. He has published essays on many other
American writers, and has contributed entries to various encyclopedias,
including the* Britannica. *His work has appeared in the* Kenyon, Southern,
and Sewanee Reviews, *the* Atlantic Monthly, *and many other journals.*

*He is known too for his studies in "American Myth"—chiefly those
of Rip Van Winkle and Pocahontas, which were included in his* Three Bags
Full: Essays in American Fiction *and have been frequently anthologized.
His 1977 book* Revolutionary Ladies—*aristocratic, Loyalist women caught
up in the war with England—won a prize in American history. His most
recent book is* Hawthorne's Secret: an Un-Told Tale, *now reprinted in
paperback. He continues work on Herman Melville—perhaps on a book
to be called* Melville's Fiction, *and* The Family Stamp.

In his present essay, it is difficult to know for certain whether Professor Young is striking the stance of devil's advocate, or entertaining serious doubts about the existence of "A Lost Generation." The marked effect of his quarrel here with the Generation's spokesman historian, Malcolm Cowley, in any case, is to force us to think far more carefully about our use of this often ill-defined concept. Was there ever such a thing as a "Lost Generation," he asks. How a "generation," how "lost"? After mentioning his general misgivings over the abuses attending such a concept, and establishing that even Cowley admits that "it was more a lucky than a lost generation," the author sets up a definite set of criteria by which to examine the eligibility of certain writers into this exclusive club. What finally holds the few exiles together who qualify, he says, was not Cowley's sense of group identity, but rather their common war experience, their exile in Paris, and a passionate devotion to writing.

* * *

If America ever really had a "Lost Generation: War, Home, and Exile" it is probably to be found in a group of cultivated, successful men and women who were truly exiled—expelled from their homes, their properties confiscated, their lives threatened till they could book passage. This was no trickle of writers and other artists, though there were a few among them. In all they were 100,000 people, and that at a time when Philadelphia, the second largest city in the British empire, was smaller than the Pennsylvania small town where this is written. They were, of course, the American-born Loyalists of our Revolution, who lost just about everything—all because they did their duty as they had learned it, and opposed the idea of colonial Independence, as did at the start virtually all Patriots, and as some Patriot leaders continued to do even after its Declaration was signed. The people born, say, during the years somewhere around 1750 really made up a generation—people in the same boat, as they took off for England, Canada, and Nova Scotia. They were not a particularly artistic group, except for a couple of painters; there were a few poets and essayists. It was not a literary age on either side. Yet where Gertrude Stein could say "America is my country, Paris my home," she was clearly found. This generation died thinking of America as its country too, but not of London or Halifax as home. They had lost both.

But "Lost Generation" means to us another group, and since the term is so widely used, at least in some circles, it might not be a bad idea to consider if there ever was such a thing. I was recently asked to do exactly that, and thought I'd best go to the library and find out. The results were mixed. There is no card in the catalogue. As for encyclopedias: the *Britannica*, old and new, no. *Grolier, Collier's, World Book,* no. *International* yes, but too skimpy to register. *Encyclopedia Americana* aha!—one column of solid information: authoritative, probably definitive, the Word:

A common but misleading designation...Origin is something Stein told Hemingway in Paris that he used as epigraph for *Sun Also Rises* and made famous. Born of experience of literate young Americans in World War I...Uprooted by war, disillusioned with ideals and traditions of own upbringing. Reaction: philosophic despair, personal hedonism. Expatriation and art to compensate. Dislike of America (Prohibition), Paris antithetical (also cheap). Pioneers: Stein and Pound. Presence of Joyce. Names of American poets and novelists in Montparnasse...Crash of the Market in '29...Henry Miller rings down curtain, only Gertrude left. Irony of tag in that Hemingway thought it nonsense; Stein got it from proprietor of a garage. Hemingway right: Renaissance of American letters in 1920s by people known as lost.

But that doesn't answer the question. The term is there, but called a tag, misleading and with a disreputable past. Worse, I had not read through the first sentence before a sense of déjà vu began hailing down: for me to say there was a Lost Generation because it's entered here means only that I said there was; fatal to the argument that those paragraphs weren't written by someone else.* But it was on the same trip to the library that I made a momentous, uncatalogued discovery. There has got to be a Lost Generation because there is a *Lost Generation Journal.* Originally out of Tulsa, Oklahoma, then moved to Carbondale, Illinois, it is edited by a professor of journalism who kept his Lost Generation Archives, like Hemingway's manuscripts, in the vault of a bank. The existence of this periodical nails down the concept; you can't have a magazine devoted to the study of something that never was.

Or can you? In his maiden issue the editor leads off with a standard discussion of the term in question, which arrives, however, at a clear conclusion: unless we mean by it a Literary Generation, the Lost one "doesn't exist"—contains "virtually no one." I never thought we meant anything else, but the editor didn't get away with his argument anyhow, and in the next issue prints a rejoinder to it by a minor member of the Generation. There was *too* a Lost Generation, he says, which "consisted entirely of Harold Stearns," who with a book to his credit arrived in Paris and became a "souse." Stearns' autobiography, originally *A Street I Know* (1935), was reissued as *The Confessions of a Harvard Man* (Paget Press, 1984), which I reviewed for *The New Criterion* (December, 1984). Stearns was not in the War, but was genuinely, totally, and willfully *lost* in Paris. Asked about his drunken, sloppy-hilarious appearance as Harvey Stone in *The Sun Also Rises*, he approved it. And so the editor of the *Journal* and his enormous staff continued bringing out a periodical that was not sure of its subject.

Just another sign of the continuing interest in the American Twenties, the nation's favorite decade. Serious concern with its writers, which began over fifty years ago with a book by Malcolm Cowley, got virtually out of

---

*What might have been added is that but for a most belated act we might never have had the term. *The Sun Also Rises* was professionally typed and ready for the printer before Hemingway pencilled in Miss Stein's remark.

control. Minor members of an alleged group became object of massive scrutiny. A recent book on Robert McAlmon is excellent. One on Harry Crosby (*Black Sun*, 1976) is brilliant. (I wrote a jacket blurb for its author, Geoffrey Wolff: "utterly engrossing...A frequently exciting, wholly satisfying book. Beautiful.") Clearly this would continue until there is nobody left to write about. *But*, I asked in 1975, were there no women in that generation—no American female writers living and loving and writing in Paris? There certainly were. The biggest development since 1975 in the subject at hand has been the outpouring of books about them. (These books underline what I have always thought the secret appeal of Paris in those years: sexual freedom.)

But to return to those writers we have long called a "generation." Were they? And were they "lost"? And what do we mean by these words? In 1973 Malcolm Cowley published a second book on the subject called *A Second Flowering: Works and Days of the Lost Generation*. On this occasion *The Southern Review* asked me to do a full-scale piece on its author and his career. This seemed a happy thought. I had been admirer of his since 1940 when I began subscribing to *The New Republic*. He is the Generation's spokesman and historian; he writes well himself. *Exile's Return* (1934) had recorded and interpreted his generation and bequeathed it to mine, twenty years later. Further, when I looked for previous works on Cowley from which I might do a little academic shoplifting I discovered there were precisely none. I was on my own.

I began by rereading that famous book, and got the idea that there was indeed a Lost Generation, though it would be unfair to stick him with that label, since he writes it with misgivings, never having found a better one. He uses the life of Harry Crosby to sum up the "themes" he'd developed, which tied his exiles together:

The separation from home, the effects of service in the ambulance corps, the exile in France, then other themes, bohemianism, the religion of art, the escape from society, the effort to defend one's originality...then the whole final period of demoralization when the whole philosophical structure crumbled from within...

The philosophical structure that crumbled had never been put together, in my opinion, but let it go. It is a fine book (and in its revised, 1951, edition even better); both participant and diarist, its author happily shared what he long ago called Fitzgerald's "double vision": he was both a drinker at the long party and the sober observer of it. I then read or reread all his other books, and finally got to the new one. It is a series of essays— some marked with brilliance, others with an over-familiarity that is simply stunning—on eight writers, to wit Hart Crane, Cummings, Dos Passos, Faulkner, Fitzgerald, Hemingway, Thorton Wilder and Thomas Wolfe. Their Works and Days make up, this time, his Lost Generation. Along the way I had bestowed a good deal of praise, along with a few digs, but toward the end I voiced an objection:

My final quibble with this book is not so much with the idea of a lost generation as with the notion of a "generation"—so far as this suggests a "group"—at all. The "sense of group identity" that Cowley imputes to his gathering of writers strikes me as mostly a myth. Beyond their contemporaneity the only thing they had absolutely in common was talent and a passionate dedication to writing, which practically all good writers have. The critic tries to attribute a considerable amount of common historical experience to them as well, but the thing that is supposed to have done most to "lose" them was the War, and of his eight writers five were never in it. Some of these people read some of the others, but by and large they did not—except by reputation—know each other well enough to nod. They had no real consciousness of any group; only Fitzgerald, the most generous, seems ever to have thought about "My Generation" at all. What had Faulkner and Hemingway to do with Cummings, Wilder, and Crane?

And so on. I did admit the fact that Hemingway and Crane were both born on July 21, 1899, and had died of their own volition—even conceded that Hemingway had a theory about Crane's suicide ("picked up the wrong sailor"). And I held off saying that some of these writers—Faulkner and Wolfe, for two—did not strike me as Lost Generation writers at all. But I did suggest that the critic had spent so much time compiling lists of American writers born between 1891 and 1905—which he began in 1951 with 224 names, and extends in this book to 385—because listing and counting obscure the fact that something else is missing: the sense of identity that makes a group a group. I dodged the question of "lost" as hopelessly vague.

Malcolm responded to me in a letter of some length. He was not as pleased as I wanted him to be with what I had intended overall as a tribute (it appeared right beside Austin Warrens "Homage to Allen Tate"; some of Cowley's friends, however, were pleased). He was, he said, in mild disgruntlement, and his main objection was right here: even if they seldom met together the writers of his Second Flowering (which he now refers to as "wartime" generation, despite his subtitle) really did make a group. Some of them were old college chums, but more they thought of themselves as brothers in arms, up the establishment. Where, he wanted to know, did I get the idea that five of his eight were never in the war?

Well, from history, or biography—specifically from Cowley. Fitzgerald and Faulkner, he goes on, were in uniform even if they didn't get overseas, and both imagined themselves dead on the battlefield. Wolfe and Crane were too young to be drafted; but they and Kenneth Burke and Matty Josephson worked in shipyards. Well again, I was never too young to be drafted, and have never worked in a shipyard, but I think things go on there that are different from war. I am committed to the importance and validity of vicarious experience, so I have to credit the combat fantasies of Fitzgerald and Faulkner as meaningful, but I don't have to consider them the same as being there in the vulnerable flesh. Mr. Cowley concludes this part of the letter, the only relevant part, by saying that he could go on and on defending his concept, and that in his book he was really thinking of a larger group, and most of *them* were soldiers.

I'm not sure that is valid, though to be sure it was Cowley himself who earlier pointed out the remarkable number of writers-to-be who drove ambulances or camions in World War I; Dos Passos, Cummings, Hemingway, Julian Green, Harry Crosby, John Howard Lawson, Louis Bromfield, Dashiell Hammett (and Cowley), among others. Thus as I pondered these matters I was slow in recognizing something more obvious: the old problem of a writer having some essays that could appear together in a book, and a publisher willing to issue it, and then through the title, and preface or introduction, writer or publisher or both trying to impose more unity on the pieces than they actually have. Thus what Malcolm is saying to me is that there *was* a Generation, but that its members were not the people he put under the heading of one this time. Without the subtitle, and the concept that is supposed to inform the book and help hold it together (and the overfamiliar material) there was nothing basically the matter.

And perhaps the trouble with me, among others, is literal-or narrow-mindedness. But it does seem to me that to qualify for membership in this group a writer should 1) have had experience of World War I—at least osmotic from having been on the scene of some of it, and 2) have spent some bohemian period in Paris. If we accept that, then of the writers in Cowley's recent collection exactly three qualify: Cummings, Dos Passos, and Hemingway. Some generation. If we ease up a little and require only one of these criteria we still eliminate Faulkner and Wolfe as a minimum.

To appreciate the importance of that war to those who were in it, most of us have to read, study. There is nothing in our personal histories that would allow us to understand intuitively. A well known novelist who *was* too young for World War II has often told me how he envies my experience of it; I would hand it to him gratis if I could, on a worn silver platter. I do not believe that my long involvement in that fracas had *any* lasting effect on me; even my hatred of the military diminishes as the years go by. All I wanted was to get out of uniform and on with other matters. My war was no watershed; there was no orgy of pleasure or relief at its passing. No Jazz Age: new problems, A Bomb, Cold War. No crash of the stock market to terminate a tidy period like the Twenties. I can't even remember any parties. The first war was very different in its effect on people, and I can offer an example of what it (and to be sure subsequent experience of a similar sort) could mean to another soldier. Its extremity is what makes the point.

Some years ago when I was going through Hemingway's manuscripts so as to order and identify those great stacks of paper I was one morning in the library of his widow's penthouse, where there were many things she had never put in the bank. In a closet behind an enormous gun, with which I believe one shoots elephants, I found a large file of Hemingway letters. These were not for me, I was into manuscript. But I couldn't help noticing the number of letters the author had written and never mailed; there were also letters that had apparently been returned after his death. Some of these were none of my business or anyone else's except his wife's, but some of them were—in particular three letters which he never mailed to me, which I deeply regret though they are full of complaints about a book on him he'd not yet seen, and bizarre (usually obscene) threats. There were other letters in part *about* me, and after I had come across about the fifth reference to what Non-Combat Characters like me cannot understand and never WILL understand I busted into the living room where Mary was at her desk and said for Crying Out Loud where did he get this non-combat stuff? I have three battle stars and a decoration. Mrs. Hemingway is very quick and she looked at me for no more than a second before saying Philip, if Ernest had known that there would *never* have been any trouble. There was a great deal of trouble, but that's not the point. He divided the whole world into combats and non-combats.

The First World War really made a difference, and the great esthetic exile that followed it was based on the previous experience of Europe, even though in most cases that had been unpleasant. Those young men were fantastically eager to get in it; I've forgotten how many times Hemingway flunked his physical (such a dream in my day!) before the Red Cross finally took him. And it was the War that did most to "disengage" them from society, and make them restless for more adventures abroad. But for the war there would have been no Twenties as we know them, and no expatriation on the scale we measure. It was a new world, which Fitzgerald with his Princeton commission and Brooks Brothers uniform described rather well: "this thing, knocked to pieces, leaky, red hot, threatening to blow up..."

Paris, my second criterion, made a difference—first of all because it was not America. I have seen a letter Hemingway wrote up in Michigan shortly after the war in which he says he was willing to die for this country but would be damned if he'd live in it. It is ironic that America should remember so warmly those who only wanted to get out. And it is seldom remarked how little they knew about their country and its cultural past. Cowley confessed for them all some time ago their ignorance of virtually all American literature before 1910, his date. There is a lot they would have liked, as many of them eventually did, in Melville, Whitman, and even Emerson, Thoreau, and Hawthorne. As late as 1935 Hemingway could dismiss *Moby-Dick* out of hand (later on he rectified that), pronounce Thoreau (whose prose he failed to surpass) "unreadable," and lump together Emerson, Hawthorne, and Whittier. I doubt that he had read one of them. A man who can claim as he did that Emerson did not know that a new classic bears no relation to old classics could not have read even "The American Scholar," most famous of the essays, which says exactly that but much better.

But, if they were getting out, why Paris? Anyone who reads books at all knows the answers to that; a single one, Hemingway's *Moveable Feast*— very minor, very beautiful—will provide many of them. But I like to think of the man who came after the ball was over, swept up the debris, and wrote the American expatriate epitaph. Henry Miller didn't arrive until 1930, and was already 38. It was a different Paris now—Quasimodo's Paris, he called it—and a different sort of American in it. The streets were cancerous to his view; he once went five days with nothing to eat. For some reason I always remember the line: "Irene [a Russian princess] has the clap, Osborn has bronchitis, and I have the piles." His adventures burlesqued the expatriate romance, the potentially tragic hero of it was now a clown. Time was that no literate American came back from Paris without an illegal *Tropic of Cancer* smuggled away in his luggage. Miller had penetrated deepest into the city and established a quite different vision of it, at once comic, anguished, and corrosive. But even he, looking back later, would remember a city whose atmosphere was "saturated with creation"; of a miserable place where he had lived for years would say "the whole street is given up to quiet, joyous work...men and women devoted to things of the spirit." If Miller could remember it that way, anyone could.

But if the experience of a particular war and of a particularly attractive city were extremely important in the lives of at least a few young American writers that does not make them automatically a "generation," nor mean that they were a "lost" one. In his *After the Lost Generation*, John Aldridge called it a generation in the "purest sense." But what makes a "generation"? First, I should think, its members should have been born at about the same time. So does Mr. Cowley, and to demonstrate that the writers of his generation were so born he worked up his list of 385 names of American writers. There is nothing objectionable about this as a hobby; it is not a bad way to keep busy without actually working. But I think the list has almost no significance. In the first place, to get it that long he has to come up with some very remarkable writers. Mathilde Eiker, Margaret Leech, and Charles Merz, all born in 1893: identify two out of three. In the second place, to get so many names he has to let the period of birth run from 1891 to 1905. It does not seem to me that anyone born fourteen years before or after I was would belong to my generation—if there were one. Further: if we took the years 1930-1944, and really scraped the barrel, would it be so hard to come up with as many names? No, it wouldn't.

For a number of people to constitute a recognizable generation, in the second place, there has to be some sense of affinity among them, a consciousness of self as part of a group, a feeling of things shared. Perhaps Cowley thinks as he does about his writers because he, at least, has exactly what it takes to belong—not just the war and Paris, but this very awareness: his first literary essay, written in 1921, was called "This Youngest Generation." Fitzgerald, too well fixed financially to live the bohemian life in France and never in the war, also felt himself part of a larger whole. But this requires a magnanimity of spirit and a degree of humility—a willingness to recognize that one is not all that unique—that these two men were blessed with and a lot of other writers lacked. "Hemingway had no feeling for the group," Malcolm wrote me. I believe it. Faulkner, Wolfe— one could make his own list of those who didn't.

As for Lost, that is a big little word, and far from clear in the present connection. If I understood *Exile's Return*, Cowley meant by it that the people he was writing about were uprooted, unattached to any region or tradition; were educated for a different world than they graduated into, and accepted no older guides to conduct. All this makes an uncertain amount of sense. But if the same observations may be made of the Beat Generation, or the nameless one of the American Sixties, then what? John Aldridge remarked that the same expatriate writers felt themselves "the specially doomed and forsaken"; this is the Poor Little Lambs-Kipling-Wiffenpoof concept. It might be found in the likes of a very early Dos Passos novel called *One Man's Initiation*, but that is lost too. Lost has many meanings, few of which apply here. "Lacking in confidence"? No. As in "no longer visible"? Scarcely. "Ruined or destroyed"? Harry Crosby, and if you include him perhaps Hart Crane. "Spiritually or morally ruined or destroyed"? In the eyes of some of their elders, it may be, or the devout. Art was the religion, morality was subject to redefinition. They were not ruined in their own eyes.

The point might be not they *were* lost but *had* lost—such things as the values of pre-war, middle class America, the virtues of their upbringing. There certainly was a Generation Gap: Hemingway and his parents presented a bottomless case, and he was not alone. Yet that things had *been* lost is still misleading, since the values had been intentionally discarded. Lost as meaning "inaccessible to good influence" expresses what the *patron* of Gertrude Stein's garage meant about his mechanic *perdue* and little else.

In fact, there is news on that score. The definitive account of how "Une Generation Perdue" came about was given for all time by Hemingway in *A Moveable Feast*, and so was his contempt for the term. The *patron* told Miss Stein's mechanic "You are all a *generation perdue*." Then she applied it to Hemingway. "That's what you all are. All of you young people who served in the war. You are a lost generation." He then dismisses "her lost generation talk and all the dirty, easy labels." But this story has now been independently annihilated by James R. Mellow in his book on Stein, and by revelations taken from the Hemingway manuscripts at the Kennedy Library by Jacqueline Tavernier-Courbin. The plain facts are that "The Lost Generation—A Novel" was the author's original title for his *Sun Also Rises*, and that when he first wrote the tale of the lost mechanic it had nothing whatsoever to do the with war. Neither the *patron* or Hemingway mentions the war. I think we should speak of "the so-called Lost Generation," or at the very least put the term in quotes.

As for the *Lost Generation Journal*, I regret having predicted in 1975 that it was about to expire. As of 1988, it has not done so, though its last issue is dated 1986. I bring you the latest word. If you'd like to subscribe the editor is Thomas W. Wood, Jr., and home plate is Box 167-D, Route 1, St. James, MO 65559.

The Harlem Renaissance:
One Facet of an Untwisted Kaleidoscope

Darwin T. Turner

Darwin T. Turner is well qualified to discuss the flowering of black literature. Born in 1931 in Cincinnati, Ohio, he received his B.A. from the University of Cincinnati at the age of 16, his M.A. at 18, and his Ph.D. at 25 from the University of Chicago. He has been producing books and articles ever since that range from Nathaniel Hawthorne's The Scarlet Letter to In a Minor Chord: Three Afro-American Writers and their Search for Identity. *He has contributed to nearly every publication in the country with articles that discuss the Black novelist, the Black educator, the Black aesthetic, and the Black genius.*

He is Phi Beta Kappa and a member of many more learned societies with a string of awards and grants that are too numerous to be mentioned. He recently received the "Distinguished Writer Award" from the Middle Atlantic Writers' Association. Currently, Dr. Turner is a Distinguished Professor of English and Chair of African-American World Studies at the University of Iowa.

Stressing the multiplicity of patterns of Black life during the 1920s Mr. Turner launches here into an examination of some of the most notable of those patterns—particularly the flowering of Black writers but stresses that a slight shift of the kaleidoscope could produce other patterns to examine. It is precisely this awareness of the diversity of Black life that leads Professor Turner to examine one facet more closely to try to determine the relative merit of a term that became a password for a whole era, the Jazz Age, or Jazzed Abandon.

Beginning by attacking the stereotyped image of Black life as one long night club tour Mr. Turner commences to describe the reality of Black life as seen by Black authors rather than white authors attempting to depict what could only be a vision in translation. Mr. Turner surmises that it was precisely the success of Black musicals that painted a picture of a people given over to abandon and exuberance that compelled Black writers struggling to define themselves in a white society to include this successful ingredient in their novels and plays and poems. But underneath these compelling scenes where inhibitions are remote lie the real issues decked out in more sober colors.

86

Professor Turner tells us to shift the focus of the kaleidoscope just a half turn to see that black writers were really examining the search for self through ancestral means, alienation from the ruling white society and defiance of that oppressive society that causes Blacks to turn against themselves and to begin aping white behavior. The scenes of abandonment then become a major vehicle for expressing one's radical self in defiance of a repressive white society where Black people's dreams outweigh their abilities to achieve them.

But it is a realistic picture and not a romantic one that Mr. Turner paints for us. Enumerating the limitations of the era, he nevertheless faces up to its true importance—that this growth of Black American writers encouraged later generations of Black writers and raised Black consciousness to a level hardly anticipated by these writers. What's more it left a mythic memory that Blacks were "talented, rebellious, proud and beautiful," that has resulted in the expansive flow of Black artists today.

* * *

Geraldine's brash cry, "What you see is what you get," is appropriate comment on the tendency of many Americans to fix their attention on only a particular aspect of Black life in America—usually the most spectacular aspect. If they would twist the base of the kaleidoscope of Black life, the multi-colored fragments would re-arrange themselves into different patterns, some of them startlingly different. But few viewers choose to adjust the kaleidoscope.

As a result, out of the many patterns of Black life during the 1920s, the dominant image emblazoned on the vision of America is the Harlem Renaissance. By the same process, from the Harlem Renaissance itself, a Jazzed Abandon has become the most memorable spectacle. James Weldon Johnson's description of reactions to Harlem summarizes the legend of the Harlem Renaissance:

It is known in Europe and the Orient, and it is talked about by natives in the interior of Africa. It is farthest known as being exotic, colourful, and sensuous; a place of laughing, singing, and dancing; a place where life wakes up at night. This phase of Harlem's fame is most widely known because, in addition to being spread by ordinary agencies, it has been proclaimed in story and song. And certainly this is Harlem's most striking and fascinating aspect. New Yorkers and people visiting New York from the world over go to the night-clubs of Harlem and dance to such jazz music as can be heard nowhere else; and they get an exhilaration impossible to duplicate. Some of these seekers after new sensations go beyond the gay night-clubs; they peep in under the more seamy side of things; they nose down into lower strata of life. A visit to Harlem at night—the principal streets never deserted, gay crowds skipping from one place of amusement to another, lines of taxicabs and limousines standing under the sparkling lights of the entrances to the famous night-clubs, the subway kiosks swallowing and disgorging crowds all night long—gives the impression that Harlem never sleeps and that the inhabitants thereof jazz through existence.[1]

Johnson continued, "But, of course, no one can seriously think that the two hundred thousand and more Negroes in Harlem spend their nights on any such pleasance."[2] So we too can say, "Surely, no one can seriously think that this picture or even the entire 'Renaissance' constitutes the totality of the patterns housed in the kaleidoscope of Black life during the 1920s."

Even if one examines only the literary portraiture of the decade, one discerns more than a single image as the minute, tinted mirrors arrange and rearrange themselves into diverse patterns reflecting the actuality of Black life or reflecting the psyches of the Black and white artists who depicted that life. A knowledgeable individual twists the instrument to view the primitivism depicted by such white authors as Julia Peterkin, Eugene O'Neill, Sherwood Anderson, Dubose Heyward, Mary Wiborg, and William Faulkner, or the exotic abandon simulated by Carl Van Vechten. But a slight adjustment reshapes those images into the cultural elitism revealed by Van Vechten and cherished by W.E.B. DuBois. Another adjustment reveals the integrationist optimism of Langston Hughes, or the pan-Africanism of W.E.B. DuBois, or the Black nationalism of Marcus Garvey. Examine rural Southern Blacks from the perspectives of Peterkin, Heyward, Faulkner, and Jean Toomer; or scrutinize the urban Northerners of Toomer, Claude McKay, Rudolph Fisher, Langston Hughes, and Countée Cullen. Smile at the enthusiastic and naive Carl Van Vechtens, Mabel Dodges, and other white patrons as they prance about with their trophies collected on safaris into the Black jungles; then scowl at the lynchers painted by Claude McKay and photographed by Walter White. Admire the "patient endurance" with which William Faulkner colored his Dilsey, but do not overlook the militant impatience that inflames McKay's poetic voice. Consider the African nationalism vaguely sketched by Cullen, Hughes, and McKay; but compare it with Hughes' poetic demands for American integration and McKay's impressionistic sketches of the damnable siren, America, that fascinates, challenges, and captivates Blacks. Excite yourselves with sexual abandon garishly painted by Van Vechten, Anderson, McKay, and Toomer; but study also the conservative, often frustrated Blacks portrayed by Jessie Fauset and Toomer. Weep for the impotent failures depicted by O'Neill and Paul Green; but rejoice with the bold, determined aspirants of Fauset and Fisher.

Beyond the literary spectrum, the images are equally diverse. The decade of the 1920s was ushered in by the triumphant return in 1919 of the highly-decorated Black 369th Infantry, which marched from the docks, down Broadway, and through Harlem, led every step of the way by James Europe's jazz band. But the decade was ushered in also by the "Red Summer" of 1919. In that year alone, according to historian John Hope Franklin, approximately twenty-five race riots in all sections of the country spilled blood on the streets of the democratic nation that, less than a year earlier, had won the war that, President Wilson boasted, would end all wars and would safe-guard democracy. Jazz was in vogue: Duke Ellington and Fletcher Henderson attracted thousands of excited people to hear their bands, and Louis Armstrong gained new fans with each performance. But poverty was in vogue also: Black migrants who could not find jobs and older residents who had lost theirs to a new influx of whites gave rent parties which remained gay as long as no one remembered that the only reason for the party was the inability to pay the rent. Occupants of Harlem for less than a decade, Blacks were buying homes for residence and for profit on a scale rivaling the stock market speculations of their white contemporaries; but hard times had already established residence in the South, as Waring Cuney revealed in "Hard Times Blues":

Hard Time Blues
I went down home
About a year ago
Things looked so bad
My heart was sore.
People had nothing
It was a sinning shame,
Everybody said
Hard times was to blame.

Great-God-A-Mighty
Folks feeling bad,
Lost all they ever had.

Sun was shining fourteen
Days and no rain,
Hoeing and planting
Was all in vain.
It was hard times, Lawd,
All around,
Meal barrels empty,
Crops burnt to the ground.

Great-God-A-Mighty
Folks feeling bad
Lost all they ever had.

Skinny looking children
Bellies poking out,
Old pellagra
Without a doubt,
Old folks hanging' 'round
The cabin door
Aint seen things
This bad before.

Great-God-A-Mighty
Folks feeling bad,
Lost all they ever had.

Went to the Boss
At the Commissary Store,

Folks all hungry
Please don't close the door,
Want more food,
Little time to pay.
Boss Man laughed
And walked away.

Great-God-A-Mighty
Folks feeling bad,
Lost all they ever had.

Landlord coming 'round
When the rent's due,
Aint got the money
Take your home from you.
Takes your mule and horse
Even take your cow,
Says get off this land
You no good no how.

Great-God-A-Mighty
Folks feeling bad,
Lost all they ever had.

For Black folks, and many rural whites, times were bad—at the very height of the Jazz Age when Scott Fitzgerald's sheiks, flappers, and Gatsbys were staging their most lavish parties. Blacks were not naive about the times. With the assistance of Walter White, a Caucasian-looking Black, the N.A.A.C.P. launched its three-decade long campaign against lynching. *The Messenger*, a Black newspaper, advocated socialism as the only solution to the economic problems of Black Americans; and *The Crusader*, another Black newspaper, denounced American bigotry in tones that a subsequent generation would believe originated in the 1960s. Recognizing the inability of non-unionized workers to withstand the arbitrary practices of the bosses, Black workers struggled to enter or establish unions: In the Brotherhood of Sleeping Car Porters, A. Philip Randolph created the most enduring of them all. Scorning any hope for Black economic or political power in the United States, Marcus Garvey, a West Indian, enlisted thousands of new followers who wished to sail the Black Star Line back to Africa. Ironically, Garvey, an actual Black from an island, won more power and financial support in America than Eugene O'Neill ever envisaged for his fictional Emperor Jones, a Black American who seizes control of a Black island.

Such awareness of the multiplicity of patterns of Black life during the 1920s justifies a re-examination, necessarily brief and somewhat superficial, of the Harlem Renaissance, particularly the literary Renaissance—to determine the reasons for its image as Jazzed Abandon, to peruse more closely the more serious themes of the literature, and to reassess the significance of that Renaissance.

If we of the 1980s picture Black life in the 1920s as a riotous night club tour, we cannot blame the best-known white writers for our misconception. Ironically, although Blacks became so popular as a subject that almost every prominent American author of the decade featured them in at least one major work, most of these authors ignored the Harlem scene in their literature. Such obvious neglect prompts speculation about the reasons: Were the authors describing the Afro-Americans they knew best? Or were they deliberately creating Black characters who would contrast with and perhaps obscure the image of the proud Renaissance-Black?

Of course, in 1920, when O'Neill's *Emperor Jones* appeared, the Harlem Renaissance was less than a flutter in the heart of Alain Locke, a Black philosopher who named the era. O'Neill cannot be accused of ignoring what he could not have been expected to see. Situating his Black on a Caribbean island, O'Neill showed how fear, stripping away civilized veneer, reduces a man—in this instance, a Southern Black—to a primitive.

The contrast between the Renaissance and O'Neill's work, however, appears in *All God's Chillun Got Wings* (1924). This drama, necessarily set in the North, describes the pathetic relationship between a Black man, who aspires to be a lawyer, and the "fallen" white woman whom he marries. The woman, betrayed and deserted by a white lover, marries the Black but becomes insane—or more insane, according to your view. The Black fails to become a lawyer partly because his wife, not wanting him to succeed, interferes with his study. The more crucial reason for his failure, however, is that, whenever he is examined by whites, he forgets whatever he knows. In 1924, the year the play appeared, Jessie Fauset and Walter White published the first Black novels of the decade: *There Is Confusion*, which centers on the lives of middle-class Blacks in Philadelphia, among them a black graduate of a white medical school; and *The Fire in the Flint*, a protest against lynching. For three years, Black musicals had been the rage of Broadway theater. Black was in, by 1924. The next year *Survey Graphic* would focus an entire issue on the New Negro; James Weldon Johnson would hail Harlem as the capital of Black America; others would call it "Mecca." Despite these events, O'Neill provided Broadway with a Black protagonist whose aspiration exceeds his ability. Whatever O'Neill's reasons for the theme, the choice of an actor to portray the protagonist could not have been more ironic. The Black who panics when examined by whites was played by Paul Robeson, all-American football player (I believe that he was the first Black selected by Walter Camp as an All-American football player), a twelve-letter man in athletics, and a Phi Beta Kappa graduate, who earned one of the highest academic averages in the history of Rutgers University.

The spectacle of Black failure was continued by Paul Green, a North Carolinian who wrote more plays about Blacks than any other white person during the decade. In 1926 Green won the Pulitzer Prize for *In Abraham's Bosom*, a drama in which Black Abe McCrannie, during Reconstruction, tries futilely to establish a school for Blacks. In the same year, 1926, W.E.B.

DuBois, editor of *The Crisis*, the voice of the N.A.A.C.P., continuing a practice intended to encourage Black scholarship, published the pictures of the year's Black college graduates. Within a few years, DuBois would proudly announce that the large number of graduates prohibited his publishing the pictures of all.

Another memorable drama of the decade was Dubose Heyward's *Porgy*, now an American "classic," a story of a Black and crippled junk dealer, who strives to win Bess, a fallen woman, from Crown, a bad, bad man. Perhaps the most appropriate evaluation of the drama comes from W.E.B. DuBois, who insisted that he did not object to the play. Then, sniffing delicately from the rarified atmosphere surrounding a New England Brahmin who was a Ph.D. graduate from Harvard and had been a graduate student at Heidelberg, DuBois explained that, although he did not doubt that Heyward's Blacks existed in Charleston, South Carolina, he regretted Heyward's failure to portray the educated Blacks DuBois associated with when he visited that city.

During the 1920s William Faulkner foreshadowed his future stature with *The Sound and The Fury*, located primarily in Mississippi, with a glance at Cambridge, Massachusetts. Faulkner's major Black character in this novel is Dilsey, prototype of "the Black who endures." Like Green and O'Neill, Faulkner probably had not read Alain Locke's introduction to *The New Negro* (1925). Locke asserted,

Sentimental interest in the Negro has ebbed. We used to lament this as the falling off of our friends; now we rejoice and pray to be delivered both from self-pity and condescension. The mind of each racial group has had a better weaning, apathy or hatred on one side matching disillusionment or resentment on the other; but they face each other today with the possibility at least of entirely new mutual attitudes.[3]

The decade ended with a production of the extraordinarily popular *Green Pastures* (1930) by Marc Connelly. Based on Roark Bradford's *Ol' Man Adam and His Chillun*, the drama seems to retell the Old Testament from the perspective of a Black child at a church fish-fry. The narrator is not a child, however, but an adult.

However distorted their vision of Blacks may have been, well-known white Americans of the 1920s cannot be blamed for the exotic image of the night-club Black. That image comes from Blacks themselves and from white sympathizers.

It may have begun with *Shuffle Along* (1921), a brilliant and popular musical, written and directed by four Blacks—Flournoy Miller, Eubie Blake, Noble Sissle, and Aubrey Lyles. In the same year, *Shuffle Along* was succeeded by *Put and Take*, another musical by a Black—Irving C. Miller, who also produced *Liza* (1923), which was followed in the same year by *Runnin' Wild* by Miller and Lyles. The beauty of Afro-American chorus girls such as Florence Mills and Josephine Baker, the exotic foreign settings, the gaiety and the frenzy of these musicals and their successors may have cultivated in Broadway audiences a taste for particular depictions of Black life. Furthermore, these musicals may have created an image difficult to change.

Although it is located in the South, Sherwood Anderson's *Dark Laughter* (1925) conjures the image of a joyful, untroubled people who, themselves freed from the need to read Freud, laugh gently at frustrated whites, who repress their own sexual desires. The image of joy continues in Carl van Vechten's novel, *Nigger Heaven* (1926), set in Harlem. Although van Vechten later proclaimed his intention of familiarizing white readers with a cultured Black society, which gives soirées and speaks French, he glamorized the Scarlet Creeper, a sweetman (a gigolo), and he depicted Black night life with an excitement certain to allure readers.

The exoticism and gaiety appear in the works of Black writers themselves. Even Countée Cullen, known to subsequent generations as a somewhat prim purveyor of high art, contrasted the warmth of Blacks with the coldness of whites, wrote atavistically of the African rhythm inherent in the walk of a Black waiter (in *Color*, 1925), and rhapsodized the wildness of the African heritage:

> I can never rest at all
> When the rain begins to fall;
> Like a soul gone mad with pain
> I must match its weird refrain;
> Ever must I twist and squirm,
> Writhing like a baited worm,
> While its primal measures drip
> Through my body, crying, "Strip!
> Doff this new exuberance.
> Come and dance the Lover's Dance!"
> In an old remembered way
> Rain works on me night and day.[4]

In his first collection, *The Weary Blues* (1926), Langston Hughes not only created jazz/blues poems but also wrote with an exuberance tending to promote the image of an uninhibited people:

> *Dream Variations*
> To fling my arms wide
> In some place of the sun,
> To whirl and to dance
> Till the white day is done.
> Then rest at cool evening
> Beneath a tall tree
> While night comes on gently,
> Dark like me—
> That is my dream!
>
> To fling my arms wide
> In the face of the sun,
> Dance! Whirl! Whirl!

Till the quick day is done.
Rest at pale evening. . . .
A tall, slim tree. . . .
Night coming tenderly
Black like me.[5]

Black novelists also contributed to the image of an uninhibited people whose lives are exotic whirls. In *Home to Harlem* (1928) Claude McKay, a Black West Indian, drowned social protest in his flood of night life—prostitutes, sweetmen, jazz, fights—as he told the story of a Black deserter from the armed services who searches through Harlem for the lost prostitute whom he loves. Succeeding novelists, such as Rudolph Fisher in *The Walls of Jericho* (1928) and Wallace Thurman in *The Blacker the Berry* (1929), seemed almost compelled to include irrelevant night club scenes as though they had become clichés of Black life.

It should not be wondered then that W.E.B. DuBois, with great alarm, used the pages of *The Crisis* to question whether writers and publishers shared his fear that Black writers were being encouraged to create derogatory pictures of Blacks. Extremely concerned about respectable images of Blacks, DuBois, twenty years earlier, had rationalized their enthusiasm—whether in work or play—as a primitivism promoted by the experience of slavery, a primitivism which would be modified when Black Americans matured into the sophistication of Euro-American society. Now that his "Talented Tenth" seemed to promote spectacles of frenzy, however, DuBois suspected that their desire to publish persuaded them to ignore the truth of Black life and to pander to whites by creating images designed to titillate.

Beneath these surfaces of gay abandon, however, are more somber issues, more sober themes which should be examined more closely. The same writers who seemed to rejoice in the enthusiasm of Black life also sounded what Langston Hughes described as "the sob of the jazz band"—the melancholy undertone of Black life, ever present but sometimes unheard by those who fail to listen carefully.

Claude McKay pictured a Harlem dancer who protects her soul from the lascivious image suggested by her dance (*Harlem Shadows*, 1922), and Langston Hughes described the weariness of the jazz pianist (*The Weary Blues*, 1926). In *The Walls of Jericho* (1928) Fisher overshadowed the scenes of night life with a quieter depiction of the romance of two working people of Harlem. Thurman tempered his scenes of night life and dances in *The Blacker the Berry* (1929) by revealing that some Blacks visit dance balls not to gorge themselves with gaiety but to discover companionship to ease their loneliness. In the same novel a white Chicagoan confirms his impression that the exotic savagery of Harlemites is grossly exaggerated by their white press agents. While his actress-sister revels in what she considers the barbaric splendor of the Black club they visit, the Chicagoan sees a generally decorous behavior which assures him that Harlemites are no wilder than the Blacks he has known in Chicago (and perhaps not as wild as the whites in either city). Countée Cullen asserted that he wrote *One Way to Heaven* (1932) to counter *Nigger Heaven* by showing the humanity of Black life in Harlem. In scene after scene, Cullen balances superficial exuberance with sober explanation: The enthusiasm of a religious revival does not obscure the fact that in attendance also are some morally respectable Blacks who are not swept away by the emotion. The heroine, a morally circumspect, hard-working woman, has attended several revivals to which she has been indifferent. A husband's illicit affair is ascribed partly to the nature of the wandering male and partly to a desire to find companionship because his wife, who has become a religious fanatic, is engaged in an affair with Jesus.

These more serious vestiges of Black life in America should not be ignored when one considers the literature of the Renaissance; for, far from being mere entertainers, many Black writers regarded literature as a means of seriously examining problems of living. Moreover, they did not restrict their examinations to problems of Blacks in an adversary relationship with white society. Almost from the first they were concerned with issues which might be considered universal if American critics were more willing to discover universality in the lives of Black people.

The interest in human conditions appears in Jean Toomer's *Cane* (1923), the work of the Renaissance which is the best known and the most highly respected in academic circles. Toomer delineates people whose difficulties do not depend primarily upon their ancestry: Karintha has matured too soon sexually; Carma lives in a society which pretends that a woman should become sexless if her husband does not live with her; Esther cannot reconcile her sexual urges with the education of a society which has taught her that "good" girls do not feel such urges; John, in "Theater," cannot adapt his idealized romanticizing into a satisfactory relationship with an actual woman; Dorris, in "Theater," dreams of a companionship that will provide a real substitute for the artificiality of the theater; Muriel, in "Box Seat," fears to defy the little-minded social regulators of the world; Avey finds it more pleasurable to be supported by men rather than to labor as a teacher in a Normal school. The problems of these individuals may be complicated or intensified by their condition as Blacks in America, but the problems would exist regardless of their race.

Jessie Fauset, the too little-known author of *There Is Confusion* (1924), *Plum Bun* (1929), *The Chinaberry Tree* (1933), and *Comedy: American Style* (1933), contrived her novels to focus on the problems of Blacks whose lives are not continuously affected by their interrelationships with whites. Most often their problems derive from their ambition or from a society excessively willing to evaluate individuals according to false criteria. In *There Is Confusion*, for example, an ambitious young Black protagonist disrupts and nearly destroys the people around her because she tries to regulate their lives according to her delusions: Because she believes that people should not marry outside their class, she interferes with her brother's romance with a young woman whose family background is different. Doing "the right thing," by withdrawing from the relationship, the second young woman then rushes into an unfortunate marriage. Because the protagonist believes that men must be trained into suitably devoted servants, she refuses to apologize to the man she loves even though she is wrong. After he apologizes in order to effect a reconciliation, she delays a response with the deliberate intention of causing him to realize that he must learn that he cannot win her too easily. She begins to realize her error only when he, jolted by her rebuff, proposes to a woman who offers him affection without reservation.

In stories which she published during the 1920s, Zora Neale Hurston of Florida explored such in-group issues as the manner in which townspeople affect individuals by forcing them to act out of character in order to maintain the respect of the mob ("Spunk"). In addition, she vividly revealed the problems which disturb male-female relationships: the alienation which develops when a naive wife is seduced by a traveling salesman ("The Gilded Six-Bits"); the tragic consequences when a self-centered husband who exploited his wife tries to replace her ("Sweat").

Black dramatists such as Willis Richardson and Georgia D. Johnson prepared domestic dramas for the Black community: the tensions between a man and his improvident brothers-in-law ("The Broken Banjo"); the pathos of a situation in which a belief in faith healing causes the death of a child.

In such ways as these, Black writers of the Renaissance explored serious issues involving Black people but not deriving primarily from the racial ancestry or from their relationship with whites. This statement, however, should not encourage a fallacious assumption that the Black writers evaded their racial identity or ignored problems which do derive from interracial conflict. To the contrary, Black Renaissance writers frequently expressed concerns which strikingly anticipate major themes identified with the revolutionary Black Arts writers of the 1960s: a search for and affirmation of ancestral heritage, a feeling of alienation from the white Euro-American world; a presentation of and protest against oppression; and even militant defiance of oppression.

Just as Black Arts writers of today affirm their African heritage, so many Renaissance writers sought identity through identification with an ancestral past. Jean Toomer sought identity derived in part from the consciousness of the slave South and Africa (*Cane* and "Natalie Mann"). As I have pointed out earlier, Countée Cullen proclaimed that the sober teachings of Christian civilization could not curb the memories and the urges which linked him with Africa ("Heritage"). Langston Hughes found pride in identification with a race so old in human history that it had lived when rivers were young ("The Negro Speaks of Rivers"). Although some of these ancestral searches may seem rhetorical rather than actual, although some of the thoughts of Africa are sufficiently atavistic to promote a concept of exotic primitivism, the quests respond partly at least to Alain Locke's urgings that Black artists search for subject and style in an African tradition.

For the Black American writer of the 1920s, however, the search for ancestry proved more difficult than for white Americans: Some Blacks, ashamed of their ancestry as slaves and as descendants of Africans whom they judged to have been savages, attempted to evolve more respectable ancestry from identification with former masters. In *There Is Confusion* Jessie Fauset suggested the problems sometimes posed by the quest for European ancestry. Moreover, Blacks who wished to affirm a Black heritage were forced to identify with a continent rather than with a particular tribe or nation. Hence, the identification sometimes became intellectual and abstract rather than personal. The problem is suggested by Hughes:

Afro-American Fragment
So long,
So far away
Is Africa.
Not even memories alive
Save those that history books create,
Save those that songs
Beat back into the blood—
Beat out of blood with words sad-sung
In strange un-Negro tongue—
So long,
So far away
Is Africa.

Subdued and time-lost
Are the drums—and yet
Through some vast mist of race
There comes this song
I do not understand,
This song of atavistic land,
Of bitter yearnings lost
Without a place—
So long,
So far away
Is Africa's
Dark face.[6]

Failure to establish psychological identity with the Black heritage and corresponding awareness of exclusion from the European heritage sometimes produced a sense of alienation comparable to that expressed by Black Arts writers today. The feeling resounds vividly from McKay's "Outcast" and "The White House":

Outcast
For the dim regions whence my fathers came
My spirit, bondaged by the body, longs.
Words felt, but never heard, my lips would frame;
My soul would sing forgotten jungle songs.
I would go back to darkness and to peace,
But the great western world holds me in fee,
And I may never hope for full release
While to its alien gods I bend my knee.
Something in me is lost, forever lost,
Some vital thing has gone out of my heart,

And I must walk the way of life a ghost
Among the sons of earth, a thing apart.

For I was born, far from my native clime,
Under the white man's menace, out of time.[7]

The White House
Your door is shut against my tightened face,
And I am sharp as steel with discontent;
But I possess the courage and the grace
To bear my anger proudly and unbent.
The pavement slabs burn loose beneath my feet,
A chafing savage, down the decent street;
And passion rends my vitals as I pass,
Where boldly shines your shuttered door of glass.
Oh, I must search for wisdom every hour,
Deep in my wrathful bosom sore and raw,
And find in it the superhuman power
To hold me to the letter of your law!
Oh, I must keep my heart inviolate
Against the potent poison of your hate.[8]

The serious themes that Renaissance writers explored most frequently, as might be expected, are protests against oppression. The presence of such themes has been obscured by three facts: 1) Many readers remember the glamorous gaiety and forget the serious comments; 2) some protests appear as brief asides rather than fully developed explanations; 3) some protests seem mild because, rather than directly assaulting whites, they adumbrate the manner in which external oppression causes Blacks to oppress themselves. The way that serious protest can be ignored is evidenced by the customary reactions of casual readers to McKay's *Home to Harlem*, which appears, even in this paper, as a prototype of a Black work that promotes exoticism. The vividly exotic spectacles blind many readers to McKay's presentation of such facts as the following: During World War I many Black soldiers who enlisted to fight for democracy were restricted to service as laborers; during the 1920s some Harlem clubs, whether owned by whites or Blacks, discriminated against Blacks by refusing them admission—except as entertainers or waiters; in many occupations Black workers surrendered their dignity to the caprices of white supervisors.

It is true that no *Native Son* burst from the Renaissance to denounce American oppression. But Walter White's novel *The Fire in the Flint* (1924) decries the brutality of lynchings, as does Claude McKay's "The Lynching." Toomer's "Blood-Burning Moon" and "Kabnis" (*Cane*) reveal the powerlessness of Blacks to protect themselves from white brutality: A successful self-defense summons the lynch mob as quickly as a murder would.

Much more prevalent is the Renaissance writers' tendency to attack oppression indirectly by showing how it causes Blacks to turn against themselves. Because color, as an evidence of African ancestry, was a shibboleth of whites against Blacks, many Blacks used color as a criterion of intra-group evaluation. In *The Blacker the Berry*, the protagonist, because of her dark skin, suffers within her family, in school and college, and in efforts to secure employment. Yet pathetically, as Thurman shows, the heroine cherishes the same criteria which have victimized her: She desires only men who are of lighter complexion and Caucasian appearance; and she undervalues herself, believing for a time at least that her Blackness is an ineradicable blot upon her record. In *Comedy: American Style* (1933) Fauset gently censured a Negro mother who values her children according to the degree of their approximation to Caucasian appearance. Walter White's *Flight* (1928) and Nella Larsen's *Passing* (1929) show the dilemmas of heroines who, repressed by the conditions of life as Blacks, attempt to improve their lot by passing for white.

In ironic repudiation of the images of Blacks as amoral beings, Jean Toomer repeatedly stressed the necessity for middle-class Negroes to liberate themselves from conscious imitation of the restrictive morality of Anglo-Saxons. "Esther," "Theater," and "Box-Seat" all reveal the frustrations of Black people, who, desiring social approval, repress their emotions, their humanness. In "Kabnis" Carrie K., fearing censure by others, represses her instinctive attraction to Lewis. Paul ("Bona and Paul") loses a female companion because of his self-conscious desire to explain to a bystander that the relationship is not lustful. Toomer's most fully developed attack on middle-class morality appears in the unpublished drama "Natalie Mann."[9] Mert, a school teacher, dies because she perceives too late that she must enjoy passion fully without concern for society's censure. Natalie, the protagonist, develops to this awareness only through the assistance of a Christ-like male who himself has experienced the rebukes of the middle-class.

Toomer was not the only writer to question the excessive effort of Blacks to conform to the standards presumed to be those of whites. The protagonist in Walter White's *Flight* is forced to leave town and, temporarily, to deny her race because Blacks will not permit her to forget that she has had a child out of wedlock: Her lover's proposal of abortion so diminished him in her esteem that she refused his subsequent efforts to marry her.

During the 1920s few writers reacted militantly to oppression with the kind of rhetoric for which Black Revolutionary literature became notorious during the 1960s. There are several reasons. A generally optimistic faith that talented Blacks soon would merge with the mainstream muted rhetorical violence and violent rhetoric. Furthermore, publishers during the 1920s did not permit the kind of language and the explicit description of violent action which became almost commonplace in later decades. Third, the publishing houses were controlled by whites. It should be remembered that much of the Black Revolutionary literature of the 1960s issued from Black publishers of poetry and in Black community drama.

Under the circumstances it is not surprising that the militant reaction often was expressed as self-defense, as in Claude McKay's well known "If We Must Die":

If we must die, let it not be like hogs
Hunted and penned in an inglorious spot,
While round us bark the mad and hungry dogs,
Making their mock at our accursed lot.
If we must die, O let us nobly die,
So that our precious blood may not be shed
In vain; then even the monsters we defy
Shall be constrained to honor us though dead!
O kinsmen! we must meet the common foe!
Though far outnumbered let us show us brave,
And for their thousand blows deal one deathblow!
What though before us lies the open grave?
Like men we'll face the murderous, cowardly pack,
Pressed to the wall, dying, but fighting back![10]

Less frequently came prayers for destruction, as can be seen in McKay's "Enslaved":

Oh when I think of my long-suffering race,
For weary centuries, despised, oppressed,
Enslaved and lynched, denied a human place
In the great life line of the Christian West;
And in the Black Land disinherited,
Robbed in the ancient country of its birth,
My heart grown sick with hate, becomes as lead,
For this my race that has no home on earth.
Then from the dark depths of my soul I cry
To the avenging angel to consume
The white man's world of wonders utterly:
Let it be swallowed up in earth's vast womb,
Or upward roll as sacrificial smoke
To liberate my people from its yoke![11]

Most often the militancy is a proud hostility towards whites. At the end of *Flight* the male protagonist learns why his father abhorred whites: They had deprived him of inheritance by refusing to recognize him as their offspring. In turn he refuses to permit an elderly white to ease his own conscience by making a monetary donation while continuing to ignore the blood relationship.

I cannot conclude without re-assessing the significance of the literary Harlem Renaissance. If it is remembered for expressions of gaiety rather than for the serious concerns of the Black authors; if it was a movement which involved only the talented artists in one segment of the Black American population, if it reflects primarily the life of only one part of one city inhabited by Blacks; if it evidences little awareness of such a significant issue for Blacks as DuBois's dream and promotions of Pan-Africanism and even less awareness of or respect for Marcus Garvey's Back-to-Africa movement: If the Literary Renaissance is so limited, does it merit serious study? Was it, as Harold Cruse has suggested, an era to be examined only as a pathetic example of a time when Black artists might have established criteria for their art but failed to do so? Was it, as DuBois stated and as LeRoi Jones insisted more forcefully later, a movement that lost validity as it became a plaything of white culture? In fact, is the very attention given to it by historians of Black culture evidence of the willingness of Blacks and whites to glorify or permit glorification of inferior art by Blacks?

Each of these allegations has partial validity. But such objections, based on idealistic absolutes, fail to consider the actual significances of the literary Renaissance.

First, in no other decade had Black novelists been afforded such opportunity for publication. If fewer than twenty original, non-vanity-press novels appeared between 1924 and 1933, that figure nevertheless exceeded the number published by commercial houses in all the years since the publication of the first Black novel, William Wells Brown's *Clotel* (1853). Even the Depression and the closing of some outlets could not dispel the new awareness that possibilities existed for Blacks who wished to write novels. The field was open to many writers, not merely to the individual geniuses— the Paul Dunbar or the Charles Chesnutt of an earlier decade. This productivity, as well as the later success of Richard Wright, undoubtedly encouraged such novelists as Chester Himes, Ann Petry, Frank Yerby, and William G. Smith, who developed during the late 1930s and early 1940s.

The literary examples and inspiration were not limited to the novel. Only a few Black serious dramas reached Broadway, but the enthusiastic establishment of Black community theaters during the 1920s furthered the creation of a Black audience for drama and promoted awareness of the need for writers to create material for that audience.

Perhaps the productivity in poetry had less significant influence because Blacks previously had found outlets for poetry: The national reputation of Paul Laurence Dunbar was known by Blacks. Moreover, poetry was still to be considered an avocation which one supported by revenue derived from other occupations. But there was hope that black writers might be able to sustain themselves partly through grants, for Countée Cullen had established a precedent by winning a Guggenheim fellowship for his proposal of a poetry-writing project.

Of final benefit to future writers was the mere fact that entreés had been established. A Langston Hughes or Wallace Thurman or Countée Cullen or, later, an Arna Bontemps knew publishers and knew other people, who might be able to assist prospective authors.

In all these senses, the Renaissance was not a rebirth but, in very significant ways, a first birth for Blacks in literature.

A second significance of the literary Renaissance is its inspiration for African and Caribbean poets such as Léopold Senghor, Aimé Césaire, and Léon Damas, who, a generation later in the 1930s and 1940s were to promote Negritude, a literary-cultural movement which emphasized consciousness of African identity and pride in the Black Heritage. More than a decade later, newer Black American writers of the 1960s looked to African Negritude for inspiration. Thus, both directly and circuitously, the Renaissance promoted Black American literature and Black consciousness of future decades.

Finally, the Renaissance has importance as a symbol. In many respects, the actuality of a culture is less important than the myth which envelops and extends from that culture. The memory that Black Americans had been recognized and respected for literary achievements, as well as other artistic achievements, established awareness that there could be a literary culture among Blacks. If the memory faded rapidly from the consciousness of white America, it did not fade from the minds of Blacks responsible for continuing the culture among their people. Marcus Garvey did not succeed in restoring Black Americans to Africa; consequently, he is remembered as a dream that faded. But the Renaissance, for Black Americans and others, has gained strength as the mythic memory of a time when Blacks first burst into national consciousness as a talented group that was young, rebellious, proud, and beautiful.

Notes

[1]James W. Johnson, *Black Manhattan* (New York: Atheneum, 1968; originally published, 1930), pp. 160-161.

[2]Ibid., p. 161.

[3]Locke, "The New Negro," *The New Negro* (New York: Atheneum, 1968), p.8.

[4]Cullen, *Color* (New York: Harper, 1925).

[5]Hughes, *The Weary Blues* (New York: Knopf, 1926).

[6]Hughes, *Selected Poems* (New York: Knopf, 1959).

[7]Max Eastman, *Selected Poems of Claude McKay* (New York: Harcourt, Brace & World, 1953).

[8]Ibid. "My title was symbolic...it had no reference to the official residence of the President of the United States....The title 'White Houses' changed the whole symbolic intent and meaning of the poem, making it appear as if the burning ambition of the black malcontent was to enter white houses in general." Claude McKay: *A Long Way from Home* (1937), pp. 313-314.

[9]Now published in *The Wayward and the Seeking: A Collection of Writings by Jean Toomer*, Ed. Darwin T. Turner. (Washington, D.C.: Howard University Press, 1980).

[10]Max Eastman, *Selected Poems of Claude McKay* (New York: Harcourt, Brace & World, 1953).

Revisiting Babylon:
Fitzgerald and the 1920s

Edward Lueders

Edward George Lueders has made the rewarding discovery that the next best thing to living through an era is to get to know someone who has. Such a formula might well lead to charges of second-hand reporting; but in the following essay Lueders proves that if the soul is discriminating in selecting its own society a fine new perspective may accrue to the reader. In the present case Lueders has selected F. Scott Fitzgerald who chronicled the Jazz Age when he was in his twenties, Carl Van Vechten, author of nineteen books as music critic, novelist, photographer, and literary humanist during his middle years, and finally Lueders himself who modestly claims an introduction to that remarkable era by virtue of having been born into it.

The claim is not extravagant. When Lueders arrived on the scene in Chicago, February 14, 1923, the party was already in full swing. And although the immediate sights and sounds of the Twenties were destined to end when he was still a child of seven, one might justifiably say that both the memory and the melody lingered on. It was, as he puts it, a natural interest: "My parents' generation—the one whose ways were passed quite directly along to me." No wonder then that he recalls so vividly a spectrum of cultural touchstones ranging from LUCKY LINDY through a catalogue of sports heroes to "the marvelous jazz music of the Twenties that captured me body and soul." Like the guest who came to the party and could not bring himself to leave, his interest in this vast assortment of memorabilia has never flagged.

That is why Lueders has subsequently devoted a part of his life and work to the fiercely experimental era of the Twenties. That is why he can approach that heady and complex decade as his special province. His passion for the jazz piano earned him a World War II assignment entertaining troops as a member of a Special Services team touring India, Burma, and China. After the war he took successive degrees at Hanover College (1947), Northwestern University (1948), and The University of New Mexico (1952), where he also served as Instructor of English (1948-52) and Assistant Professor of English and speech (1952-57). Subsequently, he has held positions as Associate Professor of English, Long Beach State College 1957-61; Professor and Chairman of the Department of English at Hanover College (1961-66); and since 1966, Professor of English at the University of Utah, where in 1987 he was named University Professor.

From *Western Humanities Review* (Summer, 1975). Reprinted with permission.

Off campus, Edward Lueders maintains musical contact with tunes from the Twenties as "a jazz pianist on a Hines-Ellington-Brubeck-Shearing kick." This proclivity combined with his abiding interest in literature account for two significant studies of the era: Carl Van Vechten and the Twenties (1955) and Carl Van Vechten (1965) which draw richly on photographs, notes and correspondence Van Vechten made available to his friend Lueders. Anyone setting out to explore the flamboyant milieu of his own birthright—or of F. Scott Fitzgerald—or of Carl Van Vechten—could hardly enjoy truer travelling companions.

* * *

Three people serve as the main sources for these backward glances at the American Twenties. Only one of them needs no introduction. That one is F. Scott Fitzgerald. No one needs any special effort to identify Fitzgerald with the so-called Roaring Twenties. For better or for worse, his name, his life, and his fiction are practically synonymous with that notorious decade.

This is not true of my second source, Carl Van Vechten, although I made a brave venture in that direction thirty years ago with a book called *Carl Van Vechten & the Twenties.* Over his long career, Van Vechten was in turn a music, a dance, and literary critic; novelist; midwife to the Harlem Renaissance; portrait photographer of celebrated Americans; and impresario of voluminous special library collections which now help us to share and understand his whole era. Van Vechten was in his forties during what he referred to as "the splendid drunken twenties," while he was writing his seven vogue-ish novels. That's two critical decades older than his friends the F. Scott Fitzgeralds. But in one sense that didn't matter, since Carl Van Vechten did not age in the customary fashion. Even in his seventies and eighties, when I knew him, he felt, as he once wrote to me, "the same as I did at eighteen." Someone—I think it was Peter David Marchant—proposed a book about Van Vechten to be called *Peter Pan in Babylon.* Very apt. The working title of my own early study of him was *More on Wine Than Oil,* a phrase taken from a particularly scurrilous passage in Rabelais which Van Vechten heartily approved.

The third source I'm going to use, though, is probably the least defensible one. Me. And obviously I need an introduction. If I were to present my own credentials, they would go something like this: I was born in February of 1923 in the city of Chicago, and my first world—the one I accepted whole, since I had no grounds for wanting (or even imagining) another one—was the world of the American 1920s. Scott Fitzgerald's world, you might say. But Scott Fitzgerald's generation was my *parents'* generation—the one whose ways were passed quite directly along to me. No doubt this helps explain my natural interest in the Twenties. It is natural enough to indulge an interest in the decade into which you were born, to which you are, so to speak, *native.*

So I admit to self-indulgence in these considerations. But indulgence is hardly out of place in a discussion of the Twenties.

Among my earliest memories, for instance, I recall a world full of heroes whose names filled the headlines of our newspapers, the morning Chicago *Tribune* and the Chicago *Evening American*—a paper which, incidentally, once fired Carl Van Vechten because, as his notice from the editor put it (at least as Carl loved to tell it), he had "lowered the tone of the Hearst newspapers." Charles A. Lindberg was a milestone, of course, and I remember a clumsy cast-iron dime-store model of his airplane, *The Spirit of St. Louis*, which had LUCKY LINDY raised in bas relief across the top of the wing— a model I would fly by extended hand around the house, making appropriate engine roars and whines while I executed steep climbs and stalls and fancy Immelmann turns on my way to Paris.

And the sports heroes: Illinois' Red Grange and Notre Dame's Four Horsemen and Northwestern's Pug Rentner during our midwestern fall, of course. But most of the year: baseball. Babe Ruth and the young Gehrig, and Connie Mack's feared Philadelphia Athletics. Closer to home, with my beloved north-side Chicago Cubs, prodigies like Charlie Grimm, Hack Wilson, Woody English, Riggs Stephenson, Kiki Cuyler, Footsie Blair, and Guy Bush.

And the marvelous jazz music of the Twenties that captured me body and soul—long before I knew the phrase had any currency beyond the jazz improvisations that could be wrung from the old Johnny Green standard with that title. Seventy-eight r.p.m. records on the polished wind-up phonograph with the steel needle, picking up and amplifying those tricky tinfoil sounds. RCA Victor, Brunswick, Vocalion, and the Okeh labels. The startling piano artistry of Earl Hines is a sharp early memory—staying up very late (was it 10 p.m.?) to hear the broadcasts from the Grand Terrace on the south side of Chicago, where Hines and his band opened in 1928 and stayed on for a decade. The exciting rumble of the reeds and brass coming on with their theme, *Deep Forest*, and then Hines' clear gymnastic piano and the shouts in the background of "Fatha Hines! Fatha Hines!" Later on, Fletcher and Horace Henderson swinging into the Thirties, and the incredible "Little Jazz," Roy Eldridge, via the late night remotes from the Three Deuces. And the first Benny Goodman trio experience with Teddy Wilson's honey-and-cinnamon perfection on the piano—which I honestly think has had as much to do with my life, my style, my method and person as anything else I can pinpoint. Well, I'll stop the indulgence while I still can. There is plenty of discovery and excitement for everybody in the music of those years, without the need of nostalgic endorsements from sentimental fans like me. And most of it is still with us on the records, thank goodness.

But I do want to summon up two more ghosts out of my own recollections of the Twenties—ghosts who will nudge me back into position to take up the Fitzgerald phenomena again. These are my personal models, my very earliest personal prototypes, for the glamorous flaming youth of the Twenties, for F. Scott Fitzgerald's scandalous flappers and sheiks: Gerry and Ed Hanskat. The Hanskats (whose name never struck me as ludicrous until now) were the fast couple, the daring and dangerous and enviable couple of my parents' set. They were also, as Carl Van Vechten once said to me flatly about Scott and Zelda Fitzgerald, *beautiful*. Gerry with her bobbed hair and boundless energy, her slight, quick boyish figure and teasing manner was something ultimate for me before I really had any reason to wonder why. And smooth Ed Hanskat, who drew everybody to him, was lean, athletic, venturesome, unpredictable, graceful, handsome beyond reason in his neat, dark-hair, smiling way. They danced the Charleston and they leaned together cheek to cheek, and Gerry would do the shimmy anytime, anywhere, and they seemed utterly gay, and I silently adored them. No doubt the fact that the Hanskat family manufactured and sold a high-class line of ladies' foundation garments added an exotic and mildly sensual note to their attractiveness for me. I remember with a remote sense of naughtiness using a slick deck of playing cards which had come as an advertising gimmick from the Hanskats' establishment. The cards had a fan-like design on the backs with the motto: STAYFORM—NOT A CORSET, NOT A CORSELET— STAYFORM. More important probably was the Hanskat family income this provided, allowing the incandescent Gerry and Ed Hanskat to drive a dashing roadster and to flaunt their devastating casualness with conspicuous style.

I evoke the Hanskats at such length to make a point. They were real. As their secret idolater, I was real. Although they share, in my retrospection, most of the characteristics exploited in the caricatures by John Held, Jr., I can never conceive of them in that artificial mold. They were, and they remain for me, beautiful people, not caricatures, not stereotypes. It is my unflinching endorsement of the art of F. Scott Fitzgerald to testify that I can hardly tell them from a host of his characters. The dilemma, of course, and probably the one these recollections should explore, is in deciding to what extent they were Fitzgerald's creation, and to what extent throughout the Twenties and beyond, Fitzgerald was, so to speak, theirs.

For the Romance of the 1920s was grounded in contradictions which Fitzgerald has come to epitomize for us in a unique combination of innocent, idealized sentiment with worldly, cynical, destructive dissipation. An unrecognized analogue for this combination which is to be found in our continuing American mores is our annual celebration of Valentines Day. Consider the two motifs of our valentines and the kind of duplicity they signal in our rites every February 14th—a duplicity whose terms I believe can be traced directly to the temper of the Twenties: first, the basic innocence of the holiday, of the pure, child-like sentimental exchange of "Will You Be My Valentine" cards; and second, the mockery of the comic valentines— rude, cynical, "liberated," and violently anti-sentimental. In recent years, catering to our latter-day sophistication, I suppose, most valentines tend to combine the two in a curiously adolescent mixture. And consider also those persistent little pastel valentine candy hearts that reappear every year, with their snappy legends right out of the Twenties: "Kiss Me," "My Pet," "Be Mine," and my favorite—now rare—"Pa's Wild."

Now, the *sentimentalist* wants his idealized yearning to go on forever. The *romantic* hopes that it won't, and enjoys the melancholy of that knowledge. Beyond both sentimentalism and romanticism, the decadent *cynic* attempts to stand clear of both, as in Oscar Wilde's pronouncement that there are two tragedies in life: not getting what you want—and getting it. Fitzgerald's work gives us the benefit of all three of these points of view, managed almost miraculously at his best, as in *The Great Gatsby*, without their getting in the way of one another.

I believe the Twenties are legitimately Romantic for us because the lasting writers of the period—I think of Fitzgerald, Sherwood Anderson, Eugene O'Neill, and Hemingway as against, say, Sinclair Lewis—were themselves true romantics: half-way, you might say, between the valentines of Gertrude Stein and those of H. L. Mencken. For these latter two were originators and prime movers, or perhaps I should say prime *voices*, in the development of an American language which was to be refined and exploited through the Roaring Twenties. And what a mixed blessing they were—Gertrude Stein with her strikingly purified, child-like incantations turning at length into closet echolalia, and Mencken with his intellectually swashbuckling style that has spawned so many ill-equipped bush-league pop imitators, from Walter Winchell and Westbrook Pegler in the Thirties down to Paul Harvey, and Howard Cosell of a later day. Yet part of the Babel in Babylon—in some ways the best part—was fashioned at the writing desks of these two prodigious American originals.

Another set of American writers in the Twenties, Carl Van Vechten and James Branch Cabell chief among them, grafted sophisticated European wickedness and decadence onto our literary stock (while both the expatriate Stein in France and Mencken with his Germanic learnings encouraged them, by the way). Yet somehow even in their work the native American strain showed through, and some kind of New World innocence and optimism—some ineradicable echo of Huck Finn's kind of worldliness—remained essential in their results.

Our contrasts with European experience and outlook continued to be instructive to writers of the Twenties, as they had been to Henry James and Mark Twain and Emerson and Hawthorne and Fenimore Cooper and Ben Franklin before them. From May, 1924, to December 1931, Scott and Zelda Fitzgerald spent five years abroad in Europe, including two extended periods of over two years each, and the whole summer of 1928 in between. The events of those years in their lives are not happy ones to recount, but their importance to the themes and perspectives in Fitzgerald's work is considerable. When he came to write his story of "Babylon Revisited," the scene was not St. Paul, or Princeton, or Montgomery, or even New York City. It was Paris. And his most comprehensive novel, *Tender Is The Night*, follows its ill-starred Americans and their Twenties-oriented illusions through Continental European settings.

I have wondered if a study of *Tender Is the Night* together with Thomas Mann's *The Magic Mountain* wouldn't reveal a great deal about the anatomy of romanticism across two centuries, along with its pathology of disillusionment and decay. Both these ambitious novels arrive at European sanatoriums seeking the cure for a disease which apparently is simply in the air. Thomas Mann's symbolic malady is the heritage of nineteenth-century aesthetic romanticism—tuberculosis (or "consumption" as they called it), a slow physical wasting away, the melancholy symptoms of which were so perversely attractive to Edgar Allan Poe, as they were to the English and French romantics and later to the Pre-Raphaelites. The afflictions in Fitzgerald's book, like those in his life, are those of twentieth-century romanticism—alcohol and schizophrenia, both of which grew out of the romantic imbalances of the twenties and which show as their symptoms a mental and emotional wasting way.

Aware of this, Scott Fitzgerald provided in his declining years what is still the best revisitation to the Babylon of our 1920s in his story of that name, and in the haunting failure of *Tender Is the Night*, and, most of all, in the mordant pieces he wrote out of his personal eclipse during the Thirties, the pieces which Edmund Wilson collected after his death and published in *The Crack-Up*.

Babylon is really a useful point of reference for Fitzgerald's Twenties, by the way. Remember that it was the Babylonians who invented money. And it is to the Babylonians that we owe our 24-hour day and our system of counting 360 degrees in a circle.

When Carl Van Vechten wrote *his* Babylon revisited as a coda to the "splendid drunken twenties"—his novel (and his last one) called *Parties* and subtitled "Scenes from Contemporary New York Life"—he patterned David and Rilda Westlake, its self-destructive, spendthrift, non-stop central characters, after Scott and Zelda Fitzgerald. *Parties* is a whirling, concentric, pell-mell novel which moves in an almost perpetual alcoholic haze. The one exception is a scene in the still center of the book when David and Rilda, waking at noon unexpectedly sober for the first time, confront each other just long enough for David to blurt out the whole plot and theme of the novel:

We're swine, filthy swine, and we are Japanese mice, and we are polar bears walking from one end of our cage to the other, to and fro, to and fro, all day, all week, all month, forever to eternity. We'll be drunk pretty soon and then I'll be off to Donald's to get drunker and we'll go to a lot of cocktail parties and then we'll all turn up for dinner at Rosalie's where you are never invited. She won't want you, and I shall hate you, but Siegfried will want you. And we'll get drunker and drift about night clubs so drunk that we won't know where we are, and then we'll go to Harlem and stay up all night and go to bed late tomorrow morning and wake up and begin it all over again.
    Parties, sighed Rilda. Parties!
    Edith returned with the cocktail shaker and glasses on a tray.

Reading such a passage, I think of Fitzgerald's terse summary in his notebooks for the whole of 1925, the year following the writing of *The Great Gatsby*: "1,000 parties and no work." Or of his character Dick Ragland in "A New Leaf": "Just when somebody's taken him up and is making a big fuss over him," we are told, "he pours soup down his hostess' back, kisses the serving maid, and passes out in the dog kennel. But he's done it too often. He's run through about everybody, until there's no one left." And I think of the pathetic paradoxes of Fitzgerald's own alcoholic charm and its devastating consequences.

As touchstones in his essays and book reviews, Scott Fitzgerald often used the work of Theodore Dreiser, James Joyce, H. G. Wells, and Joseph Conrad. He also referred to the specific background against which—out of which—each wrote: Dreiser—midwestern morality; Joyce—Dublin Catholicism; Wells—London Fabianism; Conrad—maritime colonialism. In a similar way, we can see that Fitzgerald wrote out of his own background a chronicle of the inadequacies of three prevailing motifs of the American Twenties: money, mobility, and celebrity.

Well, these are the same motifs that the Twenties themselves thought of as wealth, speed, and success. They are also, I must recognize with my own characteristic American ambivalence, the same motifs which I indulged at the start of these considerations, taken from my innocent, now almost dream-like recollections as a child in—and of—the 1920s. The only America I have known is one in which money is the keynote, although it is growing clearer to me every day that "getting and spending, we lay waste our powers." The only America I have known is one in love with, and now tragically dependent upon, its automobiles. It is a nation on wheels. A major difference between the leisurely pace and turn-of-the-century charm of Paris recorded in Carl Van Vechten's graceful novel, *Peter Whiffle,* and the American in Paris passed on to us by Fitzgerald and Hemingway (to say nothing of George Gershwin) is neatly symbolized by the ubiquitous taxicabs of the latter. And *The Great Gatsby*, of course, would be unthinkable without cars. Finally, the only America I have known is one whose insatiable appetite for celebrating its heroes is increasingly fed (and often poisoned) by the relentless illusions of image-making, of advertising, of what was once called with typical Twenties high spirits "hoopla" and "ballyhoo" and now, alas, has been solemnized and institutionalized as "public relations." I realized anew recently when I saw the latest movie revival of the old Hecht-MacArthur play *The Front Page* how much the hallmark of this established American motif was, during the Roaring Twenties as it is today, a self-serving duplicity, a stylish excess, and a fatally misplaced idealism. F. Scott Fitzgerald helped to enshrine it for us. H. R. Haldeman and John Ehrlichman and John Mitchell and Richard Nixon were some of its more recent exponents—and victims.

Babylon—a most engaging place to visit. And to revisit. But I'll tell you what: I wouldn't want to live there.

From Mayday to Babylon:
Disaster, Violence, and Identity
in Fitzgerald's Portrait of the 1920s

Norman H. Hostetler

If F. Scott Fitzgerald can be epitomized as The Chronicler of the Jazz Age, then Norman H. Hostetler, on the basis of the following essay, can be just as fairly characterized as the Chronicler of F. Scott Fitzgerald. For herein Hostetler points his pen squarely at certain ominous cultural themes in Fitzgerald's fiction frequently overlooked by literary critics and assorted nostalgia seekers who languish in more "innocent, sentimental, idealized, yet worldly, cynical, dissipated" motifs of the Twenties. Hostetler pays due respect to such ambiguities, because they are evident to all interested parties. Historically, fictionally—they are there.

What sets Hostetler apart, therefore, is his effective explorations of a sub-strata of violence in Fitzgerald's fiction not quite so apparent to the secular realist—but ultimately revealing to the probings of the cultural anthropologist. Like most good critics, Hostetler is curious about cultural artifacts primarily as they serve symbolic ends. His ultimate purpose, however, is to analyze the ultimate meaning of the symbols. Fortunately his patient psychological probing of various relationships between artifact and symbol, characterization and culture unearths a significant thematic premise: that "Fitzgerald's view of the 1920s consistently reveals the destructive side of Babylon. In an increasingly mechanized and dehumanized society, where the meaning of personal experience is more and more slipping away from the control of the individual, the pervasive potential for disaster is all too apparent. Where moral sensitivity and intellectual understanding no longer serve as guiding lights, the dark maw of violence beckons us all into a sort of ultimate escape from which there is no recovery."

This naturalistic approach to Fitzgerald's fiction is adequately documented in terms of the psychological, moral and sometimes physical demise of most of Fitzgerald's major characters—regardless of their "In" or "Out" status in the social and economic world.

Norman Henry Hostetler graduated cum laude with a B.A. in Humanities at Kansas State University in 1960. He received his M.A. (1965) and Ph.D. in English (1973) from The University of Pennsylvania. Since 1980 he has held the position of Associate Professor of English at The University of

110

Nebraska-Lincoln. Although he has concentrated much of his teaching and research on Fitzgerald and his literary compatriots, Hostetler is active in more eclectic American Studies approaches to modern literature. His interest in the Twenties, however, is anything but casuistic, being firmly rooted in a number of penetrating studies of Nathaniel Hawthorne's psychological and spiritual probings of human experience. From a more secular point of view, Hostetler is conversant with recent studies of American naturalism, both before and after Dreiser. This distillation of psychological, spiritual and naturalistic forces lends Hostetler's own explorations of the dark side of Babylon an impact that often approaches revelation.

* * *

One of the major problems the critic of the 1920s has is handling the individual and social ambivalances of the period.[1] Edward Lueders, in his essay on Fitzgerald in this volume, has addressed himself in a most insightful way to this issue by documenting the essential double nature of the period—innocent, sentimental, idealized, yet worldly, cynical, dissipated. These characteristics he perceives in both the representative individuals of the time and in the prevailing American cultural motifs of money, mobility, and celebrity—or wealth, speed, and success. This association of the personal condition with the cultural I find particularly valuable, and I would like to extend his connection by exploring, in this essay, a possible method of relating the two areas of experience through an examination of F. Scott Fitzgerald's perceptions of the relationship of society and identity.

We have a tendency to see the failure of the individual to achieve the ideal of complete personal integration as a personal failure—an idiosyncratic failure related only to the individual capability of handling money, alcohol, sex, or whatever. I think that Fitzgerald instead saw the roots of destructive individual behavior lying in the cultural condition. The basis for this interpretation lies in three remarks Fitzgerald made in his 1930s essays in which he looked back on his 1920s experiences. The first of these is in "Early Success," where Fitzgerald comments on his first published fiction:

All the stories that came into my head had a touch of disaster in them—the lovely young creatures in my novels went to ruin, the diamond mountains of my short stories blew up, my millionaires were as beautiful and damned as Thomas Hardy's peasants. In life these things hadn't happened yet, but I was pretty sure living wasn't the reckless, careless business these people thought.[2]

The second, in "Echoes of the Jazz Age," describes the experience of his friends:

By this time [1927] contemporaries of mine had begun to disappear into the dark maw of violence. A classmate killed his wife and himself on Long Island, another tumbled "accidently" from a skyscraper in Philadelphia, another purposely from a skyscraper in New York. One was killed in a speak-easy in Chicago; another was beaten to death in a speak-easy in New York and crawled home to the Princeton Club to die; still another had his skull crushed by a maniac's axe in an insane asylum where he was confined. These are not catastrophes that I went out of my way to look for—these were my friends; more-over, these things happened not during the depression but during the boom. (p. 20)

The third remark is a statement in "The Crack-up" about his personal attitude during the 1920s: "Life was something you dominated if you were any good" (p. 69). The problem here is evident. To "dominate life" is to make it conform to one's own expectations and abilities—to make it, in other words, an expression and realization of one's individual identity. But something has clearly gone wrong with this expectation when experience confirms a world characterized by disaster and violence on both individual and social levels.

By the mid-1930s, Fitzgerald was all too aware of the extent of his miscalculations regarding his own ability to "dominate life." In actuality, the reverse had occurred. Rather than impose his personality on other things, he had come "to identify myself, my ideas, my destiny, with those of all classes I came in contact with" ("The Crack-up," p. 71). He now recognized that "identification such as this spells the death of accomplishment" ("Handle With Care," p. 81)[3] because it requires an abnegation of the self.

Fitzgerald had relished playing the role of "the Author"—despite his awareness that it constituted a "false face" ("Early Success," pp. 87-88)— because it seemed to offer him the promise of personal influence in the society. He could exert the force of his identity in order to have some influence on the creation and construction of the American society in a way that the non-involved author working only through the medium of his art apparently could not.

By the time of "The Crack-up," he had come to believe that the cost of exhausting the psychological self in an attempt to create or sustain social conditions or roles is emotional, moral, and cultural bankruptcy. His real problem was not how to become the representative figure of the Jazz Age but how to avoid the limitations and exactions of that publicly enforced role. In effect, Fitzgerald was now arguing that the only significant reality for the individual is his personal identity, and that the social relationships are "real" only in the sense that they are perceived by the individual—"the world only exists through your apprehension of it" ("The Crack-up," p. 74). For Fitzgerald in the 1930s, the essential locus of life became internal instead of external.

But the fact that Fitzgerald became explicitly and personally aware of the problems of identity in the 1930s does not mean that his works in the 1920s do not reflect the same concern. "Mayday" shows how early that "touch of disaster" is manifest. Explicitly designed as a revelation of the milieu of New York on May 1, 1919, the story interweaves the fates of numerous characters whom Fitzgerald sees as culturally representative. In a drunken spree at the end of the story Philip Dean and Peter Himmel borrow the door signs and become Mr. In and Mr. Out. In and Out are useful terms for explaining social status. "In" people have wealth and social power (which are frequently the same thing)—they can, for example, control the amenities of the social system, such as the hotels and restaurants, which are the institutions most fully organized to respond to individual demands. Thus Dean and Himmel have power over waiters and elevators (only in social, not moral terms—despite Mr. Out, you can't get to heaven in an elevator). "Out" people—the two soldiers and especially Gordon Sterrett—are defined as those who do not fit the proper image of power and who therefore cannot control the amenities. They are deliberately excluded—Sterrett will not be welcome any longer by Dean, Edith, the hotel, or the restaurant. He has been labeled a failure by all of them and defined out of social existence. He is psychologically incapable of handling the inevitability of this social destruction and symbolically commits suicide, as effectively destroyed by the nature of his position in society as the soldier Keyes, who is physically incapable of handling his position and is literally pushed out the window by the mob. But the fundamental point is that just as it is impossible to separate Dean and Himmel as In and Out there is no significant difference between In and Out in terms of the *process* of social identification involved. They are meaningless without each other. Both Dean and Sterrett were originally at the same point in college. They have gone in opposite directions psychologically, but they are *defined* in terms of their places within the society—we differentiate because of appearances (Dean is separated from Sterrett at the beginning of the story by the description of their clothes) and power to control the institutions. They are therefore representatives of an identical process of dehumanization, reflected in Dean's insensitivity to Edith at the end and Sterrett's total loss of self-respect and dignity.

Reflected in this story and others are the pressures of rapid social change—industrialization, urbanization, life-styles—all the things subsumed in the concept of "The Roaring Twenties." People who are encouraged by social expectations to depend upon stable social roles for their identities are not prepared psychologically to handle this increased rate of change in social conditions. When change outside their control occurs, there is a resulting anxiety, frustration, and sense of cultural schizophrenia. This dissociation of identity and experience applies to all people who see themselves in terms of social position regardless of the particular positions they occupy. It is the resulting quality of experience that makes the 1920s seem the first part of the contemporary era.[4]

Take "Babylon Revisited," for example. The In's in that story are invariably anxious, the Out's resentful, no matter who they are—both are products of the social condition. Neither In nor Out is "earned" by any apparent success or failure of individual endeavor—intellectual, emotional, moral, or whatever—and like Hemingway, Fitzgerald argued that you never get something for nothing. The costs may be delayed or obscured, but they are very real. With the drastic change in conditions between 1929 and 1931, the people who occupy the roles of the In's and Out's reverse—but it's all the same thing. Marion locks Charlie out psychologically as totally as Charlie locked Helen out physically. Thus the nature of one's social status is perceived as fragile and accidental and subject to forces nobody can control. To leave one's identity in the hands of these forces is to invite disaster.

This tendency to define identity in terms of social position (most clearly illustrated by Tom Buchanan in *The Great Gatsby*), denies the possibility of identity in terms of love, self-actualization, morality, or any other form of fulfilling or integrating the psyche. But the repression of these personal elements of experience leads to a characteristic frustration/aggression reaction, as fatally self-destructive to the individual psyche of those apparently at the apex of the social condition as it is to those who are not. See, for example, Anson Hunter in "The Rich Boy." His apparent politeness is the actual repression of his cruelty, bred by his assumption of wealth and social power from his youth. His actual nature appears when he drinks, thereby causing him to lose physical control of his ability to sublimate his power into psychological games, and when there are direct threats to his social status, such as in his forced break-up of Cary Sloane's affair, that leads directly to Sloane's suicide.

As I have been implying throughout, there is a relationship between psychological and physical destruction, which is revealed in even minor stories. In "Bernice Bobs Her Hair" the psychological dehumanization precedes the symbolic physical cutting of hair, of both Bernice and her cousin Marjorie. Perhaps even more clear is "The Baby Party," where everybody is motivated by egotism—the psychological attempt to gain power—which is related to the all-pervasive social competitiveness. The children can't handle these psychological games and resort to violence—pushing each other down— whereupon the adults lose control, first verbal and then physical. I will have more to say on this dark maw of violence in a moment.

For Fitzgerald, something is wrong with American society, as is evidenced by the tendency of the products of that society, both personal and mechanical, to go wrong. As Professor Lueders states, the automobile is indeed the symbol of increased mobility (and also of increased alienation, I might add), but Fitzgerald also recognized the automobile as the twentieth century replacement for the railroad as the symbol of the American technological society—a relationship most evident in the auto wreck after Gatsby's party. The wheel is off, nobody is in control, the system is out of order, and the only solutions offered are irrelevant and characteristically American—the nostalgic one of put it in reverse, and the violent one of giving it more gas.

The genteel/sentimental/romantic popular cultural conditioning that Nash, Lueders, and others have identified tends to imply that there is a logical coherence to social events that will permit the individual who exhibits the appropriate personal characteristics to control the consequences of his experience—to "dominate life." As Jay Gatsby so eminently shows, this assumption is out of phase with the reality of contemporary existence. The consequence is an enormously increased sense of alienation of the individual—whether In or Out—from the community, culture, society, and self. This is heavily reinforced by the technological reduction of the individual to the services of the machine, as illustrated by the garageman George Wilson in *The Great Gatsby*. As previously indicated, the consequence tends to be anxiety among Ins and resentment and envy among Outs—both heavily repressed by efforts to find new identity through social roles. The repression creates a characteristic dehumanization of individuals—both in attitudes toward the self and toward others. This is, of course, the perfect climate for the expression of the frustration/aggression reaction through violence as the primary mode of defining relationships with others.[5]

We have already seen in "Mayday" how casual violence—the apparently random and meaningless destruction of individuals—is not idiosyncratic but symbolically related to the value of the individual in a system of socially defined roles. This is the point of connection with the "dark maw of violence" in the real world. Normally, the expression of violence is sublimated to symbolic modes—that is, we normally perpetrate violence on each other through psychological games. Psychological violence occurs when the aggressor damages the role concepts and hence the sense of self-worth of other individuals. The process results in dehumanization, which makes it easier to rationalize the use of physical force when there is a breakdown in the usual psychological patterns. "The Rich Boy" shows how the sense of loss of control leads to the outbreak of casual violence.

Herein lies the connection between the personal and the social worlds— violence has become the characteristic mode of establishing personal relationships within the social order. Indeed, it is a necessary and concomitant part of the expression of social relationships for people who take their identity from their social roles. The position of the individual within the social order then depends upon the power to define people—to establish their roles and meaning—which constitutes another form and product of dehumanization. This is an "artificial" power in the sense that it is only the product of the *position* occupied within the system (which we have seen is accidental, uncertain, and outside one's own control), as opposed to the people whose power depends upon personal ability, creativity, and knowledge (for example, Dick and Abe in *Tender is the Night*). The former group (people whose power is "artificial"—see, for examples, such characters as Marion Peters, Tom Buchanan, and Baby Warren) become defensive and destructive toward the latter group, who are seen as change agents and therefore threatening toward the system with which the former identify.

Fitzgerald establishes these relationships quite explicitly. For example, the sybaritic luxury of the Washingtons in "The Diamond as Big as the Ritz" is dependent on a deliberate policy of murder and enslavement—for Fitzgerald, you can't be poor and free at the same time, but you can't be rich and free either. Tom Buchanan in *The Great Gatsby* acts similarly as the representative of the social order. He perceives himself to be at the apex of society; for him, therefore, all change is bad news. Thus he acts as if his exploitation of the Wilsons and other people were essentially moral, because this exploitation reaffirms the power relationship between them and thereby helps maintain the apparent stability of the system from which he takes his identity. It is of course ironic that Buchanan's concept of stability results in ever increasing amounts of alienation, dehumanization, and destruction. In this society, I should note that the use of money is also a form of violence. There is no significant difference between Tom's physically breaking Myrtle Wilson's nose and his psychologically forcing George Wilson to knuckle under, whenever the latter starts to rebel, by threatening to deny him the commission for selling the car. Once again we see the relationship between the actual and symbolic acts of violence.

Hence the tragedies in Fitzgerald's real and imaginative worlds are not just personal but cultural, and the chief question that remains is, why do people continue to play these games? The answer is provided by *Tender is the Night*, Fitzgerald's final portrait of the 1920's.[6]

Few people are capable of freeing themselves from this social trap, and all are conditioned to think that individual fulfillment lies in the social arena. Dick Diver is the man of potential genius whose profession, psychiatry, provides awareness and knowledge of the importance of individual identity. He has the potential to be the great man—to create the personal identity of such magnitude and power that it is able to affect society and social institutions in a positive way. But the man who should have been capable of the supremely integrated personality becomes instead the subject of a novel of disintegration. He is broken and eroded away, his control of his identity gradually ground down by too many encounters with the external world, until there is nothing left.

The positive potential for Dick lies in his creative scholarship—more than just a skilled clinician reconstructing psyches of the rich, like Franz Gregorovius, Dick has the ability to create the profound artifact (his textbook) answerable to his own excellence. Thus the individual can retain control of his identity and powers while doing something more than selfish ego-feeding—he can offer something of positive value to other individuals in the society. In this regard, Fitzgerald's attitude in *Tender is the Night* comes very close to his final view of his role as artist in the society that I suggested earlier.

Dick Diver chooses instead to seek identity through some kind of profound, even apocalyptic, emotional involvement with Nicole, a dream of overwhelming unity that makes an individual more than an individual by expanding his identity beyond the bounds of the physically isolated personality. In Dick's terms, he "wanted to be loved." In so doing, he takes control of his identity out of his own hands and places it in the social situation. And whenever identity becomes defined by social roles and relationships, the door is open for violence and disaster.

Dick expresses a willingness to pay the price and put his great creative ability at the service of superb dinner parties and other people's problems. But he does not really understand the cost involved. Role playing demands the exercise and consumption of the creative ability.

In choosing Nicole, Dick confuses the natural and social worlds as disastrously as Charlie did in "Babylon Revisited" ("The snow of 1929 was not real snow. If you didn't want it to be snow, you just paid some money."). Dick associates Nicole with the romantic qualities of the night, the moonlight, and flowers, and through her offer of herself for only a complementary vibration from him, Dick believes that it won't cost much to have both the personal and suprapersonal worlds.

But Nicole is representative of the social world, not the natural, as is most evidently shown by her insanity—her instability is created through the social encounter and "curable" only through her return to the norms of the society as the only source of identity. Nicole is the product of the American institutions, all of which gave a tithe to her; "as the whole system swayed and thundered onward it lent a feverish bloom to such processes of hers as wholesale buying." Her insanity is not idiosyncratic but a fundamental element of the social order, where people "use" people as a convenience. It is representative of dehumanization and the use of power in the worst sense—the ferocious bourgeois mediocrity of the eater and the eaten. The characteristic nature of this world in *Tender is the Night* is that the supposedly "good" parties and people turn out to be the "bad" parties and people. Dick can't control the outcome of his actions invested in the social world. And mere endurance is not enough if it is sustained only by using people—Nicole, the psychological destroyer, and Tommy Barban, the physical destroyer, leave the world a little worse than the way it was.

Nicole is thus one of the destructive people, and her insanity simply makes her a more sensitive register of the destructive quality that resides in any involvement with representatives of the system. The situation is epitomized by the scene at the railroad station. Abe tells Nicole that he is "tired of women's world." But to Nicole's appropriate challenge, "Then why don't you make a world of your own?" Abe, who has previously been specifically labeled an "out," can only reduce the sublime to the ridiculous: "Tired of friends. The thing to have is sycophants." Nevertheless, he still knows that, in their relationship to society, the representative woman and the creative man are implacably opposed. To Nicole's ironic statement, "I am a woman and my business is to hold things together," he replies, "My business its to tear them apart"—to analyze, to understand, to alter.

Shortly thereafter, the forces of destruction that Abe has just attacked find a more receptive perch: "Dick Diver came and brought with him a fine glowing surface on which the three women sprang like monkeys with cries of relief." Immediately after that, Maria Wallis literally destroys a man, identity and all—"they had an awful time finding out who, because she shot him through his identity card." The implication is clear that very near the core of society and the social institutions lies violence and destruction, as is further suggested by the murders of Peterson and North and the recurrent references to war.

The book insists that violence is the product of a civilization—an American inheritance from the days when "you shot first and apologized afterwards." Violence is ironically described as "the honorable, the traditional resource of [Dick's] land." The inevitable consequence of the commitment of the self to the social encounter is that by the end of the book, the only two people who matter, Abe and Dick, have both been destroyed.

What is worse is that the destruction of the individual doesn't really matter to society. Nobody cares about the individuals or that destruction is the logical product of the social involvement. Even Dick acts as if violence were just an inconvenience; he leaves the railroad station "as if nothing had happened." And Nicole's reaction to the murder of Jules Peterson suggests one of the book's deepest pessimisms—that within this social situation, to care is the real insanity. Nicole, one recalls, originally "felt complicity" for the incest, but then she engaged the attitudes of society at the boarding school and "from sheer self-protection she developed the idea that she had had no complicity." Unable to involve her father or herself, she involved the entire society—"all men"—which the society, of course, at once interpreted as serious anti-social behavior. She is not finally "cured" until she abandons completely the *ideas* of complicity, of moral responsibility, of individual involvement—an abandonment symbolized by her final inability to stay attuned to Dick's moral and intellectual "interpretation and qualification"— for the amoralism of Tommy and Baby.

From the suicide of Gordon Sterrett to the hopeless moral sterility of the Warren's world, Fitzgerald's view of the 1920s consistently reveals the destructive side of Babylon. In an increasingly mechanized and dehumanized society, where the meaning of personal experience is more and more slipping away from the control of the individual, the pervasive potential for disaster is all too apparent. Where moral sensitivity and intellectual understanding no longer serve as guiding lights, the dark maw of violence beckons us all into a sort of ultimate escape from which there is no recovery.

Notes

[1]Roderick Nash discusses this issue in his chapter on "Reputation" in *The Nervous Generation: American Thought, 1917-1930* (Chicago: Rand McNally, 1970), pp. 5-32.

[2]*The Crack-up*, ed. Edmund Wilson (New York: New Directions, 1945), p. 87. Quotations from Fitzgerald's essays in this and the next three paragraphs are all taken from this book.

[3]The titles of the essays "Handle With Care" and "Pasting It Together" have been incorrectly exchanged in *The Crack-up*.

[4]The literature on this subject is too extensive to be dealt with adequately here. See, for examples of works that bear significantly on aspects of this essay, Wylie Sypher, *Loss of the Self in Modern Literature and Art* (New York: Random House, 1962), R. D. Laing, *The Politics of Experience* (New York: Pantheon, 1967), Rollo May, *Power and Innocence: A Search for the Sources of Violence* (New York: Norton, 1972), and John Vernon, *The Garden and the Map: Schizophrenia in Twentieth-Century Literature and Culture* (Urbana: Univ. of Illinois Press, 1973).

[5]There is no generally agreed upon definition of "violence," since the various emphases on physiology, psychology, or ideas depends upon one's anthropological, sociological, or philosophical bent. For examples of wide-ranging possibilities, see the numerous essays in *Violence and the Struggle for Existence,* ed. David N. Daniels and others (Boston: Little, Brown, 1970). As I use the term in this essay, "violence" means destructive aggression that inflicts damage or injury upon the physical or psychological self of an individual, or on property seen as a symbolic extension of that self. It may or may not be consciously intended or malicious; it may or may not have apparent social sanction or justification.

[6]New York: Scribner's, 1934. It is important to use the original version of the text, which conceals Nicole's illness from the reader until after she has been established as a representative cultural ideal, and therefore subordinates those aspects of her insanity that are idiosyncratic to those that are symbolic of the social condition.

Flappers and Some Who Were Not Flappers*

Elizabeth Stevenson

It is difficult to imagine a scholar better qualified than Elizabeth Stevenson to write a woman's perspective of the 1920s. Born in the Panama Canal zone on June 13, 1919, far removed from the stateside agitation for women's suffrage ratified the following year, she must have become increasingly aware of a certain ironical contrast between her own childhood and the rise of a new American feminism. Such perceptions must have been slow in fruition, however. Certainly, her early education at Atlanta's Girls' High or Decatur's genteel Agnes Scott College did not open abrupt insights into the off-beat rhythms of the Jazz Age—nor did she qualify as a flapper.

In fact, her preoccupations as a young scholar led her to write highly literate biographies and critical studies of Henry James (1949), Henry Adams (1955, 1958) and Lafcadio Hearn (1961)—traditional approaches to established cultures hardly associated with the carefree life of the new American Babylon.

Paradoxically, it was precisely Ms. Stevenson's chronological and geographical detachment that served her so well as a cultural historian. If Atlanta seems a long way from the frosted speakeasy culture of New York City, Chicago or the American colony in Paris, Ms. Stevenson more than compensates the reader with her research into women's role in the popular and not-so-popular culture of a controversial decade. Thus, despite her considerable responsibilities as an Assistant Dean of Emory University, she produced in 1967 a landmark exploration of the subject: Babbitts and Bohemians, the American 1920s.

As the title of her present essay indicates, there was considerably more contrast and variety among the women who symbolize the myth of the Twenties than many literal historians have been led to suppose. The spectrum ranges, in fact, from full-fledged flappers, whose carefree mannerisms and lifestyles are excitingly documented, to the domestic Babbittry of the American heartland. In effect, Elizabeth Stevenson has caught it whole. Her extensive reading, observation and research have produced for this anthology a dazzling array of women whose lives have both decorated and permanently informed not only the Twenties, but generations to come.

*Adapted in part, and with interpolations, from *The American 1920s*, Macmillan Publishing Co., 1967—originally published as *Babbitts & Bohemians*.

* * *

We have all been talking about the twenties. If each one of us shines the spotlight of our particular bias on the time, perhaps in the crossfire of these views we may catch a likeness of the time.

As for the age in general, it seems to me that it has become a sort of myth, and the role of women in the twenties has become a myth too. We have recreated an image of the twenties from hints in movies, popular songs, tales of parents and grandparents, and from the softening effect of the backward, nostalgic look.

The twenties, as a coherent period stretching from the end of the 1st World War to the beginning of the Great Depression, has become a blur, a kind of montage of gangsters terrorizing great cities and heedless flappers dancing the Charleston upon the tabletops of speakeasies about to be raided by lively but ineffective cops.

In contrast to the world of the speakeasies and flappers and gangsters, memory tells us also of a contrasting world of the twenties; it tells us of a great, dull, small-town space labeled Main Street or Middletown where the generation just older than the flappers, the cops, and the gangsters, are occupying the foreground and doing a respectable fox-trot at a conformable country club. It is reported that there were then also, filling in the hinterland, great numbers of sweating, underpaid farmers and their dowdy wives, clothed out of the catalogs of Sears Roebuck and Montgomery Ward, living without electricity and waterworks, unable to get their creaking Fords or rusty wagons out to the highway when the rains mired up the country roads. But this known fact has been set aside and what has been made to count for memory are other, more fortunate folk: the townspeople with new washing machines and toasters and vacuum cleaners, caught up in the life of installment buying and the emulation of the heroes and heroines of the advertisements in the *Saturday Evening Post*. (In fact, these middle Americans of the 1920s are recognizable kin to the middle Americans of today—only it is ads on television that rule our lives.) And it is the more erratic lives of the flappers which take on the glamour of distance. The flappers appeal to us as possessing a kind of feather-headed romance in their gestures.

It is now beginning to be possible to look at the contradictions objectively and to find out perhaps how much of the myth is true, how much of the truth is different from or even more entertaining than the myth, and to see the real life of people below the catch phrases: "The Golden Twenties," "The Roaring Twenties," "The Jazz Era," "Prosperity Decade," "Normalcy," "After the Great Crusade," "The Boom," "The Crash." Looking at that time steadily, and comparing it with the time before and the time after, it might be possible to see it as an age involved in a real way with the outside world it tried to deny. And the viewer might find that the short episode remains distinct, poignant, and perhaps significant. Those who deplore and those who delight in the twenties would agree that it was a fountain of life that rose into the light of a universe that had not seen its like before, that it displayed itself in some style, a new American style, and then willfully and tragically descended out of light into darkness. A whole people partook of drama, did things foolishly or brilliantly, and doing so created a recognizable mode. A careless running to extremes, a contradiction of license and oppression, of stuffiness and gaiety: the whole somehow hung together as the expression of a young people at a certain stage of development.

As for women in the twenties—

American women were more visible in the twenties than they had ever been before. They had *come out,* as one might say, in their wartime experience in the years just before the decade began. They had entertained, nursed, done factory and office work, as they had never done it before; and they were not willing to *go back in* again. The generation of the Eighties may not remember, or may not know, that women attempted to *come out* earlier in American History, in the aborted suffrage movement before and after the Civil War. But this *coming out* in the Twenties was more blatant and more general than anything that had happened before in American society.

I see women in the Twenties as playing particular roles, decreed by their society, also as breaking away from those roles, sometimes in attitudes of distortion and exaggeration. But I also see them, as human beings, sharing in making the era, in being, if one may use the expression, "creative." They helped give the time its tone.

I take the word "creativity" to mean an extra quality or dimension, and an extra talent for form, for fixing expression into a memorable shape. In the Twenties one can see a sort of national excess of spontaneity and form in automobiles moving in musical sequence along an assembly line, in a jazz band caught in an ecstasy of strict agreement played out against a loose improvisation, in the ordered confusion of the stock market on a busy day. One can see an individual excess of spontaneity and form in a writer such as F. Scott Fitzgerald or Marianne Moore ordering words to express a special meaning.

Before going on to individual women who expressed 1920s freedom and restriction in different ways, it is—I hope—interesting and entertaining to consider the phenomenon of the flapper as an expression of a certain aspect of the Twenties. Ordinary, everyday American women, responding to pressures in the twenties, became what their contemporaries called—usually admiringly—flappers.

Whether there was freedom and a new chance for all—and there was not—there existed an erroneous but cheering belief that there was change ahead. The openness of the future and the accessibility, as it seemed, of success produced a froth upon the surface of society, and many short-lived, heedless, and sometimes, graceful careers danced upon this foam of confidence. A later, more solid time that would have more real opportunity for women (or for men) would lack this effervescence, which was a unique attribute of the twenties. An English observer characterized a conspicuous part of the population: "Dancing as aimlessly as gnats in winter sunshine it brings to bear on the jolly business of being *ephemeridae* the same hard and cheerful efficiency that it uses in its money making." Observers from overseas were keen, but never got it quite right. They assumed in Americans a hard, deliberate choice in the universal career of money-making, with other choices discarded, whereas, for Americans, there was nothing else they knew, and they put into money-making the traits reserved in Europe for other careers: sports, gambling, politics, status-creation, even a kind of esthetics.

Flappers...

The most effervescent symbol of the Twenties was the flapper. She was a new American girl, a new woman, a new arrangement of the elements of sex and fashion. She no longer exists; she existed for only a few years in the mid and late Twenties, but during that short epoch she was a completely defined and recognizable type. In the Twenties she was suddenly there, it seemed and welcome.

Yet the flapper evolved. She was born perhaps in the experiences some few women had in the war of 1917-1918, when all sorts of freedoms and equalities with men occurred during the exigencies of Red Cross and other welfare work among the soldiers or particularly in the excitements of entertaining soldiers. Travel, informality, closeness of contact between the sexes in situations of danger changed the relations between men and women, at least for short periods in certain places; and some of this carried over into the period after the war, when some women began asserting themselves with impudence and self-assurance.

Mary Pickford was not a flapper, and the Mary Pickford type of sweet, confiding, shy, and yet cheerful and innocent female dominated the early, after-the-war covers and illustrations in the *Saturday Evening Post*, which may be taken as a place to watch for the flapper's arrival. A change appears first in the familiarity of the boy and girl on the innocuous covers. In a Norman Rockwell painting for the issue of March 12, 1921, the girl is more kittenish than hoydenish; her hair, her dress, her attitude, are soft and tentative, but she is unafraid and a little bold, whereas the boy whose hand she is holding—to tell his fortune—is awkward. She looks into his eyes with confidence and no assumption of consequences to her boldness. A year later, in a cover by Thomas H. Webb for the issue of May 13, 1922, the closeness of the boy and the girl, while still playful, is more self-conscious; he is standing close in an attitude of embrace, ostensibly showing her how to hold a bow and arrow; her dress is beginning to be tomboyish: a skirt and sweater, the sweater belted in leather, an Indian beaded band across her forehead. Her glance backward at the young man—awkward boy no longer—is more conscious of possible consequences of this exciting intimacy.

During 1922 and 1923 the girls in the stories wear soft, full dresses, rather awkwardly long. Sometimes the heroine in sweater and skirt wears her hair in a long thick braid down her back. Older women wear ample clothes, which denote maturity. In 1924 there is a change in an occasional cover or illustration. Out of the cover of January 5, 1924, a gambling girl looks straight at you. Her dress is the slightest, flimsiest silk, cut low and square-necked, thin straps over her shoulders. Her bobbed hair is almost hidden by a soft, wide, shirred bandeau of the same silken material as the slight, slim gown. She handles gambling counters as she sits at a table; the look she gives says that she handles her life as a gamble, too.

Dresses in many of the stories remain rather indefinitely long, but the nice young girl's position in society is infinitely free and easy; one story shows the heroine sitting at a drug counter, exchanging pleasantries good-naturedly and unselfconsciously with the sleek young man behind the counter. A boy and a girl in an Alice Duer Miller story sit at ease upon a beach. They wear the new bathing suits; his is one-piece, armless, but high-necked; hers is one-piece, reaching a few inches down the thigh, the skirt of the suit gaily and boldly striped. She has on some kind of stocking below the knees and slippers. As late as January, 1925, a cover shows a fond and fatuous portrait of a Mary Pickford girl who has long corkscrew curls trailing down to a soft and modest neckline. But inside the same issue, on the first page after the cover, there is a bold girl in a hosiery ad who seems to herald a new age. She is perched carelessly but gracefully upon a glossy mahogany table, dangling one silken leg off the edge. Her hair is softly waved and bobbed and her dress is sleeveless and short, held up by straps that look like flowers. Her slippers are slight things with pointed toes. At this moment the flapper is here, and all girls, the good ones and the bad ones, try to be flappers; the time is the end of the year 1925 and the early part of 1926. So long did it take her to come. Girls with skirts short to the knees or just below the knees become frequent if not universal.

In a story in the issue of April 3, 1926, there is a girl who is the very type: a girl seen in a careless pose, her back to us, on tiptoes, her dress hem hitting the back of her knees, her waist low and bloused. On her head is a cloche hat with a soft brim. Another story shows the same kind of girl dancing the Charleston, the caption comments,"with imagination and abandon." Girls, by this time, are shown putting on lipstick in public, confident of their own importance, and displaying a breezy independence of opinion. Many girls try to be flappers. The generic flapper is the nice girl who is a little fast, who takes the breath of staid observers with her flip spontaneity, her short-lived likes and dislikes, her way of skating gaily over thin ice. Would-be flappers are often heartless little ignoramuses, gum-chewing, vulgar, wearing ridiculous clothes, imitating a mode in second-rate style; others are overdecorated, costly, gangsters' girl friends. Many girls of the mid-twenties, however, grew up, finished school, fell in love, married, all without any whiff of the style of the type—yet bobbing their hair, doing up their hems, learning to Charleston.

By 1925 the phenomenon of the flapper was so conspicuous that many words were put on paper analyzing her. In 1920, before the full-blown type existed, Scott Fitzgerald gave a book of short stories the title *Flappers and Philosophers*. A magazine like *The New Republic*, given to the serious study of politics and economics, had space on September 9, 1925, for a piece by Bruce Bliven, an attempt to describe the new girl. Bliven thought he knew how she made up her face and what she wore and told it in a piece called "Flapper Jane."

She is frankly, heavily made up, not to imitate nature, but for an altogether artificial effect—pallor mortis, poisonously scarlet lips, richly ringed eyes—the latter looking not so much debauched (which is the intention) as diabetic...

[Her clothes]...were estimated the other day by some statistician to weigh two pounds. Probably a libel; I doubt if they come within half a pound of such bulk. Jane isn't wearing much this summer. If you'd like to know exactly, it is: one dress, one step-in, two stockings, two shoes. [No petticoat, no brassiere, of course, no corset.]

The flapper seemed the most notable new character upon the scene. She attracted the most attention. When she smoked a cigarette conspicuously on a public street, reporters made a front-page story of the incident. She rallied a whole new circle of male types around her. Her beaus, boys in Joe College clothes, or sharp young gentlemen in belted jackets and new Van Heusen soft collars, and trousers with wide flapping legs, shared her good times, learning to drink in a dry age, dancing the fox-trot in roadhouses, riding about in rattletrap flivers or expensive Marmons, going to the movies and the speakeasies, traveling across the Atlantic to a gay, superficial Europe that seemed to belong to Americans. Oddly, the particular, identifiable flapper faded away, very quickly, to be replaced, so that the fact was hardly noticed, by another. She and her boy friend, after a short season of gaiety, vanished and became a part of a solid, respectable, and inconspicuous mass of settled, older, married folks, upholding the standards of the good life as sketched in Sinclair Lewis's *Babbitt*. Flappers and Babbitts had to be rather well off. Unprosperous folk did not have the cash or time to belong to either type, so the double layer of bright young people and stuffily proper middle-aged ones was after all very thin—a two-tiered icing upon the cake of the age.

And some were not flappers...

Flappers were a category of women (who did not know they were a type, thinking that they acted entirely out of freedom) who had been warped by society into behaving in a certain way.

But allow me to name over a handful of women of the Twenties who do not fit into a category. Like the men one remembers from this time, they were individuals, more ambitious, more gifted, more stubborn about doing what they wished to do. They gained something from the increased scope which the era gave women, but they gave back much to the time, in color, charm, and achievement. They were not all noble, not all good, but they expressed themselves as well as expressed something of the spirit of the Twenties.

There is a wild variety among them. Think of the difference between Emily Post, and "Mother" Jones. Mrs. Post devoted herself to telling those on the way up the social ladder how to behave at dinner parties, what to wear, what to say, how to drink soup without disgracing themselves.

"Mother" Jones, a devoted labor agitator, went about instructing uncouth and ill-paid miners in West Virginia and Colorado how to assert their rights and make better wages and not be killed by the guns of the hired goons of the mine owners. The inside of the jails which "Mother" Jones frequented would have had little use for the manners which Mrs. Post inculcated. Both women were useful in and to the decade. And in a way both Mrs. Post and "Mother" Jones decorate the time.

Women could be as bizarre in politics as their menfolks. There was not only a "Pa" Ferguson in Texas politics; there was a "Ma" Ferguson, and they were both, in succession, governors of the state.

There were not only clever, unscrupulous men who exploited fears and prejudices to bring the Ku Klux Klan to a new growth of life in the twenties. There was Elizabeth Tyler, who was the organizing genius of the movement in this time.

There was, of course, a great supply of women of the middling range, more or less happy in their home-making, longing perhaps for expression, but rarely finding it, of whom an early prototype was Sinclair Lewis's Carol Kennecott in *Main Street* and a later one, Dodworth's wife in the novel, *Dodsworth*. If the twenties was a decade which allowed these women to escape conformity, there was still enough force and weight in opinion to make these accomplishers pay a stiff price for escaping from housewifery.

Equality being easiest in the arts, one can begin with the entertainers. Three to be mentioned, among many others, were Black women, the one who called herself simply Bricktop, a second Josephine Baker—two who went to Paris and helped convert Europeans to the delights of American song and dance; a third was Ethel Waters, who began a long career at this time upon the domestic stage.

A dazzling handful of singers, comedians, actresses, and a nightclub hostess added to the joy of life. Libby Holman sang the blues, Colleen Moore and Clara Bow embodied "flapper" virtues in the movies. Adele Astaire and Marilyn Miller danced on the Broadway stage with dazzling verve, making audiences feel younger and better. Fanny Brice created a double persona, a wistful, awkward child, droll and irresistible in simplicity and a poignant singer of "he done me wrong" songs. Texas Guinan was a phenomenon as a nightclub hostess. The young Edmund Wilson took the trouble to write an admiring essay about her: "this prodigious woman, with her pearls, her glittering bosom, her abundant beautifully bleached yellow coiffure, her formidable trap of shining white teeth, her broad bare back behind its grating of green velvet, the full blown peony as big as a cabbage exploding on her broad green thigh." And her genial greeting, "Hello, sucker!" to customers introduced them in comradely fashion to a world they knew to be a fraud but with Texas Guinan in control, one which they knew they would enjoy.

The wife of F. Scott Fitzgerald, Zelda, was not quite a dancer or a writer, although she tried to be both. She was a sort of magnified flapper and pursued a hectic career in public places, trying to live every day at the pace of a Charleston; like the twenties, she came a cropper, and she is remembered.

Two young writers appeared upon the scene, and in their own persons embodied much of the times. Dorothy Parker was better known for her witty conversation during the days of the Round Table at the Algonquin Hotel than for her writing. The seriousness of her viewpoint, underneath the wisecracks, sometimes escaped the notice of her contemporaries. Her stories and the verse have had survival value. Her first collection of verse, *Enough Rope*, appeared in 1926. Anita Loos managed to look like a pretty, light-headed friend of her heroine Lorelei Lee of the book *Gentlemen Prefer Blondes*, published in 1925, and which even a philosopher, Bertrand Russell, and a Supreme Court Justice, Wendell Holmes, confessed they enjoyed.

Writers much admired in their own time, suffering something of an eclipse today, helped free women from personal shackles by the independent way they lived as well as by their writing. Edna St. Vincent Millay's *Second April* (1921) and *A Few Figs from Thistles* (1922) and other volumes published during the twenties, possess some of the perfume of the time. Elinor Wylie's verse, *Nets to Catch the Wind* (1921), and *Trivial Breath* (1928), as well as her highly mannered novels, *The Venetian Glass Nephew* (1925) and *The Orphan Angel* (1926) show craftsmanship and care coming out of an allegedly careless age.

A poet more considerable than either of these writers made her way slowly. Marianne Moore's first book of poems, *Observations*, was published in 1925. She came to New York after teaching at the Carlisle, Pennsylvania Indian School, lived at the YWCA on Lexington Avenue, worked at the New York Public Library and at the end of the decade edited the *Dial* magazine. Disciplined, intellectual, inventive in patterns of words and thoughts, Marianne Moore was to rank in later decades as a thinking poet.

Young writers of fiction like Elizabeth Madox Roberts and Caroline Gordon brought new areas of American living into public consciousness and set standards for excellence in style. Willa Cather, who had begun writing before the decade achieved its own style, published her four most solid novels during this time: *A Lost Lady* (1923), *The Professor's House* (1925), *My Antonia* (1926), and *Death Comes for the Archibishop* (1927). Edith Wharton went on grandly producing first rate work in a career that had had its beginning in Theodore Roosevelt's presidency. Among several volumes of fiction published in the twenties, *Hudson River Bracketed* (1929) was one of her more accomplished novels.

Gertrude Stein attained her greatest influence in this period as an encourager of young writers and as a collector of modern art. Her writing caused scandal but also caused the "booboisie," as H. L. Mencken called them, to take notice. As influential as Stein, but without the encrustations of ego, Sylvia Beach, a young American woman who kept a bookstore in Paris, Shakespeare & Co., mothered and sistered any number of aspiring writers. Both women were a part of the American invasion of Paris. However, they were fixed stars there and influenced many who simply visited.

In journalism, Mary Heaton Vorse was a brave reporter of the dark side of American life, writing about strikes, riots, and dire poverty in such textile towns as Gastonia, South Carolina. Dorothy Thompson was another journalist who began her long career in this period by going to Russia for a first hand view of that new culture. Her book, *The New Russia*, was published in 1928.

Eva Le Gallienne, actress and director, enriched the legitimate theater. Creating and directing her own Civic Repertory Theater, she revived plays by distinguished European playwrights and put them on the American stage for the first time. She gave Broadway the benefit of a scholarly and sophisticated approach to play producing.

In the visual arts, there were a number of painters, sculptors, and photographers at work, who happened to be women. Georgia O'Keefe, painting into her eighties, was in an early stage of her career in the twenties, beginning to see objects in a way no one had ever seen them before, and to put them on canvas—ostensible flowers, barns, red or purple hills—giving them a new meaning in her paintings.

Cecilia Beaux was painting. Peggy Bacon and Wanda Gag were painters and illustrators of high distinction. Dorothea Lange and Bernice Abbott were using cameras as artists in pictures which ranged from private expressions of mood to a stark kind of reporting. Anna Moses (Grandma Moses) was working away quietly within the vision of her New England hills and woods and houses.

In various fields, other persistent women made a mark. Constance Rourke brought out her *American Humor*, (1931) a perspective on American literature which was to be a landmark in criticism. Helen Lynd had an equal part with Robert Lynd in the sociological study, *Middletown* (1929) which tells us what middle America was like in the twenties. Esther C. Goddard was Robert Goddard's research and photographic associate in his experiments in rocketry and space flight, at a time when such work as theirs brought on them only ridicule. Jane Addams continued her leavening of the slums of Chicago and wrote a second volume about this experience in *Second Twenty Years at Hull House* (1930). Margaret Mead began her field researches in the South Seas and published *Coming of Age in Samoa* (1928) and *Growing up in New Guinea* (1930). Amelia Earhart, after serving as a nurse in the war and as a social worker in Boston, began her exploits in flying and her solid work in encouraging commercial aviation. She was the first woman to fly the Atlantic, and the first person to fly a long stretch of the Pacific.

I have simply enumerated these women. I have not tried to explain why the twenties made it a good time for them to work. It is obvious that there was a new spirit of work among them, a willingness to risk themselves for ideas of various kinds. If I might hazard a guess, I would say that the contradiction of the twenties made it possible for these individuals to achieve something of their own. The solid base of assumed prosperity (the family or home town which was there in the background, out of which most of them came and to which, in hard times, they might go back) that solid base, not understanding them, yet gave them something real to react against and to depend on and was a help to these scorners of Babbittry. And in addition, the other side of the twenties, the margin of freedom which this time of mental and economic lassez-faire possessed, gave these bright aspirers room to be themselves, to try new things, the illusion that there was time and place for their books and pictures and exploits to go on forever.

I hope that I have at least indicated that the decade of the twenties was a period of more variety than we often assume. The flappers were a poignant symbol. The harder-headed, if not harder-hearted women who achieved in many different vocations, were as real as the flappers. They have had a lasting influence on our thinking, on our manners, on the character of American civilization. We are where we are today, in part, because of them. We might venture further on, if we emulated their spirit.

The Flapper:
Hollywood's First Liberated Woman

Patricia Erens

The '60s, like the '20s, proved to be an era when the rights of people were paraded and individuals felt not only the need but the compulsion to prove their individuality and uniqueness. Minority groups usually benefit from the self consciousness of an age and women finally began to emerge as individuals in the '20s and re-emerge in the '60s. Naturally this upswing has produced social scientists to study and analyze and catalogue it, and for the first time in our history women are studying women as important contributors to social development.

Patricia Erens' field is women in film. In addition to her responsibilities as a Professor at Rosary College, Illinois, she has written four books: The Films of Shirley MacLaine, Sexual Stratagems: The World of Women in Film, The Film Career of Akira Kurosawa *and* The Jew in American Cinema. *She has contributed numerous articles in leading film magazines. In 1974 she co-chaired the prestigious festival* Films by Women/Chicago 74.

In her paper "The Flapper: Hollywood's First Liberated Woman," Patricia Erens explores the film and literary traditions that led to the creation of the flapper and the women writers who popularized this new image. Seen as a kind of synthesis between the passivity of Sleeping Beauty and the spunkiness of Goldilocks, the flapper emerged from these three precedents: the virgin who was always pure and demure, the vamp who was seductive, erotic, outside the norm and always defeated, and the child-woman who behaved in just the way her name suggests. The flapper always relied on a man to "save her" but she had more energy and verve than the virgin type.

Through an analysis of the movies of the Flapper Era Ms. Erens shows that the main qualities of the flappers were their youth, health, vigor, and energy. It was the commencement of the cult of youth, and the flapper established herself as independent and socially liberated, rebellious of established authority. This is not to say however that the concerns of the flappers were worthy of their energy. Much of their vigor was spent in trying to get a man or unravel the good girl vs. bad girl subplot which leads to getting a man. Interestingly enough the movie public was ambivalent toward the flapper. Applauding her energy and appeal at the beginning, the audience felt morally justified when the flapper heroine was cleared of the "bad girl" charges and her frivolity gave way to depth of feeling. The flapper gets her man.

Oftentimes in the movies the flapper must be in some way punished for her independence before she "gets her man" but this in no way led her to concern herself with anything other than herself. There was no thought of social responsibilities and the flappers for one small moment lived only for self liberation, amusement, and men.

* * *

In 1920, 35,000,000 Americans went to the movies every week. That figure represented one out of every three people and that was only the beginning. With the introduction of sound in 1927, ticket sales soared to 57,000,000 a week. By 1929, 80,000,000 tickets were sold weekly, meaning that better than one out of every two people saw a movie each week of the year.

Stars rose and fell. Girls poured into Hollywood hoping to find fame and fortune. Lucille le Sueur becomes Joan Crawford. Kathleen Morrison becomes Colleen Moore. Anita Dooley becomes the exotic Nita Naldi as Theodosia Goodman had become Theda Bara a generation before.

Stars were hired at immense salaries only to kick back a third to producers. Writers channeled a portion of their fees to directors and movie budgets were not infrequently looted. Assuredly, all was not as it appeared in the fairy tale stories on the silver screen.

Behind the scenes were scandals involving sex, murder, rape and drugs. 1921 saw the end of the careers of several silent stars, most notably Fatty Arbuckle, Mabel Normand, and Mary Miles Minter. But, Hollywood knew the value of sex and seduction at the box office. These themes were popularized by the spicy domestic dramas of Cecil de Mille in the early twenties in films like *Male and Female* and *Forbidden Fruit.*

Eventually a hue and a cry from an outraged public caused Hollywood to move towards self-regulation. In 1922, producers hired Will Hays, Harding's sober Postmaster General, to head the Motion Picture Producers and Distributors Association. De Mille turned from domestic dramas to religious epics (not without orgy scenes, however) and von Stroheim had to keep his sophisticated decadence in check.

In 1927, Warner Brothers astounded the world with "talking pictures." Producers called it a passing fad, but audiences clamored for more. Sound changed the face of Hollywood and brought to a close what many have called Hollywood's Golden Age (and what others have seen as a primitive, incomplete art form).

There is no doubt that the image which best captured and typified this era was the flapper. There were other images to be sure: Mary Pickford experienced continued popularity in the roles of child women through 1926 and at the other end of the spectrum, Greta Garbo, the *femme fatale,* achieved immediate success with her first films in the mid-twenties. But Pickford belongs to another era, the age of Griffith and Victorianism and Garbo was a European import who possessed an unfathomable mystery which intrigued, but eluded American audiences.

On the other hand, the flapper was an American creation—young, fresh, honest and healthy. In an article written for *Motion Picture Magazine* in 1927, Margaret Reid stated, The term "flapper" has become a generalization meaning almost any *femme* between fifteen and twenty-five. Some five years ago it was a thing of distinction—indicating a neat bit of femininity, collegiate age, who rolled her stockings, chain-smoked, had a heavy "line," mixed and drank a mean highball and radiated "It." Reid goes on to credit F. Scott Fitzgerald with the creation of the term in his book, *This Side of Paradise*, published in 1920.

Although Fitzgerald provided the name, there were other writers, especially women authors like Elinor Glyn, Anita Loos, and Rachel Crothers, who helped develop the image of "the new woman." Glyn, an out-spoken British novelist, set the stage as early as 1907 with her book, *Three Weeks*, which glorified adulterous love. It was a small sensation on both sides of the Atlantic.

Basically what Glyn proposed was the restoration of romance into the lives of married people. As a champion of this cause, she advised millions of women through lectures, newspaper columns, and a book entitled, *The Philosophy of Love*, on how to stay alluring, elusive, mysterious and unpredictable. This may seem corny and commercial today, but in the years before and during the twenties, it went a long way in helping the ordinary housewife gain a sense of self-identity and independence. I should emphasize that what Glyn was proposing was not necessarily sexual allure.

In her most famous work, a short novella published in *Cosmopolitan* in 1927 entitled *It* (which gave rise to a film of the same name and also established the career of Clara Bow—the "It" girl). Glyn explained, "It is a strange magnetism, why even a priest can have it."

In her person Glyn represented the new woman. Arriving in Hollywood in 1920 at the age of fifty-six after an unhappy marriage and several affairs, she worked for Paramount and MGM as scriptwriter and producer for eight years, exerting tremendous power over her films. She hand-picked Clara Bow for the role in *It* (both had red hair) and appeared in the film herself. Though her characters exist for love and excitement, her personal life was devoted to work and agitation.

Anita Loos is less influential than Glyn on the flapper image, although her life also was exceptional. While still a teen-ager, she began writing scenarios and scripts for Biograph. Between 1912-1915, she turned out 105 story ideas which were primarily used by D. W. Griffith. By and large these pieces were no credit to women's lib; however, the female characters were usually spunky and her plots moved. Her contribution to the life of independence and pleasure is best developed in *Gentlemen Prefer Blondes* written in 1925 (filmed in 1928) which H. L. Mencken claims "makes fun of sex, which has never before been done in this grand and glorious nation of ours."

On the stage, Rachel Crothers depicted flappers as well.

Accordingly, the flapper was not a Hollywood invention; her origins reach back into literature and drama. However, her popularization was definitely related to the movies, which not only depicted her exploits, but also visualized her dress, carriage, gestures, responses, etc. Although all the films were silent, her usual witty remarks were sprinkled throughout on inter-titles.

Margaret Reid's definition of the flapper seems a little disappointing for those who are looking for the equivalent of today's NOW woman, yet Reid is by and large accurate. The film flapper was not a political agitator, but she was liberated—to a point.

In her search for good times she demonstrated ingenuity, independence, and a sense of self-worth. Seldom was she intimidated by established authority. If most of her efforts were reserved for getting a husband, at least she was going to enjoy herself first.

To accomplish this usually meant going against the established traditions inherited from the preceding Victorian era. The differences become immediately apparent by comparing the values of parent figures and their flapper children, especially in a film like *Dancing Mothers*. The freedom the flapper sought was a direct threat to the older generation.

Lingerie parties, scanty attire, drinking, smoking, frenetic dancing and all-night socials may not seem serious today, but it was open rebellion in the twenties. Molly Haskell, author of *From Reverence to Rape*, summed up the situation as follows, "the flapper's main objective was social, rather than intellectual, liberation."

At this point it might be useful to look at the flapper in contrast to the female images that preceded her—most especially the virginal Victorian heroine of the pre-war period and the vamp which emerged with Theda Bara's debut in *A Fool There Was*, 1915.

The pre-war films emphasized the virtues of innocence, joy and ladylike behavior. Married women were often child-women who depended on the protection of their husbands, who in Griffith films seem constantly in danger of being raped. Mature women in these films were not above blushing coyly or jumping up and down in childlike fashion.

With the decline of this image came the rise of the vamp. Seductive and exotic, she exuded almost hypnotic powers over men whom she led astray by promises of sex—implied, but not shown on the screen. In the end, she was always defeated. Simultaneous with this lady of the night was the child-woman, best depicted by America's sweetheart, Mary Pickford. During the post-war period, she won acclaim in films like *Little Lord Fauntleroy*, *Pollyanna*, and *The Little Princess*. Sporting blond, cork-screw curls, she managed to continue these roles into the twenties when she was well beyond thirty.

Although neither the virgin, the vamp, nor the child-woman were suitable images for the twenties, all contributed to the blossoming of the liberated woman, the flapper. Lillian Gish, Griffith's definitive actress, may have been delicate featured, but she had back-bone, nerve, courage, and anger. She also used her head. The vamp, though too exaggerated to draw imitators from the female audience, did counter the prevailing mores of the time. However, not only did she pay for it, but she always stood outside of acceptable society. Lastly, Mary Pickford, sentimental to the hilt, did show ingenuity and intelligence, rebelling against the fussy manners of the day, not afraid to get dirty and always capable of getting out of a jam.

Given this heritage, the film flapper arrived on the scene ready to raise a little hell before she settled down to married life. In a sense she was the answer to the American male's dream—combining qualities of both the dark vamps and the golden haired princesses. She promised much, yet in the end proved moral enough to make marriage feasible. Thus men were able to have their cake and eat it too. This speculation is supported by a quotation by Alan Jenkins, cited in a book called *The Twenties*, "Amid all the instant sex and apparent permissiveness, girls were still put on pedestals, from which they frequently descended to become playmates." It is noteworthy that most of the popular flappers of the day were brunette, like the vamps, and even Joan Crawford had dark hair in her early flapper films.

The flapper differed from the vamp in that she was recognizable as the girl next door, or down the block, or at the office. Different actresses represented different social classes and different styles. Clara Bow was usually lower or lower-middle class, often playing roles which allowed the average American girl to identify with her and to dream. In her films she played a manicurist, usherette, waitress, cigarette girl, taxi driver, swimming instructor, and salesgirl. Interestingly, her jobs always brought her into contact with men. As a manicurist in *Mantrap* (1926), she worked in a barber shop. Even as a salesgirl in the lingerie department, she was visited by more men than women buyers. Also, these jobs provided ample opportunities for touching members of the opposite sex.

Clara Bow's roles held out the hope to millions of women that they could hold their own and have fun, even without the benefits of family money. Not so concerned with her reputation as the middle class miss, Bow was willing to take risks, often to defend others. In her films she demonstrates a genuine concern for those around her. Her full cheeks and rounded body imply a soft heart and good natured liveliness devoid of all malice or ultra-sophisfication.

Colleen Moore represented the young collegiate, a more upper class flapper, and closer to the Fitzgerald model. Basically a comedienne, Moore's films are full of good fun and lively activities. More spoiled than Clara Bow, she is accustomed to getting her own way and proves a match for her beaus on the tennis court as well as the dance floor. Though not remembered to the degree of Clara Bow, she set the vogue with *Flaming Youth* (1923). As Marjorie Rosen points out in her book, *Popcorn Venus*, *Flaming Youth* caused a mild revolution fashion-wise, influencing the trend towards loose dresses, high hemlines and bobbed hair.

If flappers did not succeed in affecting fundamental changes in society, they did at least put on the face of revolution and declare the younger generation a group apart.

Constance Talmadge represented the epitome of upper class sophistication. She is the flapper deluxe—witty, graceful, up on the latest books as well as the latest dances. As depicted in *Lover From Paris*, she is more concerned with her reputation than the other flappers.

Lastly, Joan Crawford rose to fame as a dancing flapper in MGM films like *Our Dancing Daughters*. Headstrong, hell-bent to get ahead, she added a note of tragedy to her roles, reminding us of a Zelda Fitzgerald.

In addition to these actresses, there were other flappers whose names are no longer remembered—Alice White, Sally O'Neil, Eleanor Boardman and, of course, Gloria Swanson and Tallulah Bankhead, who are remembered for other images. Also, there is the great American actress, Louise Brooks, who established the type on the German screen and is best remembered for her films made in Europe, such as *Pandora's Box*.

Hollywood's attitude to these young heroines was somewhat ambivalent. While they glorified the antics of these stars and even encouraged public images to match the screen roles, the flapper did not always get off without some criticism or set-back. Money hungry Crawford dies in an auto accident at the end of *Sally, Irene and Mary*. In *Dancing Mothers* the sympathy goes to the dutiful, middle-aged wife who maintains great dignity in contrast to the flighty antics and insensitivity of her daughter Clara Bow. To some degree this was a result of restrictions imposed by the Hays Office.

Often incidents are left vague, as in *Dancing Mothers* where Clara Bow stays out all night. Was she sleeping with a man or dancing the Charleston? Some films were out and out morality tales. In *Our Dancing Daughters* Crawford asks, "What's wrong with me? I'm decent, no cheat. Men like trickery and lies." But in the end she gets her man and proves that the flapper can taste all of life and be virtuous too.

Respectability was still to be honored. Clara Bow does not succeed in getting the boss until her name is cleared for suspicion of having and supporting an illegitimate child in *It* or alters her behavior in *The Wild Party*. Bow may gain our sympathy for kindly caring for her neighbor's child and staunchly claiming it as her own, but she does not win her man until her virginity is established. In the end morality is more meaningful than humanity. Thus the film flapper seldom champions the rights of her less fortune sisters or seriously questions the masculine supremacy of society. She did not use her economic resources to establish an independent existence as Beatrice Hinkle advised in her tract "Against the Double Standard," but she did gain self-confidence.

The films show little female solidarity until the end of the decade in a movie like *The Wild Party* (1929). Perhaps compassion and understanding were allowed to surface because the film was directed by a woman, Dorothy Arzner. In the thirties more films would express close relationships between women, especially as they worked towards a common goal. The backstage musicals and the film *Marked Woman* (1937), a story of a group of prostitutes who help indict a Lucky Luchinao-type character, are examples in point.

On the whole, the flapper is out for herself. Usually she is the sole star, supported by a cast of male admirers. In films where there are more than one romantic female, the women are often depicted as jealous antagonists. Dedicated to living life to the fullest, the flappers were not dedicated to any causes beyond themselves. Even the sympathetic mother in *Dancing Mothers* comes to accept this attitude.

As Clara Bow represents the epitome of the flapper, it is worthwhile to look closer at her image. In most pictures Bow portrays a working woman. As her work is usually rather menial, she demonstrates no sense of commitment. On the other hand, she also demonstrates no desire to find a more meaningful job.

In all films Bow is interested in men. Romance becomes a game. The titles of two films are revealing: *Mantrap* (1926) and *Get Your Man* (1927). The idea is to set up a situation so that the man chases her. For this she is not opposed to being the initiator or using special tactics. These include using legs and eyes—two sure-fire weapons. Bow was particularly adept at winking and batting her eyes, a virtue Glyn had emphasized in her writings. There is a beautiful scene in a film with Colleen Moore called *Ella Cinders* where Moore practices eye expressions as she dreams of becoming a Hollywood star. In the film she wins a photo contest and a trip to Hollywood, a story with many allusions to the life and career of Clara Bow.

Early flapper films played up the childlike, boyish qualities of women. This is especially true of Bow who was short and round faced. Again, titles reflect the direction of the films: In 1926 Bow made *Fascinating Youth*, *Kid Boots*, *The Runaway*, and *Two Can Play*. Unquestionably, the youth cult began in the roaring twenties. Bow's childish, sensual qualities were best displayed in another 1926 film, *Dancing Mothers*, where she played the role of Kittens. As the decade progressed, however, Bow became more hard-boiled. The sassy repartee of *The Wild Party* is a forerunner of sharper, more sophisticated dialogue in the talking films of the next decade.

All flapper films have at least one dance sequence, although production numbers are rare except in Joan Crawford films. Movement is the key feature of the flapper style—frenetic energy, jumping and touching. These qualities most aptly apply to Bow. In a book entitled, *The Celluloid Sacrifice*, Alexander Walker describes her as follows: "her highly individual way of projecting sexiness was by touch: she was always touching her man lightly and fleetingly, seldom lingering, as if she found it stimulating to break contact and come again."

Primary plot developments center on getting a man. Secondary developments concern unraveling misunderstandings. This usually means discerning the difference between what Bow appears to be and what she really is. The discrepancy lays the foundation for the good/bad girl, which has become part of the American cinema ever since. As it turns out, Bow didn't have an illegitimate baby in *It* nor did she have an extra-marital affair in *Mantrap*, nor sleep with her boyfriend in *Wings*.

Although Bow wears seductive clothes, she never transgresses certain mores; these are stronger in the earlier films. For instance, when her date tries to kiss her in *It*, she responds by calling him a "minute man." The moral code in *The Wild Party*, a later film, is more flexible.

Throughout her career, Bow showed a strong sense of self-worth and confidence. Possessing cool, she always had the perfect response as well as tremendous resourcefulness. The car scene in *The Wild Party* and the dress scene in *It* are two examples. In addition, as heroine, she was usually fearless, always frank (if not totally honest), and mostly a good sport, even when she lost her man. Despite a streak of selfishness and a failure to confront greater problems of the day, she and the other flappers—real and fictional—did take important steps towards feminine independence and liberation. What they lacked in seriousness, they made up for with enthusiasm. Perhaps the final word is that in the confused world of the roaring twenties, they possessed that unique quality which Glyn had called "it."

A brief analysis of one film, *Dancing Mothers* (1926), provides an illustration of how various elements mentioned in this paper operated on the screen, especially iconographic images, archetypal situations, and implicit codes of behavior.

The film opens on the deck of an ocean liner returning from Europe to the United States. On board are Catherine Westcourt (Clara Bow) and her father Hugh (Norman Trevor). As Catherine, called Kittens throughout the film, Bow possesses the classic characteristics embodied in the image of the flapper.

She is young and unmarried. Her behavior reflects a childlike attitude, spontaneous, physical, irresponsible, and self-concerned. In addition, there are seductive overtones to her personality. Others, especially her parents, tend to indulge her whims.

The first shot of Kittens, wearing a white, fur coat, reveals her soft, curly hair (bobbed short) and her girlish face. We see her stroking a cute, fluffy dog. Both her coat and the puppy suggest her sensual nature. When the dog jumps off her lap, she immediately pursues it, thus demonstrating one of the key characteristics of the flapper—her constant motion.

On her merry romp she meets the film hero, Gerald Naughton (Conway Tearle). Self-possessed and confident, she introduces herself, possessing no compunctions about being the initiator. Always she remains sweet and poised.

When the ship docks at New York harbor, Kittens runs to kiss her mother (Alice Joyce), whom she refers to as Buddy. In contrast to Kittens, Ethel Westcourt is a large, stately woman, who possesses great reserve and dignity. A montage sequence reveals that she once had been a successful actress who abandoned her career in 1907 to marry Hugh Westcourt and to raise a family.

The next scene shows Kittens and her current beau, Kenneth, out on the town. Kittens wants to visit The Pirate Cafe, a speak-easy which features menacing decor as a means of titillating the customers. The cafe also provides drinks and dancing for its upper-class patrons. The cafe scene furnishes an opportunity for the flapper to demonstrate her frenetic energy. Always, Kittens' eyes are darting around, taking in every last drop of excitement. The scene in the cafe is interspersed with cut-aways to her mother, who remains home alone.

Despite the illicit overtones of the speak-easy, Kittens appears wearing a full, white dress which implies her essential innocence. She is contrasted with her father's mistress (seated in another part of the cafe), who is dressed in a dark, slinky dress which marks her as "the other woman." To emphasize the iniquity of Hugh's relationship with his female companion, he slips her money, which she openly rejects. However later, she clandestinely accepts it. This overt demonstration of duplicity is exempletive in that duplicity signifies the ambivalent moral attitude of the filmmakers towards the flapper character. Flappers are initially presented as positive figures who live by new moral standards. Later the appealing characteristics are recodified and the flapper either reforms or is punished. Other women in the film who exhibit similar moral standards are portrayed as immoral and destructive. Sympathy shifts from scene to scene.

Jealous of Kitten's attention to Gerald, who has also arrived at The Pirate's Cafe, Kenneth threatens to tell her father. Unperturbed, Kittens replies, "Go ahead; he is right over there." Such a remark evidences the degree of control Kittens exerts over her male companions. This factor is particularly prevalent when the flapper comes from an upper-class background.

In the next scene Ethel reveals her concern about Kittens' relationship with Gerald, whom we presume is unacceptable because of his age and also his participation in the demi-monde. In response to Ethel's request that he speak to Kittens, Hugh replies, "The youngster of today can take care of herself. Things have changed since you were a girl." At first, this statement seems to be the moral message of the film, especially as Kittens and her father have thus far dominated the story. Only later, as the attention shifts to Ethel, do we re-interpret this sentiment as false.

Following the evening at The Pirate's Cafe, Ethel is visited by Mrs. Mazzarene, who convinces her that their lives are not over and that they have as much right to pleasure as the rest of their families. Ethel agrees to accompany Mrs. Mazzarene to The Roof Club as the first step in her commitment to a new life. A cut to The Roof Club reveals Hugh with his female companion. Shortly thereafter, Kittens and Gerald arrive. Taking Gerald aside, Hugh asks him to stop seeing Kittens. Gerald agrees, claiming no romantic interest of any kind. Ethel arrives, determined to seduce Gerald away from her daughter. The comings and goings in this episode are reminiscent of French farce.

Hugh is shocked to find his wife on his own turf. A triumph for women's liberation occurs when Ethel refuses to return home with Hugh. She claims that when she stayed home as a dutiful wife and mother, she lost him to these clubs. Now, she too will try "the high life."

The next episode constitutes the turning point with regard to audience identification and sympathy. As prearranged, Ethel goes to Gerald's apartment for tea. She appears looking beautiful and dignified. Gerald is infatuated and tells her she is the first good woman he has met. She too feels the stirrings of emotion and agrees to return for dinner. After she departs, Kittens arrives. She takes a small drink and becomes very giddy. Her childish, spoiled behavior reflect a lack of any deep emotion, thus showing her up to disadvantage in comparison with her mother.

When Ethel returns, Kittens hides in an adjoining room. Gerald again declares his love and tenderly kisses her. Ethel's face registers love, anger, and guilt. Kittens barges into the room and is shocked to discover her own mother. Her response is sarcasm, followed by laughter and tears. Again, her behavior fails to command our sympathy.

Following this climax, the film quickly comes to a resolution, as Ethel prepares to leave for Europe—alone. Although Gerald proposes marriage and Hugh and Kittens plead with her to stay and offer to reform, Ethel refuses. She charges her family with gross selfishness and states that henceforth her first duty will be to herself. Thus said, she sails out the front door and drives away like Nora in Ibsen's *The Doll's House.*

Although *Dancing Mothers* is certainly a unique film, especially in its portrayal of the older woman, its treatment of the flapper is characteristic of the period. At first gay and appealing, by the film's end, she is shown to be merely frivolous and empty headed. The film ends with her declaration to reform.

Lemon, Jelly, And All That Jazz

John W. Parker

John "Knocky" Parker (1918-1986), internationally renowned jazz pianist and silent film scholar, has played concerts with his All-Star Jazz Band throughout America and in England and France. His career began as early as 1935, when after graduation from high school he became a staff pianist at radio station WBAP, Fort Worth, Texas, playing radio programs and recording with the Light Crust Doughboys (Vocalion, Columbia, and Bill Boyd's Cowboy Ramblers Bluebird, Victor) from 1935 to 1942. After graduating from Texas Christian University in 1942, he earned his M.A. from Columbia University and an Ed.D. in American Studies from the University of Kentucky. He taught English at the University of Nevada, Columbia, Kentucky-Wesleyan College, George Peabody College (where he also received an Ed.S. degree), and Methodist College in North Carolina. He served as Chairman of the Department of English at both Kentucky-Wesleyan and Methodist College. In 1963, Knocky became a Professor of English at the University of South Florida, where his tandem interests in music and film were comfortably balanced. He accumulated a fabulous series of silent motion pictures, including most of the extant Chaplin and Keaton films, and since 1950 recorded for such prominent record companies as London, Paramount, Riverside, Audiophile, and Concert Disc.

"Knocky" Parker joins author and artist Rudi Blesh, and Professor Edward Lueders, in critical commentary on the music of the Jazz Age. Parker's specific task here was to reconsider the development of jazz as an art form, and to recall something of the background that went into making Chicago the capital of the twenties. He reviewed some of the personalities and songs that made the decade memorable, and examined the fate of New Orleans Dixieland and the country blues when they became big business under the aegis of record and radio, and sheet music enterprises. In analyzing the musical patterns of the period against their cultural background, Parker shows us an age in which, as Hemingway had complained to Fitzgerald, youth refused to grow up. Parker describes the spirit of "rapturous freedom" when youth seemed endless as evidenced in the dances, song titles, and slogans of the time. Yet, he says, all that carefree exuberance was based upon sheer illusion. What seemed imperishable was terribly ephemeral. Significantly, explicit in the songs written all through the decades since the Twenties, the

140

the retrospective image Americans have of the period is as illusory as the dreams of the age itself.

* * *

All through the decades since the twenties, America has tried to recapture that happy era when youth seemed endless, with springtime forever and lovers found no tomorrow but just tonight—"If I Could Be with You One Hour Tonight," "Tonight You Belong To Me," "Save Your Sorrow for Tomorrow." Among the many things the world will never see again, however, is this rapturous freedom of the twenties. No matter how hard we try to recapture the spirit by reviving the songs, the dances, the costumes, the slogans, or the carefree exuberance of that never-never land that already seems long ago and far away, we cannot.

Even now the stars of the twenties are still luminous with their imperishable glow: the indefatigable Mae West, Loretta Young, the Mills Brothers, Louis Armstrong, Astaire, Crosby, Wynn. Paul Whiteman and Jean Goldkette still echo on recordings the same arrangements they made famous over five decades ago. Somehow, in the old songs played the same old way, we can still recapture something of the golden age, the jazz age, when it was "not raining rain, you know, but raining violets."

One of the first attempts to revive the roaring twenties was as early as 1931, when, after the 1929 debacle, a song in George White's *Scandals* implored:

> Life is just a bowl of cherries,
> Don't take it serious;
> Life's too mysterious.

The bereaved were comforted by a reminder of this world's transiency:

> You work, you save, you worry so,
> But you can't take your dough when you go—go—go—[1]

The song reviewed the fall of kings, Ozymandias, and added a suggestion of Emerson—"Things are in the saddle and ride mankind"—combined with the philosophy of Mehitabel—"*Toujours gai,* there's dance in the old dame yet!"

> So keep repeating, "It's the berries,"
> The strongest oak must fall.
> The sweet things in life to you were just loaned,
> So how can you lose what you've never owned?
> Life is just a bowl of cherries,
> So live, and laugh at it all.[2]

This reversal of "Thanatopsis" failed to assuage the temper of the thirties, however, and the answer was in another song, "The Thrill is Gone," from the same show. And in the next year themes such as "There is oh, such a hungry yearning burning inside of me"[3] and "I've Got a Right to Sing the Blues" ushered in bleak houses and hard times.

In this chapter, though, I should like to reconsider the development of jazz as an art form and to recall something of the background that went into making Chicago the capital of the twenties; to review some of the personalities and songs that made the decade memorable; to examine the fate of new Orleans Dixieland and the country blues when they became big business under the aegis of record, radio, and sheet music enterprises; and to see what happened to the musician when his Frankenstein brought him under its control.

The story of jazz music in the twenties began, perhaps, in 1917 with many New Orleans musicians leaving their city of a million dreams and looking for a home. In that year the Mayor of New Orleans, acting on orders from the Secretary of the Navy, closed Storyville in the French Quarter; and the shift of the New Orleans jazzmen to the Windy City was the first step toward Parnassus. The wartime factories and big-city mills had already imported masses of workers from the country, and the revolt from the village was in full sway. All trains led to Chicago, and the Illinois Central carried its passengers in droves, either in the parlor cars and pullmans in the grand manner, or in the box cars and cattle cars in more indigent lounges. All headed for Chicago, where on

> ...State Street, that great street,
> I just want to say, just want to say,

They do things they don't do on Broadway,[4] and so, from 1917 to 1923 over five hundred thousand migrants settled in Chicago, south of the loop between the Lake on the east and the cattle yard on the west. The song "How Ya Gonna Keep 'em Down on the Farm" certainly proved true, and service men coming home knew that they could lose their blues on

> ...State Street, that great street,
> The street that Billy Sunday could not
> shut down.

As early as 1910 and 1911 such musicians as Freddy Keppard and Tony Jackson had already appeared in the big city for a series of limited engagements, and had remained as harbingers of happy times ahead. In 1913 the Chicago *Defender* called attention to the new art:

Have you heard Emanuel Perez's Creole Band? Have you heard that wonderful jazz music that the people of Chicago are wild about?[5]

In 1918 King Oliver's Creole Jazz Band opened at the Royal Gardens, and the overture was over; the first brilliant scenes in the history of jazz were underway. The King was a pioneer, and he wrote back to his friend Buddie Petit:

> If you've got a real good blues, have someone to write it just as your [sic] play them and send them to me, we can make some real jack on them. Now have the blues wrote down just as you can play them it's the originality that counts.[6]

The music was New Orleans, and under the influence of sterling musicians playing in the old familiar idiom, anyone sensitive to the logical sequence of the folksy form and arrangement could join right in the ensemble and follow right along.

When Lil Hardin, a young lady who had come up from Memphis to study, received a hurry-up call to join the Creole Jazz Band, she sat down to play, and asked for the music, only to be told that there was none. As to the key the piece was in, she was advised, "Never you mind. G'wan and hit it, gal." There was nothing to do but to hit it.[7]

At King Oliver's Dreamland Cafe opening in 1920, Johnny Dodds, a New Orleans lad who had arrived in Chicago that same evening, appeared on the bandstand, unwrapped a clarinet from a long roll of newspaper, and at once established for all time the pattern for all successive clarinetists playing Dixieland solo or ensemble. Later on Johnny's little brother, Baby Dodds, joined the band on drums, and on the night of July 8, 1922, young Louis Armstrong landed at the I. C. station downtown about eleven o'clock and went directly to join the great Oliver at the Lincoln Gardens. As Louie described his arrival:

> When I was getting out of the cab and paying the driver, I could hear the King's band playing some kind of a real jump number. Believe me, they were really jumpin' in fine fashion. I hesitated about going inside right away, but finally I did.[8]

King Oliver was the leader of the first jazz hierarchy. He and Armstrong on cornets; Honore Dutrey, trombone; Johnny Dodds, clarinet; and a rocking rhythm section with Lil Hardin, piano; Bud Scott, banjo; Bill Johnson, bass; and Baby Dodds, drums, established the form for Dixieland groups for all time. Not even the other musicians themselves, though, could understand how, without any apparent cues at all, Joe and Louis could suddenly stand up and play elaborate harmonic breaks. Armstrong later explained:

> ...King and I stumbled upon a little something that no other trumpeters together ever thought of. While the band was just swinging, the king would lean over to me, moving his valves on his trumpet, make notes, the notes that he was going to make when the break would come. I'd listen and at the same time, I'd be figuring out my second to his lead. When the break would come, I'd have my part to blend right along with his. The crowd would go mad over it![9]

Such a performance required a wonderful ear and a remarkable ability of improvisation.

The siren song of this new music caught the ear of many another wonderful musician who came under the hypnotic influence of these new songs from the delta. And so, just as there had been in New Orleans a second line of youngsters following the bands, anxious to learn, so too in Chicago young musicians watching avidly for new phrases and intonations were quick to absorb the harmonies and melodies of this new style. Before Oliver learned how to send tunes to Washington for protection, many songs in his repertoire were copyrighted under different names and even recorded by alert young Chicagoans who realized that what they heard could be a moneymaking proposition. As Jelly-Roll Morton put it, "Some blues is played; some is wrote; and some is just tooken."[10]

The greatest influence on all the musicians, either then or now, was the great Jelly-Roll Morton, who upon the advice of his good friend, Tony Jackson, had appeared in Chicago in 1907 and again in 1914 and 1917 during tours. He returned in 1922 at a time when New Orleans jazz was flourishing everywhere. Everywhere he went, his tunes and ideas—played by Freddy Keppard, King Oliver, Doc Cooke, Jimmy Noone, Erskine Tate—were taking the town by storm. At the Melrose Brothers Music Store was a big banner hung out front, "Wolverine Blues sold here," and the time was right for Jelly-Roll to assert just how good he was and then to sit down and prove that he was right on every count. When Jelly walked into the Melrose music store, he took the first step in what was going to be, ultimately, the corporation control of jazz, with the composer and the artist turning over their tunes and talents to the magnates of the business world.

The Melrose Brothers are important names in the jazz of the twenties. They were two young men from Kentucky who had started a little music store right across from the Tivoli Movie Palace. Tipped off by Jessie Crawford as to what tunes were to be featured on the organ, they stocked up on the music, and their business was promising. Ted Lewis suggested that they establish tie-ups with the new Negro music on the South side, and they became the first major publishing house of the new jazz, blues, and stomps, with Jelly-Roll Morton, the New Orleans Rhythm Kings, and King Oliver as their outstanding stock in trade. After Melrose published the Morton tunes, Jelly-Roll became a big success; likewise, the Melrose Brothers moved from a dirty shop to palatial headquarters. Alan Lomax quotes Lester Melrose:

Listen, mister, Jelly-Roll wouldn't have been nothing if it hadn't been for Melrose. We made Jelly and we made all the rest of them. We made the blues. After all, we are here, and where are they? Nowhere...I took my chances on some of the tunes I recorded being hits, and I wouldn't record anybody unless he signed all his rights in those tunes over to me.[11]

The Melrose boys succeeded in the business world; Oliver and Morton and Leon Rappollo of the New Orleans Rhythm Kings died in extreme poverty. In 1937 King Oliver, stranded with a band in Savannah, with high blood pressure, pyorhea, $1.60 in a dimes saving bank, and a job working as janitor from nine a.m. to midnight, wrote his last letter to his sister,

> Now my blood has started again and I am unable to take treatments because it costs $3.00 per treatment and I don't make enough money to continue my treatments. Now it begins to work on my heart. I am weak in my limbs at times and my breath but I can not ask you for any money or anything. A stitch in time save nine. Should anything happen to me will you want my body?[12]

Back in 1921, just fifteen years earlier than King Oliver's letter to his sister, the Chicago *Defender* had reported,

> King Oliver set Los Angeles on fire. He was offered all kinds of inducements to stay, and the highest salary ever offered anyone. All Los Angeles says he's the greatest, and some hot babies have been here the past year.[13]

The great Jelly-Roll Morton, penniless and friendless in the forties, was still outlining his plans to sue the Music Corporation of America and the American Society of Composers, Authors, and Publishers when he died in 1941. His last letters to his wife tell a sorry story:

> I received the check from Melrose. $52.00. I seen a lawyer. He advised me not to cash it, so I will institute a suit against them. I was depending on that to send you home. Now I will have to wait a little longer. Thanks for the prayers....
> ...My breath has been very short like when I had to go to the hospital and have been spitting blood and many other symptoms too numerous to mention, but I am some better this morning.[14]

Make no mistake about it, though; Jelly was always the greatest of them all. Even Victor records billed him as the "Number One Hot Band." No other jazz musician ever displayed so much finesse and delicacy, so much elegance and grace. His compositions have a magnificent feeling for form. His piano background brought out the beat in all his performers. As Jelly himself said about his band, "Good, Hell, it's perfect." And back in the twenties, the Charleston boys and the red-hot mammas would stop for a moment, even in their wildest dissipation, to pay homage to genius whenever Mr. Jelly Lord would flash his diamond-studded tooth in a dazzling smile, and sing a paean to his prowess:

> Oh, Mr. Jelly Lord,
> He's the royal of that old keyboard,
> Just a simple comer,
> Now at home, as well as abroad,
> Why, they call him Mr. Jelly Lord.[15]

The success of a musician—in the twenties as well as now—is dependent upon the success of the businessman. The musician creates a product which the businessman, the public, the critics and reviewers, attempt to fit into their society. As the musician is led to adjust his work to the demand of the public, he compromises his art accordingly. The businessman obtains further concessions before the final product is thrown upon the open market. It is the responsibility of the sales manager to reconcile the music to the traditions of the society for which it was created, to guide the artist in his selection of styles that might best fit a given time and place in order to receive maximum acceptance. The transmission of the form—disc or paper, and the physical attractiveness of the product—label, jacket, or cover, are all important factors. The manufacturer then is responsible for the tradition of the art, for its acceptance by the critics and reviewers, and for directing the demand of the public toward the object in view. Patronage dates back to ancient balladry, and payola is as old as Adam. There are questions about selection of record or sheet music company, about press relations and radio (now t.v.) and the right night club appearances, about the ballyhoo of reviews and criticisms, about fads which might boost sales, and about the problem of short-term or long-term values and sales survival. The encomiums accumulate after the musician has paid the supreme price, when it is no longer possible for him to create more work like the first. Only when his life has passed into a distorted legend can his work be appreciated in a universal sense and understood in historic perspective.

There is no doubt more truth than fiction in Lester Melrose's remark that Victor's manager threw him out of the office when he first proposed recording Jelly's jazz. Jelly-Roll, like so many other musicians, desperately needed management, and the Melrose brothers certainly managed him. They rated Joe Oliver, though, as the most important musician of the twenties because of his ability to meet the public deferentially. Too, both Melrose boys remarked about the difficulty of transcribing and arranging Jelly's music. No one knows now just exactly how much music Jelly knew; Elmer Schoebel and Mel Stitzel arranged the published orchestrations. Omer Simeon and Albert Nicholas have both remarked about the skeleton arrangements that the Red Hot Peppers worked out in the studio in collaboration, and the legend that survives suggests that Jelly knew little about writing, or for that matter, reading music.

Victor in Chicago, though, was only one of several recording companies servicing the jazzmen of the midwest and southwest areas. Paramount Records was a subsidiary of the Wisconsin Chair Company at Crafton, some fifty miles north up Lake Michigan. The company sold home furnishings, and the directors thought that a record subsidiary would help sell their phonographs. They set up so-called "New York Laboratories" in Port Washington, Wisconsin, and rented Chicago studios on the second floor over a music store at Jackson and Wabash. Mayo Williams, a booking agent, acted as director of what was called "race" recordings and as the controlling force of Chicago Publishing Company, which printed the successful blues of the Paramount, Broadway, Gennett, Q.R.S., Banner, Regal, Argo, and Emerson record labels. As agent for both artists and recording companies, and as director of a publishing firm, Mayo Williams was an important person for blues singers to know.

There was a ready market for the Paramount blues records. The gangs of workers in Chicago and Detroit found full expression of their sentiments in the country blues sung by Blind Lemon Jefferson from Dallas, or Blind Blake from Jacksonville.

Blind Lemon Jefferson had been born blind in a small town, Wortham, Texas. Begging on the street with a guitar seemed the only profession open for a poor blind country boy, and Lemon had a real gift in his fingers. When he was twenty, he moved to Dallas and walked up and down the streets of deep Elm night and day, playing and singing the blues:

> I stood on the corner; my feets were soaking wet,
> I haven't seen anybody look like my baby yet.
> I stood on the corner and almost bust my head,
> I couldn't earn enough money to buy me a loaf of bread.[16]

Lemon was booked as a blind wrestler, and, since he weighed well over two hundred pounds, he survived the falls. There was no getting around it, though; he amused the public and lived on the small change tossed his way. Too, he learned all the work-songs, hymns, city and country blues that were offered by the streets and brothels of Dallas and Fort Worth.

Sometimes he would journey to Waxahachie or Corsicana to play and sing all night for a country brawl from eight to four a.m., and by the time he hit Chicago in 1925, he was ready for the big time. In four years he recorded eighty-one blues and became Paramount's outstanding artist. One advertisement of his records in the Chicago *Defender* carried a picture of upreared snakes with a big shaky title, "That Black Snake Moan," and the description,

Heads up! black snakes—weird, slimy, creepy—e wonderful subject for a wonderful Blues hit, and "Blind" Lemon Jefferson sure makes Blues history on this great Paramount record. You'll never quit playing this one when you hear that moan. Get it at your dealer's, or send us the coupon today. Be sure to ask for Paramount No. 12407.[17]

A coupon in the corner contained a listing of numbers with space for name and address and the directions,

Send no money! If your dealer is out of the records you want, send us the coupon below. Pay postman 75 cents for each record, plus small C.O.D. fee when he delivers records.[18]

These coupons poured into the home office by the thousands, and the pressings—1600 a day—kept the Paramount machine busy from early morning until after dark. Sam Charters in his fine book, *The Country Blues*, says that after every session the company would have waiting for Blind Lemon a few dollars, a bottle, and a prostitute. The blues he sang, as well as the life he lived, were earthy and to the point:

> Peach orchard Mama, you swore nobody'd pick
> your fruit but me,
> I found three kid men shaking down your
> peaches free...
> One man bought your groceries,
> Another joker paid your rent,
> While I was working your orchard and giving
> you every cent.[19]

Lemon's last record, "Empty House Blues," was made in February, 1930. He left the studio saying that he was to sing at a house party, and walked out into the drifting snow. Stories were that he left a party too drunk to find his way and froze to death sitting in the gutter. Some said that he was sitting waiting for his car and driver, but that they never found him.[20] His body was taken back to Wortham, Texas, and buried in an unmarked grave in a valley of Johnson grass and two gnarled oaks:

> Oh, there's one kind favor I ask of you,
> Yes, there's one kind favor I ask of you.
> Just see that my grave is kept clean.[21]

Little has been written about one of the major contributions to jazz, the skiffle and string groups from as far southwest as El Paso and Houston to as far southeast as Nashville or Louisville. In the big colored districts, remarkably raffish street bands would appear playing home-made or souped-up instruments such as a washtub bass, washboard drum, kazoo, comb, jug, mandolin, banjo, guitar, violin, harmonica, whistle, or even steel guitar with the broken neck of a bottle producing an eerie slide. Whereas young New Orleans musicians had cut their teeth on handed-down wind instruments, the Negro pawnshops in Memphis or Dallas made available to would-be street musicians inexpensive stringed instruments that had been a part of the western culture since the Spanish and Mexican ranchers. And so in Texas and Tennessee bands like the Light Crust Doughboys and the Memphis Jug Band were putting out wilder, hotter versions of "Bugle Call Rag" and ragtime-stomps than tame ensembles like the Benny Goodman group ever dreamed of. The young performers in the skiffle, string, and jug bands played with exuberant conviction and a sense of audience immediacy that the Virtuosi di Roma might envy, and right out in the middle of deep Elm or Beale Street some nights would be heard the most honest-to-goodness truly toe-tickling music since the Pied Piper of Hamelin. Columbia Records was one of the first major companies to invade the South with portable recording units, and the 14,000 series that resulted included a treasury of southwest swing as full-blooded and hot-bellied as anything the New Orleans or Chicago schools had ever played. One of the records,

"The Dallas Rag," by a Mozartian string quartet, the Dallas Jug Band (mandolin, banjo, guitar, jug), contained such superb articulation on the jug as to make the Budapest String quartet cellist envious of its dynamic tone.

The distinction between the city blues and the country blues sometimes blurs. The country blues artist is primarily self-taught, with an undisciplined approach to restrictions of time or tone. Mainly, he makes up his blues as he goes free-wheeling along. The city blues instrumentalists or vocalist will be more objective and will sing the required beats to the bar and intonate accuracies of pitch. The Bessie Smith who, according to legend, early in her recording career stopped singing and yelled out to the director, "Hold on a minute while I spit," was pretty country. The Bessie Smith, though, who sang "Alexander's Ragtime Band" on a later record date had become fairly citified. Her tutor, Ma Gertrude Rainey, retained the best of the country tradition, even when she appeared with a well-rehearsed tightly-knit little band, her own Rabbit Foot Minstrels.

Ma was a strutter and a shouter; "Selling that Stuff" was one of her tunes and her main concern, and her art, either in person or on records, came through clearly. When Ma and her Rabbit Foot Minstrels pulled into Chattanooga, Tennessee, sometime before 1920, Bessie Smith joined the troop and became Ma's most famous protege. Barnstorming through the gin mills, honky tonks, and bordellos of the South gave Bessie an apprenticeship that made her songs about her responsibilities, troubles, and frustrations the strong expression of a tough, robust woman who, though downhearted, could sing with conviction, "I've got the world in a jug and got the stopper in my hand."[22] How powerful she was is told by Sy Oliver who, while working a stage show in Baltimore, heard Bessie tell the boys one day, "Watch me walk one today." During the show, she concentrated her performance of "Empty Bed Blues" on one man in the third row. Then, in the middle of the song, the man, trance-like, followed her up and across the stage and finally down the steps back to his seat from the opposite side.[23] Bessie had hypnotized her victim and, as she had said, had "walked" him at her will. Albert Nicholas says that on an early record date Bessie pointed to the microphone and told the engineer, "I don't need that old thing." Bessie could sing over and drown out the loudest swing band going and her voice had a vitality and a ring of sincerity unequalled by any other singer. Between 1923 and 1933 she sold ten million records. She could never understand, however, why her show "The Harlem Babies" was booked in Negro theatres on the south side while Ethel Waters appeared before large audiences in the loop and took the town by storm. Mrs. James P. Johnson, the wife of Bessie's favorite pianist, once remarked, "Bessie would come over to the house, but, mind you, she wasn't my friend. She was very rough."[24]

Bessie's personality was like her singing—raw and pulsating, brutal and violent, vigorous and powerful. The very factors that made her an attractive, uninhibited singer made her unattractive socially. The same brashness that harmed Jelly proved to be Bessie's undoing. Other singers with production numbers and dramatic backdrop played to greater success, and by 1933 she found herself down and out. The great Bessie who once received a thousand-dollar advance against a five per cent royalty for her recordings was eventually forced to give house rent parties in Harlem in order to pay for her room. Tragedy touched her closest associates, too. Big Charles Green, the instrumentalist on "Trombone Cholly" and "Empty Bed Blues" was found frozen to death on a Chicago doorstep; Joe Smith, the great cornetist in "Lost Your Head," "Baby Doll," and "Young Woman's Blues," died of tuberculosis in a mental asylum. Bessie herself was killed in an automobile accident near Clarksdale, Mississippi, in 1937. Louis Armstrong said of her,

> She used to thrill me at all times, the way she could phrase a note with a certain something in her voice no other blues singer could get. She had music in her soul and felt everything she did. Her sincerity with her music was an inspiration.[25]

Such country performers as Blind Lemon, Ma, and Bessie, brought jazz to the honky-tonks; the next step was the channeling of this power into small chamber orchestras and then into large bands from which chamber settings of trumpets, saxophones, or rhythm could be featured. The large orchestras helped to draw the attention of the commercial business interests to an art form that could be chained and exhibited for night club and hotel exploitation. With a personable front-man affably waving his baton, the rotogravure groups out front could enjoy an occasional sortie by a jazz member of the ensemble, provided of course that he was surrounded by musical cliches a la mode. Naturally the orchestras were commercial and played all the latest hits, dressing them up for a sophisticated clientele—"I love my wife, but oh you kid!"—and featuring each section in a stereotyped block format. A typical arrangement of the twenties would consist of the brass playing the straight lead with a few filigrees from a jazz soloist, then saxes and trumpets together playing the verse in harmony with just enough drum push-beats to break up the monotony, and then a little jazz by a couple of virtuosi backed with hot, full rhythm section—then a twenty-three skidoo vocal with a few more toned-downed ragtime fill-ins in the background, and at last the hottest soloist of all tooting tutti above the band full-chorded and hallelujah, the whole piece ending in a Charleston-coda on the cymbals. The arrangements, plus the threat of hostility from the leader when he turned an evil eye on an offender, disciplined the band. The main emphasis was the melody, plus any gimmick that might help identify the group: rippling rhythm, wide-vibrato by the saxophones, bubble inundation, or—sometimes—an emphasis on very brief fill-ins by a number of jazz musicians buried in a debris brightened only when they occasionally forced their way to the surface for a fresh burst of air. These soloists were important, especially when they could be taught to keep their place, but it was a hard life. Some of them—like Bix Beiderbecke or Eddie Lange—could not read well and had to memorize the entire book, and retaining a complete repertoire took a great deal of memory work, but the boys who could read would always help those who could not, and somehow they all made out. The exacting ensembles and mechanical contrivances became, finally, more than any sensitive musician could give—or take—and the best (such as Beiderbecke or Lang) gave up the ghost, or, like Miniver Cheevy, kept on drinking and embalmed the old pieces in alcohol, still looking over the four-leaf clover that they'd overlooked before.

In the twenties song-writing also became a syndicated business. Radio turned commercial in 1922, and by 1924 coast-to-coast hook-ups were successfully established. Radio piracy of the wave length became so chaotic that the Federal Radio Commission was established to arbitrate the difficulties. Talking pictures quickly made the silent film obsolete, and the record manufacturers and song producers were quick to syndicate with radios and movies, and by the late twenties the music business had become a multi-million dollar affair illustrating the sorry saga of humanity on its downward march.

The songs themselves captured attention, too, from the news events of the day. The discovery of the tomb of Tutankhamen in 1922, for instance, helped to popularize further an interest in the far East which had been picking up momentum all through the century and which exploded full-blown in the literature and popular songs of the twenties. It was an English novelist, Edith M. Hull, a writer of novels hotter even than the asbestos Elinor "It" Glyn, who hit the jackpot with *The Sheik*, and who created in her title character a hero and a trade-mark that was to become in our time the symbol of an insatiable pleasure-ridden world. Rudolph Valentino in *The Son of the Sheik* catered to a palpitating audience which even he was not titillating enough to satisfy, and he burned out quickly in 1926, leaving behind him a long long trail the likes of which we will never see again.

Vaudeville got hold of a song celebrating the infamous Arabian amorist and inserted a one-line refrain, "without no pants on" between the already-formidable-enough statements in such a manner as to make even the "It" girl blush.

> At nights when he's asleep,
> Into his tent I'll creep,
> The stars that shine above
> Will light our way to love—[26]

is as plain a recital as one is apt to get, even in this age of nymphets and baby dolls. The impetuous sheik has indeed turned out to be an implacable hero-image.

Arabia though was only the beginning of a junket that was to tour extensively through the East in the Oriental Twenties. The titles themselves are enough to indicate the interest: "Borneo," "Chong-Ho Comes from Hong-Kong," "Chant of the Jungle," "Pagan Love Song," "Bound for Morocco,"

"Moonlight on the Ganges," "Down in Jungle Town," "Hula Lou," "On The Beach of Waikiki," "Yaks Eula Hickey Dula," "Underneath Hawaiian Skies," "So Long, Oo-Long, How Long You Gonna Be Gone," "Egyptian-ella," "Dardanella," "Palasteena," "Song of the Islands," "Oriental Fantasy," "In a Little Grass Shack at Zealakaua," "Abbe Dabba Honeymoon," "Timbuctoo," "The Japanese Sandman," "On a Chinese Honeymoon," "China Boy," "Yellow Dog Blues," "When Buddha Smiles," "Bagdad," "Mandalay," "Ukulele Lady," "Hello, Alcha, Tawaii," "The Desert Song," "Diga Diga Do," "Nagasaki," "Underneath the Russian Moon," "Kalua," "Wang Wang Blues."

The theory was to take a far-away name mentioned often in the papers—the Dardenelles of World War I—and to add a feminine suffix, and you'd have "Dardenella," "Egyptian-ella," "Palasteena." The songs told stories peculiarly American, reviewing the concerns of the day, such as avoirdupois:

> Ella was a dancing queen who started getting
>   fat,
> And every day found two pounds more on Ella—
>   poor Ella—
> Pretty soon she found she lost her job be-
>   cause of that,
> And what was worse—she lost her fellow.
> And so she sailed to Egypt to forget,
> But ah!—she made a hit, and she's there yet.
> If you hear of a queen who can shim and shake
> Till she makes you think that you're in a
>   quake,
> They're talking about—Egyptian-ella.[27]

One song satirized the debutante for her dilettante accomplishments:

> Lena was the Queen of Palasteena,
> How she used to play her concertina.
> She'd play it day and night,
> She'd never get it right,
> She'd play with all her might,
> And how they'd love it—want more uv it—
> I heard her play it once or twice,
> Oh, murder! Still it was nice.
> She was fat, but she got leaner
> Shovin' on her concertina,
> Lena from Palasteena way.[28]

"Dardanella" was one of the earliest examples of boogie woogie, a continuous *basso ostinato* supplying a pseudo-Oriental atmosphere, and the treble consisting of an ascending chromatic scale returning by descending circuitous thirds. The lyric too combined eastern and western cultures; yet in spite of the setting, "We'll build a tent just like the gypsies of the Orient," the social mores remained singularly puritanical, "For there'll be one girl in my harem when you're mine."[29]

Another subject which was popular with the songwriters was the South. The same audience that bought the records of Bessie Smith and Blind Lemon wanted to hear about their sunny Southland:

> Born where the waving corn
> Greets you every morn from every side,
> And where a candid hand
> Makes you feel so grand and filled with pride,
> It's the Southland that I mean,
> Where the air is all serene...[30]

In the twenties, moreover, trains were all bound south of the Mason-Dixon line: "Dreamy Alabama," "Carolina Sunshine," "On Miami Shore," "Swanee," "Dear Ole Southland," "My Sunny Tennessee," "Ten Little Fingers and Ten Little Toes Waiting Down in Ten-Ten-Tennessee," "Tuck Me to Sleep in My Old Kentucky Home," "Wabash Blues," "Carolina in the Morning," "Georgia on My Mind," "Loving Sam, the Sheik of Alabam'," "On the Gin-Gin-Ginny Shore," "On the Bam-Bam-Bammy Shore," "Rose of the Rio Grande," "Way Down Yonder in New Orleans," "Charleston," "I'm Goin' South," "Louisville Lou, the Vampin' Lady," "Sadie Green, She's the Vamp of New Orleans," "My Galveston Gal," "Mexicali Rose," "Alabama Bound," "When the Midnight Choo-Choo Leaves for Alabam'," "Headin' for Louisville," "Florida, the Moon, and You," "Hello, Swanee, Hello," "Away Down South in Heaven," "Mississippi Mud," "There's a Cradle in Caroline," "Caroline Moon," "Dusky Stevedore Down on the Swanee Shore," "Cryin' for the Carolines," "Lazy Louisiana Moon."

Sometimes these songs of the South—to prove literacy, perhaps—resorted to spelling: "M-i-double crooked letter-i, double crooked letter-i, double humpback-i, Mississippi, floating down to New Orleans,"[31] "I'd give the world to be in D-i-x-i-even though my—"[32] One song was even orthographic—"It's round in the ends and high in the middle, it's O-h-i-o-."[33]

Another interesting motif recurrent in these songs of the South echoes the Grangers' antipathy to the railroad. The high price of tickets is the same theme that caused the Chattanooga choo-choo boarder of the forties to declare, "I've got my fare with just a trifle to spare," albeit enough for "dinner in the diner, ham and eggs in Carolina,"[34] One impetuous passenger, moreover, deplored the railroad schedule:

> Oh, I just can't wait for the choo-choo
>   train,
> I'll hop aboard an aeroplane,
> And I'll be in my Dixie home again
>   Tomorrow.[35]

The "Two Tickets to Georgia" passenger of the thirties showed complacency in the conversation, "How much do I pay? O.K., G-a."[36] The traveller of the Midnight Choo-Choo in 1912 affirmed, "I'll be right there; I've got my fare."[37] The footworn Alabama passenger of 1925 referred to the belligerence of the railroad company in the line, "I'll give the meanest ticket man on earth all I'm worth to put my tootsies in an upper berth."[38] The comment "meanest ticket man" has ominous overtones indeed, and the phrase "all I'm worth" implies both that pullman tickets are awfully expensive, and that the traveller himself is not worth very much. "When the Midnight Choo Choo Leaves for Alabam'" mentions "that rusty-haired conductor man" as if red-headed conductors were especially noxious, and continues infelicitously,

> I'll grab him by the collar,
> And I'll holler,
> "Alabam'! Alabam'!"[39]

The irate passenger headed Alabamaward is the ironic completion of the migration north fifteen years before, only the big noise from Illinois is drastically more foreboding.

As the gangster made his way South to continue the reconstruction, however, the southern lady was out to make far more destructive conquests.

The time was long past when the girl would plead with her paramour, a B-and-O brakeman who had thrown her down, that she would do the cooking darling, she would pay the rent, she knew that she had done him wrong. In the twenties Alice had come out of the kitchen and had changed her role considerably. Mom had taken over new territories—see Philip Wylie— and she was out to prove not only equality but superiority as well, as man was at her mercy. Theda Bara of "Kiss me, my Fool" fame had suggested the pattern for the *femme fatale*, and the incendiary red-hot mamma and her cool, hard-hearted partner, Hannah, were worthy antagonists of man:

> I saw her on the beach with a great big pan,
> there was Hannah Pouring water on a drowning man!...
> An evening spent with Hannah sitting on your knees
> Is like flying through Alaska in your B. V. D.'s!
> Hard-hearted Hannah, the vamp of Savannah, G-a.[40]

Georgia featured another scintillating siren, "Sweet Georgia Brown," on whom no gal made had got a shade, whose two lips were hard to beat, and who made them all sigh and want to die—

> I'll tell you just why,
> And you know I won't lie—not much—
> It's been said she knocks'em down.
> When she comes to town,
> Since she came, why it's a shame

How she cools'em down.
Fellows she can't get
Must be fellows she ain't met—
Georgia names 'em; Georgie claims 'em,
Sweet Georgia Brown.[41]

Feminine dominance of mankind, though especially strong in the South, flourished nationally. Rose of Washington Square, for example, who had been around a long time, had

...those Broadway vampire lashed to the mast,
She's got no future, but oh, what a past![42]

Sally, missing for some time from her alley, no less, had convinced her man pretty adequately before she took off. As he put it,

No matter what she is—wherever she may be,
If no one wants her now, please send her back to me.[43]

Susie wore her man out. He himself admitted,

We went riding; she didn't balk.

Back from Yonkers I'm the one who had to walk.[44] The sheet music of "If I Had You" back in 1928 bore the headline, "The Prince of Wale's favorite song," and contained the prophetic lines,

I could be a king, dear, uncrown'd,
Humble or poor, rich or renowned,
There is nothing I couldn't do if I had you.[45]

One philosopher bewailed that wedding bells were breaking up that old gang of his, but the details of mankind's domesticity were listed more specifically elsewhere,

He's washing dishes and baby clothes,
He's so ambitious he even sews.
Have no regret, folks,
That's what you get folks,
For makin' whoopee.[46]

The courtier was really on the spot—"Aggravatin' papa, don't you try to two-time me...I'll cut you down, and I don't mean maybe."[47] One poor old guy had to see his mamma every night, or he couldn't see mamma at all. Another Hairbreadth Harry had to smile when his girl did, sigh when she did, and cry when she did, before he could be happy. In song after song, mankind was truly taken into tow:

> She likes to bill and coo,
> I never liked to bill and coo,
> But she likes to bill and coo,
> And that's my weakness now.[48]

The heroine of the day was Little Coquette, A Hemingway-Fitzgerald type who, with a "certain little cute way of flirtin'," had her victim under instantaneous control the instant he looked into "Them There Eyes."[49] Furthermore, she permeated his entire existence:

> You're the cream in my coffee,
> You're the salt in my stew,
> You will always be my necessity,
> I'd be lost without you.[50]

And what finally happened to the indomitable ladies of the evening: Sadie Green, the vamp from New Orleans, Louisville Lou, Hard-Hearted Hannah, Black Eyed Susan Brown or her sister Georgia? One meets such a charmer in many of the songs of the 1930's or in any Hemingway tale, psychoanalyzing herself in a cabaret somewhere:

> Night and day
> Under the hide of me,
> There's an oh-such-a-hungry yearning
> Burning inside of me.[51]

One of Duke Ellington's most famous blues of the thirties with lyrics by Andy Razaf reviewed the denouncement of the twenties' belle a decade after her riotous fling:

> They say, in your early life romance came,
> And in this heart of yours burned a flame,
> A flame that flickered one day, and died away,
> And so, with disillusion deep in your eyes,
> They say that fools in love soon grow wise,
> The years have changed you somehow.
> I see you now
> Smoking, drinking, never thinking
> Of tomorrow, so nonchalant,
> Diamonds shining, dancing, dining
> With some man in a restaurant.
> Is that all you really want?
> No Sophisticated Lady, I know
> You miss a love you lost so long ago
> That when nobody is nigh, you cry.[52]

Obviously, jazz could sometimes contain several hidden meanings, and an enthusiastic coterie avidly defend the music. Paul Whiteman had said, "The difference between "The Song of India" and "The Memphis Blues" is purely geographic.[53] Transcending time and place, composers blatantly went about bringing the classics up to date. One writer, for instance, suggested that Schubert needed syncopation and pep, and offered to put the finishing touches to the unfinished symphony. Chopin, Beethoven, Rimsky-Korsakov all reappeared with lavish retouches, improved and modernized within an inch of their lives. There was no getting around it—the twenties had plenty of class, one way or another:

> Edie was a lady,
> Though her past was shady
> Edie had class, with a capital-k.[54]

The twenties were self-confident, if anything. Victor had Paul Whiteman; Brunswick had Red Nichols—each attempting to out-do the other with lavish, portentous twelve-inch records of some fragile vehicle that could barely bear the brunt of such an onslaught. Gershwin wrote classical stuff, and the high-class pianists played swanky jazz. Ostentation ran amuck.

The stock market crash of 1929, however, meant a changed way of life. The art of the jazz age could no longer conceal, like the picture of Dorian Gray, the ravages of corruption. When the buying on time fell due and the payment on demand was ordered, the twenties' imitation of life—the concept of a paper moon sailing over a cardboard sea, or of the paper doll that one could call one's own—changed abruptly. The jazz age was over, and the tempo of the thirties brought about new patterns of culture.

Notes

[1] Lew Brown and Ray Henderson, "Life is Just a Bowl of Cherries" (New York: De Sylva, Brown, and Henderson, 1931).

[2] *Ibid.*

[3] Cole Porter: "Night and Day" (New York, Harms, 1932)

[4] Fred Fisher: "Chicago" (New York, Fred Fisher, 1922).

[5] Chicago *Defender*, Nov. 14, 1913.

[6] Cited in Frederic Ramsey Jr., and Charles Edward Smith, eds., *Jazzmen* (New York: Harcourt, Brace and Co., 1939).

[7] *Ibid.*, p. 163.

[8] Cited in Nat Shapiro and Nat Hentoff, eds., *Hear Me Talkin' to Ya* (New York: Rinehart, 1955), p. 163.

[9] *Ibid.*, p. 104.

[10] This quotation was given to me by Al Rose.

[11] Alan Lomax, *Mr. Jelly Lord* (New York: Duell, Sloan, and Pearce, 1950), p. 186.

[12] Cited by Ramsey, Jr., and Smith, p. 90.

[13] *Ibid.*, p. 69.

[14] Cited by Alan Lomax, *op. cit.*, p. 250.

[15] Jelly-Roll Morton, "Mr. Jelly Lord" (New York: Melrose Bros., 1923).

[16] Blind Lemon Jefferson, "Long Lonesome Blues" (Paramount 12354, 1926).

[17] Dec., 12, 1926.

[18] *Ibid.*

[19] Blind Lemon Jefferson, "Peach Orchard Mamma" (Paramount 12859).

[20]Sam charter, *The Country Blues* (New York: Rinehart, 1959), pp. 66-72.

[21]Blind Lemon Jefferson, "See That My Grave Is Kept Clean" (Paramount 12608).

[22]Bessie Smith, "Down Hearted Blues" (Columbia G1503).

[23]Jacket of Della Reese's "The Story of the Blues" (Jubilee 1095).

[24]Cited by Shapiro and Hentoff, p. 242.

[25]Nat Shapiro and Nat Hentoff, *The Jazz Makers* (New York: Rinehart, 1957, p. 140.

[26]Henry B. Smith, Francis Wheeler, and Ted Snyder, "The Shiek of Araby" (New York: Waterson, Berlin, and Snyder, 1921).

[27]Walter Doyle, "Egyptian-elle" (New York: Leo Feist, 1930).

[28]Con Conrad and J. Russel Robinson, "Palasteena" (New York: Shapiro, Bernstein, 1920).

[29]Fred Fisher, Felix Bernard, Johnny S. Black, "Dardanella" (New York: McCarthy and Fisher, 1919).

[30]J. Russel Robinson and Con Conrad "Tomorrow" (New York: Waterson, Berlin, and Snyder, 1921).

[31]Bert Hanlon, Benny Ryan, Harry Tierney, "M-i-s-s-i-s-s-i-p-p-i" (New York: Am. Jerome, 1916; assigned 1916 to Leo Feist).

[32]George Gershwin and Irving Caesar, "Swanee" (New York: Harms, 1919).

[33]Alfred Bryan and Bert Hanlon; "O-h-i-o" (New York: Jerome H. Remrick, 1922).

[34]Mack Gordon and Harry Warren, "Chattanooga Choo-Choo" (New York: Leo Feist, 1941).

[35]Robinson and Conrad, *op. cit.*

[36]Joe Young, Charles Tobias, and J. Fred Coots, "Two Tickets to Georgia" (New York: Irving, Berlin, 1933).

[37]Irving Berlin, "When the Midnight Choo-Choo Leaves for Alabam'" (New York: Waterson, Berlin, and Snyder, 1912).

[38]Bud De Sylva, Bud Green, Ray Henderson, "Alabamy Bound" (New York: Shapiro, Bernstein, 1925).

[39]Irving Berlin, *op. cit.*

[40]Jack Yellen, Milton Ager, "Hard-Hearted Hannah" (New York: Ager, Yeller, and Bernstein, 1924).

[41]Ben Bernie, Maceo Pinkard, and Kenneth Casey, "Sweet Georgia Brown" (New York: Jerome H. Remick, 1925).

[42]Ballard MacDonald and James F. Hanley, "Rose of Washington Square" (New York: Shapiro, Bernstein, 1920).

[43]Clifford Grey and Jerome Kern, "Sally" (New York: T. B. Harms, 1921).

[44]Bud G. DeSylva, "If You Knew Susie" (New York: Shapiro, Bernstein, 1925).

[45]Ted Shapiro, Jimmy Campbell, Reginald Connelly, "If I Had You" (New York: Robbins, 1928).

[46]Gus Kahn, Walter Donaldson, "Makin' Whoopee!" (New York: Donaldson, Douglas, and Gumble, 1928).

[47]Roy Turk, J. Russel Robinson, Addy Britt, "Aggravatin' Papa" (New York: Waterson, Berlin, and Snyder, 1922).

[48]Bud Green, Sam H. Stept, "That's My Weakness Now" (New York: Shapiro, Bernstein, 1928).

[49]Maceo Pinkard, William Tracey, Doris Tauber, "Them There Eyes" (New York: Irving Berlin, 1930).

[50]Bud G. DeSylva, Lew Brown, Ray Henderson, "You're the Cream in My Coffee" (New York: DeSylve, Brown, and Henderson, 1928).

[51]Cole Porter, *op. cit.*

[52]"Sophisticated Lady" (New York: Gotham Music, 1933).

[53]This remark was made to the author by Paul Whiteman at the Frontier Centenial, Fort Worth, Texas, summer, 1936.

[54]Bud G. DeSylva, Richard Whiting, Nacio Herb Brown, "Edie Was a Lady" (New York: Harms, 1932).

American Humor in the 1920s

Lawrence E. Mintz

Since taking his Ph.D. at Michigan State University in 1969, Professor Lawrence Mintz has earned an international reputation in the field of American humor. A Woodrow Wilson Fellow in 1966-1967, and a Visiting Professor in American Studies at the University of Paris III in 1975-1976, his expertise has taken him abroad numerous times as a lecturer and panelist for seminars on the American character and American Humor, in Britain and France, as well as Hungary, Czechoslovakia, and Portugal. Professor Mintz's edited collection of essays, Humor in America, *was published by Greenwood Press (1988), and he has published several articles, chapters in books, and reviews and presented conference papers on American popular literature, television, comic strips, and many aspects of humor. He is on the advisory board of the* Journal of Popular Culture. *From 1974 to 1984, he was an editor of* American Humor an Interdisciplinary Newsletter, *and he now serves in a similar capacity for the new international journal,* Humor. *Professor Mintz's work-in-progress includes a study of American humor since 1963 and a research project dealing with the image of Europe and Africa in American theme amusement parks. Teaching and lecturing opportunities in Portugal and Czechoslovakia as well as with visiting teachers from Hungary and Germany has led to a recent interest in developing new approaches to teaching American Studies abroad.*

Professor Mintz's analysis of the "golden" age of American humor would be invaluable to this anthology if only to demonstrate the amazing quantity and diversity of humor produced during the 1920s. In literature, theater, film, the graphic arts, newspaper and magazine journalism, and variety entertainment, the author shows us that the Twenties marked the peak of comic writing in this country—representing a "flowering of satire and parody and sheer nonsense that has never been equaled before or since, a galaxy of our greatest funnymen gathered at one transcendent moment." But the greater value of Mintz's essay is that as a medium that is always close to basic human emotions and cultural tensions, humor proves a particularly apt method for capturing the moods of the age, and for understanding its pervasive emotional and intellectual climate. This value is enhanced when one considers that humor deals with just about every subject of human importance—sex, race, ethnicity, politics, class-consciousness, family matters, urban and rural life-styles, technology and industrialization.

Mintz views the Twenties as a decade in which humor figures prominently not just as a resume and a culmination "of all the traditions of the past," but a "transitional period in which the evolution of American humor toward darker, more serious self-criticism becomes clear and defined." In fact, as a humor marked by deliberate iconoclasm, sarcasm, pessimism, and hostility, it provides an unnerving reflection of escalating tensions and a darkening of mood that culminates in cultural collapse. It is a highly deflationary humor, necessary to penetrating the naive materialistic and hedonistic illusions of the age, and to serving as an outlet for anti-democratic cynicism.

Mintz sees that factors of growing urbanization and industrialization are keys to the new self-deprecating humor that develops in the '20s, and which marks an important change in national self-perception. Reacting to the "future-shock" of the twentieth century—urbanization, industrialism, technology, bureaucracy, sharpened class distinctions, changes in family and sex roles, and an increasingly heterogeneous and crowded society—the new humor reflects not only the failures of democracy, but a nation of individuals increasingly depersonalized, inept, vulnerable, and dominated by gadgets and machines. The image of the "little man," the loser whose power is "drained to zero," becomes emblematic of the nightmare of the American dream rather that its fulfillment, a nightmare whose darkly comic reflection has become even more pertinent in the present age.

* * *

The first few decades of the twentieth century are often considered to have constituted a "golden age" of American humor, and while the precise chronological boundaries for the period are subject to debate, the decade of the 1920s would figure prominently in any such designation. Corey Ford's encomium provides an unrestrained, but not atypical appraisal: "The early twenties marked the peak of comic writing in this country, a flowering of satire and parody and sheer nonsense that has never been equaled before or since, a galaxy of our greatest funnymen gathered together at one transcendent moment, like a configuration of planets which would not occur again in a life time."[1] The criteria for claiming that this age was "golden" usually include the quantity and diversity of the humor produced, its unusually high quality—defined variously as a predominately high standard and/or the existence of an unusual number of comic "geniuses" and "great works"—and its pertinence, both to the traditions of American humor and to the zeitgeist, or the emotional and intellectual climate of the era.[2]

The case for quantity and diversity is without doubt the easiest to establish. Even a most abbreviated listing of the humor activity during the period reveals an enormous amount of material produced in the widest possible variety of comedy genres. An annotated bibliography of twenties humor in literature, theater, film, the various graphic arts, newspaper and magazine journalism, and variety entertainment would easily fill the pages of a very thick book. For the student of the period as well as for the student of American humor, the sheer bulk of available examples is as intimidating as it is provocative. Literally hundreds of writers poured out daily, weekly, and monthly columns and short stories for the newspapers and for the many magazines which were devoted—or at least readily receptive—to humor, such as *Life, Vanity Fair, Judge, The New Yorker, The Saturday Evening Post, The Smart Set,* and *American Mercury.* Works published originally in these and other similar sources provide many of our humor anthologies with samples from the huge outputs of such writers as Ring Lardner, Dorothy Parker, Robert Benchley, Corey Ford, Franklin Pierce Adams (FPA), Don Marquis, Frank Sullivan, H. L. Mencken, Frank Moore Colby, Wolcott Gibbs and many, many others, and one might well add to this list the names of the more highly regarded, "serious" writers such as Ernest Hemingway, F. Scott Fitzgerald, Sinclair Lewis, and Sherwood Anderson for their short humor and satire contributions. Over 150 college humor magazines flourished, serving as a training place for many of the later professional humorists and feeding an anthology of their offerings, *College Humor,* which sold as many as 800,000 copies per issue at its peak.[3] The newspapers and magazines also boasted a profuse display of humorous graphic art, the former hosting the many comic strips such as "Krazy Kat," "Barney Google," "The Gumps," "Thimble Theater," "Bringing Up Father," "Mutt and Jeff," and "Boob McNutt" to name but a few, and the latter encouraging the art of the social cartoonists and comic illustrators like Peter Arno, John Held, Jr., and Gluyas Williams.

At the theater one encountered scores of light social comedies every year, over twenty from George S. Kaufman and his various helpers alone during the decade, for example, the humor of the many variety revues such as Earl Carroll's *Vanities* and Florenz Ziegfeld's *Follies,* numerous musical comedies, and the lively offerings of vaudeville, burlesque, and other variety entertainment forms. Such comedians as Bert Lahr, Ed Wynn, Bert Williams, Will Rogers, Fanny Brice, Eddie Cantor, the Marx Brothers, and almost all of the important comedy stars of the mass media of subsequent decades were to be found polishing their business in the popular theater during the twenties, alongside hundreds of lesser known creators and interpreters of American humor.

And then, of course, there were the movies. According to many of the critics who deal with the subject, silent film comedy alone could qualify the decade of the twenties as a "golden age of comedy."[4] Their emphasis is usually largely qualitative and devoted to their trinity—Chaplin, Keaton, and Lloyd (sometimes generously expanded to include attention to a few of the higher angels like Harry Langdon or Laurel and Hardy)—and it perhaps properly obscures the fact that scores of other comedians were churning out literally hundreds of silent screen comedies each year during the peak years of the period (1914-1929).[5] Toward the end of that period, silent forerunners of the romantic comedies which would characterize the sound film comedies of the thirties and forties (or for that matter, film comedy to date for the most part) evolved, adding the work of such artists as Douglas

Fairbanks and Ernst Lubitsch to the more familiar formulae of silent film comedy. The roll call could go on and on—for film and for the other genres in which humor flourished during the twenties—but quantity alone does not argue sufficiently the case that humor is particularly important to the period. We will have to engage matters more complex and more important than a mere listing of the sources available for study.

Establishing that the "golden age" humor was of an unusually high quality would add considerably to the contention that humor is an important aspect of the decade, but as those of us who teach courses in American humor know all to well, discussing the quality of yesterday's humor is difficult, often even painful! However the thesis that the humor of the twenties and thirties is superior to that which preceded it and followed it is encountered frequently (interestingly enough, every generation seems to produce critics for whom the humor of the present is a pale copy of that which immediately preceded it), and it has become almost a common-place that an unprecedented number of comic "geniuses" were at work in the era. Among the names often presented to advance this claim are those of Benchley, Marquis, Thurber, Lardner, White, Herriman (creator of "Krazy Kat"), Chaplin, Keaton, Lloyd, Lubitsch, and the Berts Lahr and Williams. To be sure, my undergraduate students do begin to perk up a bit when our historical survey of American humor moves beyond the haze of the nineteenth century into the partial clearing of the early twentieth, but only a small percentage of the humor of the "golden age" remains truly effective today. The comic masters and their masterpieces are surely the tip of the iceberg, and while a relative aesthetic judgment perhaps bolsters the claim somewhat, one must be wary of generalizations based upon a sampling of material that is not representative of the whole. For Jesse Bier it is the genius of the "golden age" that prompts his praise of the period and his view that the subsequent decades represent a "fall" of American humor (p. 204). For others like Dorothy Parker, herself a candidate for the honors heaped upon the humorists of the time, the celebrated wit of the Algonquin group was, in retrospect, largely pointless, frivolous, and forgettable.[6] Perhaps it is simply unjust to apply the tests of time and of universality to a form of communication which is so topical and inherently ephemeral. It would be more fruitful to turn to the question of comic pertinence, or aptness to the era in which it appears.

But here too some interesting and perplexing theoretical problems must first at least be raised, if not solved. For those of us who are interested in the use of humor as a cultural source, it is indeed tempting to designate the humorist as the "conscience of the twentieth century," as Norris Yates does by using that phrase as the subtitle for this book, *The American Humorist,* or to declare that the iconoclastic, irreverent, cynical, wild, aggressive, exuberant spirit of the humor of the period is a metaphor for the zeitgeist, as did some of the early social, cultural, and intellectual historians of the twenties. Unfortunately such a simplistic, off-handed declaration is no longer acceptable—contemporary historians have been made all-too aware of the dangers inherent in the selection of a limited range of artistic expression as a summation of a period's basic "spirit." As Roderick Nash puts it in his indispensable account of the history of the twenties, "the spirit of an age, a traditional and worthy goal of intellectual history, is not a single entity but a many-faceted complex of ideas."[7] The artist is not necessarily a representative of public opinion or mood; his works are not necessarily popularly received, and when they are the reasons why are not always clear. We know far too little about the motives and functions of artistic expression to assume automatically that there is a conscious, deliberate perception of the implications that we, the critics and historians, read into the works of a previous era.

Dealing with humor as a source only complicates the matter. Great minds have been trying to explain the phenomenon of humor at least since Plato, and there is still no generally accepted definition of the term, much less a solid understanding of how it works. We are only beginning to investigate the psychology and the sociology of laughter; even if the records did tell us what we needed to know about what was popular with whom, we would still be far away from knowing whether the audience laughed with or at a comic persona, whether laughter indicates an identification with the comic butt or a sense of superiority over him, whether the humor was perceived to be a confrontation with reality or an escape from it into impossible, more palatable fictions. Generalizations which seek to explain the humor of a particular period are further complicated by the absence of uniformity of the material. Paradox, ambiguity, and ambivalence are always present. Finally one faces the realization that the continuities in American humor from its earliest expressions to the present are as evident, as real, and as important as any changes and evolutions we may discover.

Recognition of the problems outlined above must inhibit the use of humor as an index to the popular sentiment of an era, but there are reasons why we should not permit them to do so totally. To begin with, the more traditional materials which are used for intellectual and social history have their own weaknesses and inadequacies, particularly when it comes to dealing with moods, values, attitudes and concerns rather than "hard data" and observable phenomena. At their best they offer us a colorless, and therefore incomplete picture, or they present as motive the intellectual rationalization of elite and public spokesmen which is often obviously self-conscious, contrived, and self-serving. Humor is a mercurial source, but it does have two advantages: it is employed to deal with just about every subject of importance—sex, race, ethnicity, politics, class-consciousness, family matters, urban and rural life-styles, technology and industrialization, and anything else that mattered, and it does so in a way that is emotional, value-charged, spontaneous or at least not consciously momentous, and highly personal.

The historians of American humor who have designated the twenties as part of a "golden age" have not been shy about attributing the humor of significant social factors. Jesse Bier's explanations are typical:

...we are forced to diagnose the interwar period as a time of increasing ambivalence and tension. These are factors of the highest theoretical significance, along with whatever it was that the *zeitgeist* had provided. The pull between antidemocratic cynicism and deflationary devices, on the one side, and the democratic character of an extensive comic choral effort, on the other, is striking; the ambiguity between skepticism and desperate faith is clear; the paradox of darkening content and full joyous technique is indisputable...

In the *American Humorist,* Norris Yates discusses the factors of growing urbanization and industrialization as keys to the new humor-vision that develops in the twentieth century,[8] as does Albert McLean, Jr., who, in his book *American Vaudeville as Ritual,*[9] discusses the "new humor," a term which "generally indicated a humor that was more excited, more aggressive, and less sympathetic than that to which the middle classes of the nineteenth century had been accustomed." In my own article, "American Humour and the Spirit of the Times," the central thesis is that there is a significant difference between the tone of nineteenth and twentieth century humor, and that that difference might reflect an important change in national self-perception.[10] For Enid Veron, in her anthology *American Humor,* the rise of the "little man" humor (which will be discussed below) "signifies a widespread cultural collapse."[11]

All of these accounts, and the many others which share their basic approach, seek to interpret changes in the humor which reflect the "end of American innocence" thesis. To summarize, and unfortunately to over-simplify, the argument, American humor is viewed as having essentially a pro-democratic optimism in its early years—an egalitarian enthusiasm that makes self-congratulation as much a part of its nature as self-criticism. The argument should not be accused of ignoring the fact that there was a considerable amount of satire directed against the common man during the early years, or that the spirit of "antitheticism," to use Bier's term for a relentless assault of the *status quo* verities, was positive rather than negative in tone (see Bier, pp. 2-3), but it does emphasize the rise of the commonsense *hero* and the basically "good-natured" thrust of the pre-twentieth century material. The more modern humor, it must be agreed, retains many of the stylistic and thematic characteristics of the humor which precedes it, but it displays a distinct drift toward pessimism, hostility, conflict and even despair. Reacting to the "future shock" of the twentieth century—urbanization, industrialism, technology, bureaucracy, sharpened class distinctions, changes in family and sex roles, and an increasingly heterogeneous and crowded society—the "new humor" reflects our concern that "the promise of American life" is not likely to be fulfilled in the near future, if ever, and it helps us to cope with that concern by revealing a capacity to survive our weaknesses, by contrasting highly exaggerated victims with our own less glaring faults, and by applying the palliative of laughter to the wounds of doubt and fear. These changes in the humor are seen to be evolutionary rather than revolutionary, it must be noted, and the many ambiguities and ambivalences that one finds in the sources prevent us from overstating our conclusions, but the thesis has considerable merit and important cultural implications.

Central to the case for an evolution in fundamental premise of American humor is the development of the "little man" character out of the wise fool and the commonsense philosopher of the nineteenth century humor. As Norris Yates demonstrates persuasively and instructively[12], the "little man" is clearly a lineal descendent of the wise fool, a character-type who has been important to humor since at least the time of the Old Testament (eg. "Ecclesiastes"), but he is also undeniably different from his ancestors. To again summarize a long, complex, and important matter, the wise fool in American humor evolves from a negative portrayal, by foreigners and by native elitists, of the common man as buffoon and barbarian, to an ambivalent characterization of the naif as an innocent, likeable, but not entirely admirable representative of the truth, and finally to a pro-democratic, confident depiction of the common man as commonsense philosopher, a simple, honest, experientially-wise archetypal hero.[13] As Yates reveals further, beyond the commonsense philosopher stands the "solid citizen," another character type portrayed ambivalently and ambiguously since he can be used positively to represent a commonsense philosopher who has risen to a position of respect and authority or he can be used negatively to reflect pomposity, stoginess, and conservative deviation from the principles of the common man as hero. In this latter role, the "solid citizen" is the commonsense philosopher grown too big for his britches, the *eiron* who has become an *alazon*, to use Northrop Frye's terms. Commonsense wisdom is thus shown to be inappropriate and inadequate in the more complicated modern era; the philosopher's confidence, sense of security and well-being, and practical optimism are anachronistic.

A good literary example of the process of the decline of the "solid citizen" and his evolution into the "little man" is Sinclair Lewis's 1922 portrait of George F. Babbitt. Babbitt is certainly, externally at least, a "solid citizen," prosperous, influential, conservative, yet in his self-image a democratic rather than an aristocratic individual. In many respects he represents a commonsense philosopher who has "made it" to a position of respect and responsibility in the community—the common man triumphant. But as Lewis's devastating portrait shows so effectively, Babbitt's solidity is as firm as his "exceedingly well-fed" body. Underneath his pose, Babbitt is actually weak, confused, dominated, and unhappy. He proclaims, as a good American democrat, that he is a free individual in control of his own destiny, but as the novel develops he discovers that he is at the mercy of his friends, neighbors, social associates, family, business partners, circumstances, and his own lack of will-power or of a genuine sense of direction. Externally he seems to be a culmination of the "American Dream," but he is really a reflection of its nightmare.

Basically the "little man" is weak, confused, and insecure. As Yates puts it, "he is *dominated*—by gadgets, by his boss, by his associates on the job, by the problem of maintaining a home, by his wife and children" (p. 355). Such "little men" are the central figures of twenties humor in all of the media, but their appearance in the domestic comic strips—which from 1917 to 1929 dominated that genre—provides us with the clearest, most simple portraits of the stereotype. Caspar Milquetoast (whose name has come to represent the type), the chinless Andy Gump, Barney Google, Boob McNutt, Happy Hooligan and a host of other losers become formulaic representations of the failure of the common man, and if their roots are clearly with the negative fools, boobs, con-men, trickster, and other nineteenth century comic characters, their descriptions and the settings in which we find them are contemporary to the time in which they appear. A description of Happy Hooligan illustrates the type: "his amorphous face, his resigned smile, and the empty can that serves him as a hat plainly stamp him as a victim. He is the quarry of children, the target of hooligans, a goat for all and sundry. His tribulations are as ludicrous as they are pathetic, and while he manages to survive, his ephemeral triumphs are only illusory."[14] Stephen Becker's portrait of Barney Google amplifies: "Barney Google was a man who had great difficulty paying the rent, keeping a job, accumulating prestige, or establishing himself as any kind of responsible citizen. His adventures were those of the fool, the dupe, the pawn of society."[15] The "little men" of the comic strips are often of blue-collar backgrounds—some like Jiggs of "Bringing Up Father" are self-made millionaires but most are far from wealthy—but their plights are not merely matters of class, or even of ignorance and a lack of intelligence. Like the later, post-twenties Dagwood Bumstead—perhaps the most familiar of the lot—the comic strip "little men" are usually reasonably well-employed, housed and fed adequately, and otherwise unstigmatized if undistinguished, but they are beset by everyone and everything, and they seem to go about their lives with a total air of vulnerability. As Coulton Waugh puts it, "man were not so much mice, as soft-bellied baby rabbits. Their brains were feeble, their will power drained to zero."[16]

Popular literature, during the twenties, contributed liberally to the establishment of the "little man" formula. While scores of writers mined the vein, perhaps Robert Benchley's "normal bumbler," or "white-collar neurotic" provides the most sparkling gems. Whether trying hopelessly to complete a simple household task like fixing the furnace,[17] or to catch a fish,[18] or to deliver the hilariously incompetent treasurer's report for which he became famous,[19] Benchley's self-deprecation was both devastating and revealing. If the comic strip caricatures might be judged to be too abstract to be readily identified with, the every-day believability of Benchley's persona was inescapable.

Film comedy's legion of "little men" offers yet further insights into the importance of this image. The paradox of employing the incredibly skilled athletes and acrobats to depict ineptness, clumsiness, awkwardness, and perpetual near-disaster is itself fascinating, but that the paradox is carried over into the themes of many of the best silent comedies is even more important. Silent film comedy was peopled with simple losers—comparable to those of the comic strip—from its inception, but during the twenties a more complex, ambiguous persona emerged. The "little man" is sometimes an ironic victor, in all of the genres, surviving the various threats and dangers to which he was exposed, sometimes even triumphing over adversaries who are much more imposing. These ironic victories can probably be paralleled with the naive fool's ironic exposing of the truth despite his ignorance and foolishness—as "God's Fool" he has a special protection and guidance. But in the film comedies, especially those of the greatest artists of the medium— Chaplin, Keaton, and Lloyd—the "little men" are often ironic heroes as well as ironic victors. Despite their obvious smallness, weakness, and vulnerability, they often demonstrate a cleverness, agility, and quick-witted courage that allows them to prevail. As Andrew Sarris points out in a recent, perceptive article, "Lloyd, like Keaton, was ultracompetent...,"[20] and Chaplin's tramp is also often observably superior to his foes. These three artists created characters who take on formidable tasks without (much) flinching, and while it is equally true that they do not often overcome directly—their is rather a kind of back-door, accidental triumph—they do display many positive traits. In films like Keaton's "The General" and Lloyd's "Safety Last," the "little man" is very close to being genuinely triumphant, though it must not be overlooked that their triumphs come after considerable peril and signs of weakness and that, particularly in the case of Keaton's endings, they are rarely if ever unrelieved (eg. Keaton "wins" his primary battle in "Cops" and in "The General" but he loses as far as his love interests are concerned).[21] Chaplin's tramp is often, but not always defeated in his primary goals, however he is never defeated by life. He retains his dignity, confidence, and jaunty optimism as he walks off into the sunset twirling his cane. Even in "Easy Street," though, it must be remembered that though he defeats the bully and brings law and order into the community, he has succeeded by employing cowardice and guile and even his agility is doubted by his falling over a chair immediately after he has downed his enemy for the last time. In short the film "little men" are still clearly "little men," but they emphasize the survivability and the ironic potential for success of the character, with a little bit of luck, determination, and cleverness. These themes do not reverse the motif's meaning; rather they suggest an optimistic, or at least less negative version of it.

The "little" man is belittled, as it has been suggested above, by nature, technology, bureaucracy, fellow men, and his own unfitting combination of arrogance and ineptness, but it is the war between the sexes and the conflict within the family that inhibit, ultimately, his possibilities for growth. If the illusion of the "little man" as a romantic success and a hero in the eyes of those who love him could be maintained, he might be redeemed. But in twenties humor courting brings aggravation rather than pleasure, and marital becomes martial at the blink of an 'i'. Once again we must remember that the basic motif of this humor is neither new nor unique. As Bier notes, there has been a "rampant misogyny" in all of our humor (p. 21), and the heartbreaking tease, the termagant wife, and the ungrateful, unmanageable child have been stock characters from Franklin and Irving to Alan King. But here too we can see an escalation of tension and a darkening of mood which may indeed be significant. There is a coexistence during the decade of light, silly, casual fun with romantic encounters and domestic contentiousness, and more serious examinations of the state of the relations between men and women.

While the jokes and cartoons of the humor magazines seem more to celebrate the spice of sexual conflict—sort of a "vivre la difference" spirit— the short stories of such writers as Ring Lardner, Don Marquis, Dorothy Parker and others are often more ominous. Parker's poems, in "Enough Rope" for example, and her short stories such as "The Sexes," or "Glory in the Daytime,"[22] express more despair and disgust at the seemingly inherent and permanent inability of men and women to communicate and to cooperate sanely, and if Parker's often discussed particular biography suggests that she might not be a representative figure, one can parallel her treatment of the theme with stories and poems of Marquis, Lardner, and Thurber, as well as with such contemporary developments as those which allow Carol Burnett to kill off two husbands—one with dynamite and the other with poison—in one hour of prime-time television. As for the family, stories such as Lardner's "The Love Nest" and Benchley's "Christmas Afternoon" are just two among many that might be examined for their portrayal of an iconoclastic approach to domestic bliss.[23]

Among the many interesting developments in the humor dealing with women during the period, the comic characters created by Mae West and by Anita Loos are perhaps the most interesting.[24] West's self-confident, self-reliant charmer—perhaps better known from her films of the thirties, but already established in the theater during the twenties in such plays as *Diamond Lil*—is in some ways antithetical to the pessimism and negativism of the "little man" characters. West's persona owes a great deal to the sexy ladies of vaudeville, burlesque, the revues, and perhaps even to the mood of earlier Southwestern humor. She is quite different from the vacant and silly flappers of the cartoons of John Held, Jr. and others, though she shares their hedonism and their materialism, among other characteristics. Loreli Lee was created by Anita Loos, in a short story, to represent the dumb, crass, but beautiful chorus girls whose popularity diminished male interest in such likeable, intelligent, worthy types as the author, but like the wise fools whom she so resembles at times, Loreli was received as a positive as well as a negative character.[25] Her naive honesty, absence of self-delusion, open desire to enjoy herself and to use others as they would use her make her admirable rather than reprehensible, and by the time Loos added some complexity to the caricature for the novel version (1925), Loreli had become one of the more interesting female characters of American humor.

The cultural commentaries of writers like Anita Loos and the others mentioned in this essay was not entirely—or even predominately—self-conscious. The humorists of the twenties were either professional comedians whose motives were to make money by making people laugh, or they were popular artists who were expressing themselves without making much of a claim to social significance (there were exceptions, of course, notably Mencken who overrated the importance of his olympian pronouncements). Even where the iconoclasm, sarcasm, pessimism, and hostility was deliberate and conscious, it usually reflected the artist's personal dissatisfaction rather than a judgment of the era, but this does not make it less important. Humor is a medium that is initially casual, off-handed, and overlooked; it is created and consumed without much analysis (which is not to imply that a great deal of thought and effort does not go into the artistic aspects of it), yet it is always close to basic human emotions and concerns. Chaplin and co. were not the first clowns to mix pathos and piercing human observation with pratfalls and slapstick, and if their encounter with humor led them to more complexity than one might expect, they were not the last to do so either.

The twenties is obviously much more than a decade of humor, just as it is more than "the roaring twenties" or any other such simplistically designated period. But it is a decade in which humor figures prominently. Jesse Bier calls the interwar humor "a resume and a culmination" of all of the traditions of the past (p. 280) and it is that; twenties humor includes important examples of all of the major trends of American humor, both stylistically and thematically. But the decade may also be seen as a transitional period in which the evolution of American humor toward darker, more serious self-criticism becomes clear and defined. The humor of the twenties certainly points to contemporary American culture as definitely as it does to the culture of the past. Students of the era would do well to examine humor as a source of insight into its character, and certainly students of American humor must consider the twenties as a crucial decade for its development.

Notes

This article has been published in a similar form in *Thalia* IV:1 (Spring, Summer 1981), 26-32.

[1]*The Time Of Laughter* (Boston: Little, Brown, 1967), pp. 2-3.

[2]see Chapter VI, "Interwar Humor," in Jesse Bier, *The Rise and Fall of American Humor* (New York: Holt, Rinehart and Winston, 1968).

[3] Dan Carlinsky, ed., *A Treasury of College Humor* (New York: Random House, 1971), p. 12.

[4]see, for example, the accounts of the silent film comedy era in Gerald Mast, *The Comic Mind* (New York: Bobbs-Merrill, 1973), and Raymond Durgnat, *The Crazy Mirror: Hollywood Comedy and the American Image* (New York: Delta, 1972). Other critics making similar claims include Walter Kerr, James Agee, and Gilbert Seldes.

[5]Kent D. Estrin, Forward to K.C. Lahue and Sam Gill, *Clown Princes and Court Jesters: Some Great Comics of the Silent Screen* (New York: A. S. Barnes, 1970), pp. 10-11.

[6]John Keats, *You Might as Well Live: The Life and Times of Dorothy Parker* (New York: Simon and Schuster, 1970), p. 287. Parker's quoted comment is directed at the spontaneous wit of the Algonquin friends rather than at their artistic endeavors, and on the following page she seems to share the view that the humor of the "good

old days" was superior to that of the present, but she does seem to have regarded the humor to be an inadequate and frivolous response to the era.

[7]*The Nervous Generation: American Thought, 1917-1930* (Chicago: Rand McNally, 1970), p. IX. See also pp. 1-4.

[8]New York: Citadel, 1965

[9]Lexington: University of Kentucky, 1965, p. 107. See particularly, chapter 6.

[10]in *It's a Funny Thing, Humour*, Anthony Chapman and Hugh Foot, eds., (London: Pergamon Press), pp. 17-22.

[11]New York: Harcourt, Brace, Jovanovich, p. 202.

[12]Yates, op. cit., esp. pp. 20-28.

[13]There are several good studies of the wise fool character as it appears in European and American literature. For a brief survey, see the first two chapters of my unpublished dissertation, "Brother Jonathan's City Cousin: The Wise Fool in Urban Social and Political Satire," Ph.D., Michigan State U., 1969.

[14]Pierre Couperie, Maurice Horn, et als, *A History of the Comic Strip* (New York: Crown, 1968), pp. 22-23.

[15]*Comic Art in America* (New York: Simon and Schuster, 1959), p. 91.

[16]*The Comics* (New York, Luna, 1974), p. 192.

[17]*Chips Off the Old Benchley* (New York: Harper, 1949), pp. 149-162.

[18]*Ibid.*, pp. 123-124.

[19]in Louis Untermeyer, ed., *A Treasury of Laughter* (New York: Simon Schuster, 1946), pp. 38-40.

[20]"Harold Lloyd: a Rediscovery," *American Film*, II:10 (September, 1977), 28.

[21]see Mast, op. cit., on the Keaton endings, pp. 137-140.

[22]*The Portable Dorothy Parker* (New York: Viking, 1944, 1976).

[23]*Haircut and Other Stories* (New York: Scribners, 1922), pp. 104-122. Benchley, in *A Sub-Treasury of American Humor*, E. B. White and Katherine White, eds. (New York: Coward-McCann, 1941), pp. 248-250.

[24]my appreciation and understanding of West and Loos owes a great deal to the dissertation research of one of my graduate students, Zita Dresner.

[25]see Anita Loos's autobiography, *A Girl Like I* (New York: Viking, 1966), for a discussion of the reception of Loreli Lee.

Freud and the Roaring Twenties:
From the General to the Specific

Ralph Von Tresckow Napp

Dr. Ralph von Tresckow Napp's diverse educational background in the related areas of psychology and sociology has taken him throughout the world as a respected lecturer and consultant. His numerous publications, including his book entitled Breaking Down the Barrier, *have focused upon contemporary problems in human adjustment that have allowed him to integrate extensive teaching and scholarly experience in sociology, American Studies, psychology, and modern history. Professor von Napp became versed in Freudian psychoanalysis while doing Post graduate work at the University of Munich from 1951 until 1957. He continued to achieve distinction in this special pursuit through clinical work in group psychotherapy at the Western Virginia State Hospital, and through group marital psychotherapy with Dr. Ali Jarrahi in Winston Salem, North Carolina.*

What becomes rapidly apparent to us through Dr. von Napp's assessment is that the easy generalizations about Freud's influence upon the 1920s that have reached us today are, at best, only slightly trustworthy. Pertinent to the collective portrait of the age as depicted in this anthology, we are shown clearly that the misreading and misuse of Freudian psychology during the 1920s serves as a perfect mirror reflection of the gross self-indulgence and tragic illusions of that age. The people in America reached out for psychoanalysis like a new religion. The loss of traditional religious zeal opened the door to Freud as a source of new answers and spiritual salvation. In fact, explains von Napp, perhaps no man since Christ has captured the American scene as Freud did. Yet the popular conception of Freud as an authoritative justification for sex without love, for licentiousness and perversion, did more to augment the post-war spiritual emptiness than to fill it. Such distortion merely vindicated the animalistic behavior of an immediate-gratification patterned people living in a sensate culture. The final irony of Freud's misunderstood intentions is that the real sexual education Freud offered Americans in the Twenties—one that emphasized moral responsibility—and one that may have helped people make the difficult adjustments of the period, did not reach them at all.

The author of this paper personally experienced Freudian psychoanalysis himself while a student at the University of Munich.

172

* * *

Freud, as a monumental individual to whose legacy America is forever indebted, can not be given enough recognition in these few pages. Even though many different religions and philosophies have long dealt with similar approaches to curing mental illness, particularly such teachings as mid-eastern Sufism, Freud was perhaps the first contemporary psychologist to realize and verify that most deep emotional problems can not be resolved by intellect alone. America increasingly turned to Freud's teachings as a solution to many of its difficulties in the ever existent social lag though many modern psychologist today have denigrated him with a superior air, for being archaic, forgetting that he was a Christopher Columbus of psychiatry in his time. Weston LaBarre, the Duke University anthropologist, says, "It is true that the classical theory of Freud is in some ways 'culture bound'; but this conveniently correct criticism has too often been exploited to rationalize turning out books on a psychology that has sometimes disenchanting things to say about man."

Especially since the Twenties Americans have been salvaged for new life through the analysis basically derived from the Freudian school of thought. Even today, however, after fifty years of enlightenment, the great majority of Americans still consider mental illness something slightly shameful, to say the least, view psychiatrists with a combination of fascination, malice, and ignorance and feel compelled to repress or outright conceal awareness of relatives who are in the hands of the "head shrinkers."

In answer to those who see Freud as an unscientific atheist, David Riesman replies, "I believe Freud has done more than any other psychologist to stimulate the scientific study of religion—something that William James was unable to accomplish." Even though some people still consider Freud a religious disbeliever he nevertheless led many people into searching for their souls, which eventually led many of them back to God. Freud could, no doubt, be called an ethical neutralist; and it would certainly not be far from the truth or unfair to call him amoral at least in his research and objectivity. From the early Twenties on too many American parlor analysts have been misguided and in turn have misguided others into thinking that all that Freud discussed was animalistic sexual activity. (This has become one of the greatest intellectual deceptions of our time.) On the contrary, Freud was "religiously" concerned with sublimating the libido into fields of constructive endeavor. He constantly insisted that the sexual drive in itself does not necessarily always find satiation in bed. The sexual drive must more often be channeled in directions adequate to a full life since man, like no other animal on earth, can not survive without sublimation. In fact Riesman states, "Freud viewed work as an inescapable and tragic necessity."

Not only must Freud be recognized as a great contributor to American culture but he must also be seen as a great teacher of men, the likes of Jung, Adler, et al, all products of his genius and today famous in their own rights even though differing with Freud on many issues. Furthermore, Freud was constantly concerned with suffering humanity whenever and wherever he found it. Erik Erikson best expresses this basic concern of Freud's with, "All these tormented people, then, whether addicted, depressed, or inhibited, have somehow failed to integrate one or another of the infantile stages, and they defend themselves against these infantile patterns— stubbornly, wastefully, unsuccessfully." For those familiar with Freudian psychoanalysis it becomes quite obvious that Erikson's quotation is literally a page out of the teachings of Freud clearly and simply.

It seems to me that historically the main thrust of Freudian psychology actually began in the 1920 s even though Freud introduced his writings in Europe sometime earlier. This thrust came at a time when America was in the throes of a post war explosive change. There was, at this time, a growing need to supplant the loss of religion with some substantive explanation and salvation. There was also a need to introduce new answers to old problems in a society that had become sensate and materialistic as never before. America was getting itself "psyched-up" for the electric shock that was to be the treatment for thousands of tortured souls in the future. Many Americans in the Twenties felt guilty in breaking away from the Church and puritanical morality. In order to repair their damaged psyche, while unable to return to Christ for forgiveness, they reached out for psychoanalysis as a surrogate—at least those who could afford it.

When Freud was introduced to America, before World War I, only a small select group of intellectuals actually understood him and his theories. A.A. Brill was perhaps the first to translate Freud, with much enthusiasm, to the American public. Much of Brill, however, was hardly comparable to the brilliant English translation of John Strachey in England. As a matter of fact, Brill's overemphasis on the sexual aspect misled many Americans into thinking that was all that Freud intended. In reality Freud had much more to offer, even though sex and the libido were focal terms in his psychoanalytical endeavors. On Freud's visit to this country, before the Twenties, he was probably amazed at the susceptibility of American minds, especially to the sexual freedom he seemed to offer them. By the early Twenties such intellectuals as Walter Lippman, Max Eastman, Henry F. May, Frederick Lewis Allen and a host of others had prepared the American public for the impending sexual revolutionary shock wave that was to finally inundate this country from east to west and north to south. William E. Leuchtenburg called this period "The Revolution in Morals." Many Americans, however, are inclined to interpret morals as only pertaining to a sexual aspect of life which, of course, it is not, even though this essay is primarily concerned with the sexual from the Freudian point of view, especially its impact on the Twenties.

In order to emancipate Americans from their sexual "hangups" it was first necessary to emancipate women sexually. The hypocrisy, however, of the existing double standard was replaced by an accent of abusing and using women as public symbols of sex as probably no modern nation had done before. Though women had been used as sexual targets long before the Twenties, it took the post World War I years to bring this exploitation into focus through the writing of Freud; which incidentally was most decidedly not Freud's intention. In this respect, one is reminded of Marx in that Marx most likely had not intended to see communism evolve into its present form in a nation he was not particularly attracted to anymore than Freud had intended sex to become licentious, as it did, in a nation he hardly knew. Though many Americans finally were to know Freud better than he ever was to know Americans, the popular thrust became a perversion of the true purpose of Freud. For example, Freud would most certainly be amazed today at the sensate advertising and entertainment based on suggestibility that hardly diminishes sexual frustration even though stimulating one's interest in sex.

The Twenties most likely convinced Sorokin, the Harvard sociologist, that his analysis of America's sexual behavior coincided with his "sensate theory" in that each culture ultimately goes through cycles of sensual behavior and America was now at its peak in the cycle. But it took Freud, in the Twenties, to help push America nearer to the brink.

Americans had long anticipated a way out of their varied prohibitions. Feeling "naughty" about their breaking the prohibition laws, they indulged in a deceptive sexual catharsis that seemed to touch their very souls. "For after all," said the American, "What is more sacred than the womb from whence we all came and which we all pursue in the act of intercourse?" They further thought that if they could resolve their sexual frustrations they could also resolve all other frustrations.

In the early Twenties Brill gambled on the acceptance or rejection of Freud's teachings in America when he first lectured to women on masturbation, until that day a strongly forbidden subject for public conversation. Instead of being shocked by such public disclosures on sex, Americans broke out into a sweat of sexual mania. By the end of the Twenties there was hardly anyone "in the know" who had not heard of Freud and his new terminology. The four letter words were rapidly replaced with intellectual gusto by such terms as ego, superego, id, libido, coitus, etc. Leuchtenburg likened Freud to the automobile, i.e., being in reach of everyone.

As the "Roaring Twenties" gushed out its feelings, for better or for worse, sex out of marriage was tempting all kinds of people in all kinds of relationships. The acceptance of pre-marital sex was not so difficult to understand especially after so many American males had been exposed to the liberal views of "Gay Paree" during World War I. Extra-marital sex, though for many just as tempting, was more forbidden fruit and at first dangerous to openly tolerate. Mencken, however, took the early risk, as had a few others in his time, predicting that adultery would become just as popular as illicit drinking.

As the moral foundation of the American family began to shake, an emerging declaration of sexual independence was being felt throughout the land. The loss of religious zeal had opened the door to Freud and somehow Americans in the Twenties unconsciously found it very convenient to link him with a materialistic sensate way of life acceptable to those who had been confused in the dungeons of their minds, particularly those feeling guilty over sexual desires. Freud's insistence that neurotic behavior was the result of sexual pulsations became a popular way of justifying one's feelings. Psychology now became the discipline for an entire nation on the brink of Dante's Inferno. The sharing of strange sexual thoughts with others was now allied with examining one's own subconscious. Dreaming was no longer the only way to fantasy and even nightmares became sexual sources of competition during the cocktail hour spiced up with the double entendre. Perhaps the Twenties are responsible for releasing some of the most frightening goblins from a Pandora's box long bolted to the past. Too many Americans took Freud's views to mean that sex without love was more intellectual; and to deny one's commitment to another was simply a game people would play, forgetting that one of the players could and usually did get injured in such psychological melee. Sexual athletes began to compete for honors in pictures and words as never before in American history. The twisted view of sex that prevailed most certainly influenced future Americans who today are wondering how they got on the couch in the first place. Freud had not meant for any people to sanctify sex as they had religious practices. One could say that the American sexual pagan was born in the throes of the emerging Twenties. Sexual rights were being confused with sexual rites. Authors such as Hemingway, O'Neill, Anderson, Lawrence and others became increasingly popular as they were read with a kind of mutual lust for the legendary "forbidden fruit." Even racial barriers continued to crumble more flagrantly in the bedrooms where formerly this desire had been reserved only for houses of ill repute. The myth that Freud could solve all woes of the American psyche was inflated out of proportion to reality. The popularity of Freud was as intense as most of the extreme ways Americans have always taken life. The "either-or" attitude began to weave its way throughout the pattern of American culture so that today if one doesn't "do it" one is a so-called "square," a figment of archaic imagination. There was, however, a sane element during these years that held a torch of truth which was to burn in support of Freud's sound theories, theories that were to hold up under years of disappointment, criticism and bitterness. Perhaps no man since Christ captured the American scene as Freud did. Others, since his time, have certainly tried but have seldom come close to such social influence.

The cultural forces swept Freud into the main stream of American life and in so doing ripped him from the weakening grip of his European origin, especially noticeable after the debut of Hitler. On the surface people were free as never before, i.e., free of inhibitions too often stimulated by "bath-tub-gin" or some other similar stimulant of that time. Their surface gaiety, however, was usually shortlived, as were other forms of extravagant living that the Twenties so violently introduced. Before the leak in the dike of plenty began artists were turned loose in all directions. The destiny of men like Picasso was already rooted in the Freudian libido, as were others who could be considered as long repressed heroic sexual figures. In very odd ways America became a tragic society in the Twenties, tragic in that it expected so much, for so many, from so few. One must conclude that the over-all importance of Freud should be obvious in that his sexual breakthrough did emancipate many a tortured soul and continues to do so in spite of the exaggerated and over-demanding expectations that no one but God could fulfill. The pendulum of American thought has swung back and forth, frustrated again and again as to where Freud should be placed in the American cultural base. Many academic empiricists have tried desperately to rule out the teachings of Freud forever because they themselves have been troubled by the human flaws in Freud. More balanced minds have accepted Freud for what he is: not an answer to all man's woes but a pioneer in the fields of pain and sorrow, a man of conviction who could see all men, one day, becoming more autonomous agents in not only sex but in all other phases of life, men who would not need sex alone to justify their existence, men who would someday have a greater control of their basic drives and in so doing control their destiny enough to reach the stars themselves!

Now that we have dealt sporadically with the general impact of Freud on the Twenties, let us look at his specific impact on the American family during that time.

As sex infiltrated the daytime as well as the playtime consciousness, job-mindedness diminished. The sexual drive of Americans in the Twenties began to systematically distract family members from other interests that were once of greater value, which in turn led them into a deceptive trap. As Americans became possessed by sex and the connotations thereof, as seen in advertisements, pornography, conversation, dress, looks, and arts, a paradox developed in that they became more inhibited in the light of serious thought particularly linked with discussion. This ambiguity made mutual trust difficult. One was not sure whether the participating discussant was advancing a form of seduction physically (or vicariously) or on the other hand seriously projecting impersonal thoughts for dissolving the sexual problem in question. On the other hand, sex did begin to serve as a kind of antidote to boredom and apathy. Today, we often apply this observation, in extreme psychiatric situations, suggesting, in specific cases, that the key to restoring the patient's health is to be found in his last fixation on sex. John Griffin in his participant-observer study, *Black Like Me*, depicting Blacks' sex life in the deep South, found this to be evident among the poverty-stricken males who had nothing left in life but the sexual opportunity of overpowering the female as often as possible, since in actuality he was inferior to her in all other aspects of life. Specifically she was permitted by the white establishment to out-earn and out-rank him in their servitude to the white world. Further evidence of this may be found in such literature as the *Mind of the South* by Cash, *Deep South* by Davis and Gardner, and *Children of Bondage* by Davis and Dollard. Freud himself, however, implied time and time again that such a sexual relationship could not survive indefinitely. We might suggest at this point that students today of Masters and Johnson and the like had best take note.

Evidence appeared more and more in the Twenties to justify a generalization that monotony of marriage could be interrupted by a varied sexual program. The emphasis on sex to assist in keeping mates together became a by-line. Though one's attractiveness was being increasingly equated with being "sexy," many a person failed to understand that hidden Freudian concepts were also at work below the threshold of consciousness, arousing an Oediups Complex that led many to marry for reasons unknown and often unrelated to the veneer of the body beautiful as seen in the eyes of the beholder. Reference should be made here to Robert Winch's excellent book on complimentary needs, *Mate Selection*.

The competition in sex that most likely began with a furor in the Twenties also, most likely, placed great emphasis on the "other-directed" characteristics Riesman wrote about much later in his book, *The Lonely Crowd*. Such vignettes as, "...he does not want to miss, day in day out, the qualities of experience he tells himself the others are having," serve possibly as a sexual interpretation of American thought then as well as now. Sexual competition was surely in full swing by the time the Twenties had died out. America has never been the same in that it has become a land of extreme contrasts in terms of sexual attitudes. Lowry perhaps says this best in his book, *Communism and Christ*, with the statement, "There can be no question that ours is a sensate culture in Sorokin's sense. The thrust toward the sensate remains very powerful and is abetted by modern communications and an omnipresent and almost omnipotent commercialism. The final phase of sensate development seems to be absorption and obsession by the sexual."

We are far advanced in this phase. American culture is sex-drenched to a degree without precedent in history. This is not because we are especially sensual as a people. We are probably less so than the Germans, the Russians or the French. but we are very vulnerable psychologically because we are still half-puritan, and on our other side we are romantic rather than realistic. America motion pictures illustrate most neatly both sides of this analysis: our sensual suggestibility and our romanticism. The popularity of sex has developed into a public type of voyeurism to such an extent that females today in America are seen as sexual targets first before they come into focus as human beings. Americans in the Twenties began to develop a hypocritical superiority about sexual autonomy. The avant garde took little cognizance of the fact that promiscuous petting without orgasm was developing into an unhealthy way of life. Ira Reiss states, "...although American women are more virginal than Swedish women, they are still more promiscuous sexually." In other words, Americans approve of petting as a morally accepted pattern of behavior as long as actual coitus does not occur. The Swedish author, Brigitta Linner throughout her book, *Sex and Society in Sweden,* offers a strong cross-cultural argument in support of the American, Reiss.

The sexual education that Freud offered America in the Twenties did not reach the academic world as quickly as the popular one, and as a result a cultural lag developed that continues to exist to this day. Freud, more or less, warned the American family as early as the Twenties that the 3 Rs in sexual education were: the right to breast feeding, the right to toilet training without fanatical coercion, and the right to love without being threatened out of any disciplinary motive. Erikson, years later in reference to toilet training, stated, "Where the anal character in our culture approaches the neurotic it often appears to be a result of the impact on a retentive child of a certain type of maternal behavior in Western Civilization, namely, a narcissistic and phobic overconcern with matters of elimination." In comparing Western Civilization in this matter with other parts of the world he states, "Our Western Civilization, however, has chosen to take the matter more seriously...it is assumed that early and vigorous training not only keeps the home atmosphere nicer but is absolutely necessary for the development of orderliness and punctuality." Somehow Freudian sexual education was badly twisted to such an extent that the natural intent of sexual behavior never did take hold. That sex permeated all facets of life did not necessarily emancipate the American public. Instead it did the opposite in that the preoccupation with sex distracted many a mind from other valuable aspects of life. Riesman states, "To be sure women still use sex as a means to status in spheres controlled by men." This comment further illustrates the point Eric Bern makes in his book, *Games People Play.* Perhaps Americans never did get the message Rilke, the German poet, offered: "Aren't lovers forever reaching verges in each other?" Instead the sexual game became a popular one to flaunt before the eyes of the old guard as if to say, "Shocking—but what are you doing to do about it?"

The popular front is most likely not aware of the fact that Freud also wrote anthropologically. His classic contribution to the field of anthropology was *Totem and Taboo* in which he dealt with sexual connotations of interest to all scholars on the international scene. Murdock, the American anthropologist, reinforced Freud's works, as did the British anthropologist Malinowski, by revealing to the western world that man is not monogamous by nature and that of the 554 social systems accounted for in the world 419 permit a man or woman to live with more than one spouse. What the people of the Twenties failed to grasp from the pages of Freud was that sex is a moral responsibility in all cultures. All cultures control sex to survive and no culture particularly approves of children out of wedlock, though most make better adjustments than we do, in the Western World, when such situations occur.

The Roaring Twenties strongly reinforced the paradox of sexual freedom on one hand and the glamor of sex and marriage on the other. The two extremes were bound to collide somewhere and sometime in our short history, which is in evidence today. The American male set his female on the road to sexual freedom and is now appalled at the results. Since the Twenties Americans have increasingly felt unwanted as mates, since they are now so often unwatched. The Philip Wylie form of "momism" portrayed in his book, *Generation of Vipers,* strongly suggests that the Freudian Oedipus Complex has castrated many an American male no matter how often they resort to bedroom gymnastics. The Twenties perpetrated the popular view that a man was a man if he could swing from bed to bed, woman to woman, again and again. Virility was equated with being a "he man" at the expense of the artistic way of life that other cultures never permitted the misinterpretation of Freud to supplant.

The competition of the flesh in such contests as the beauty parades must trace its history back to the Twenties and Freud. The Madison Avenue boys practically at once saw a ploy they could profit from in their exploitations of sex. The target they chose was the female body, personified, which has since become the cheapest, most available and non-imaginative means of selling almost any product. The sadness is that the American male in being so seduced doesn't have the satisfaction of knowing or even enjoying it. Riesman's reply to the sexual hyperactivity of men is that, "their outward appearance of aliveness may mask inner sterility." Erikson, in looking at the entire scene from the Freudian point of view, states, "But he certainly never advocated that men or women should treat one another as objects on which to live out their sexual idiosyncrasies." Sex has been decidedly a constant paradox in American history with the radicals on one hand and the reactionary puritans on the other. Since Freud's influence in the Twenties sex has become a commercial commodity of unrelenting proportions.

In conclusion, as mentioned earlier, the brevity of this essay can hardly do Freud justice. It is hoped, however, that some further insight of his impact on the Roaring Twenties has been adequately made for such an anthology as this one. I am sure that those of us who have undertaken the often painful experience of Freudian psychoanalysis, are aware how fortunate the world is that such a man appeared when he did, regardless of the now apparent misinterpretations. Not only has his method of soul searching saved many from an ongoing tortured existence but his analysis has opened the way toward a more understanding and autonomous sexual life for countless others.

Perhaps the most negative aspect of Freud's psychology has been its pseudo-intellectual popularity, the very popularity, that made Freud a household word. Unquestionably, popularity has opened many doors where Freud might never have entered, but in the long run those very doors have been opened to a flood of innuendos devastatingly misleading and utterly dangerous to the true meaning of sexual autonomy. Until Freud there was little if any relief from a psychologically unhealthy cycle of life. A man was born somewhat into a fate of adjustment or maladjustment. If he were too sensitive in an abnormal environment he often broke. Few adequate solutions were available other than a total prison-like confinement or temporary relief, if at all available. Since Freud, the chains that hold maladjusteds often can be broken, sometimes forever. If America has only this alone in Freud to appreciate, it is in itself enough for any one man to have offered in his lifetime!

References

It would be more than redundant to list the various references by Freud and on Freud in this paper. Some of my material, however, came from two specific papers of mine: The "Popular Cultural Effect of Freud on the American Family" presented at the Popular Culture Association in the South, Fifth Annual Meeting in 1976 at the University of Tennessee and "Sex and Some Contradictions in Marriage" (A Marital Psychotherapeutic Approach to Sex) presented at the Sixth Annual Sociological Research Symposium in 1976 at Virginia Commonwealth University and published by same.

In addition to other authors and their works recognized throughout, I wish to express my special appreciation to the following authors and their enlightening material as they first appear in this paper: Weston LaBarre, *The Human Animal*, (Chicago, 1955), David Riesman, *Individualism Reconsidered*, (Glencoe, 1954), Erik Erikson, *Childhood and Society*, (New York, 1963), William E. Leuchtenburg, *The Perils of Prosperity*, 1914-32, (Chicago, 1958), Pitirim Sorokin, *Social and Cultural Dynamics*, (Glencoe, 1959), Ira L. Reiss, "Premarital Sexual Standards in America, (Glencoe, 1960), David Riesman, *The Lonely Crowd*, (New Haven, 1950), and George P. Murdock, "World Ethnographic Sample," *American Anthropologist*, 59: 664-687, 1957.

The 1920s and the 1960s:
Lost or Found Generations?

Roderick Nash

Roderick Nash began his teaching career in the northeast where he was raised but after obtaining his B.A. (Magna Cum Laude) from Harvard University, and his M.A. and PH.D., from the University of Wisconsin migrated to southern California (University of California at Santa Barbara) where he teaches history and environmental studies. Mr. Nash is active in many scholarly historical societies as well as environmental societies such as the Sierra Club and The Wilderness Society. It was these two related interests that cast Mr. Nash in such an enviable position in 1966.

As an environmentalist in a time when that was not yet a popular cause and as an historian teaching at the University of California at Santa Barbara he had his finger on the pulse of the heartbeat of the American sensibilities and was able to gauge its ebb and flow. What Mr. Nash was able to witness firsthand was that although the 1960s was an age of disillusionment with traditional values and structures it was a time that conversely began to build and organize its own values, its own structures.

With history as his guidepost Mr. Nash evaluates the new lights of the 1960s. Like the 1920s he tells us, a war has caused a climate of disillusionment. There has been a fundamental disorganization with the result that some of those members of society who feel lost and alienated retreat deeper into the safe pocket of old values and traditions and some re-examine the old propositions and begin to create new ones.

It is with those that throw away the old values that Mr. Nash concerns himself, those that the more traditional members of society refer to as being "lost" was really discarded, so that the generation should more aptly be labeled the 'found' generation. What these seekers found was an energy level and a sense of self that far exceeded that of previous generations.

The self oriented direction of the decades preceding the '20s and the '60s and ironically following them was now directed toward challenging and changing what was perceived as intellectually and spiritually restrictive. The new intellectual freedom of the '20s and the '60s led to changes in the literature, the music, the mores and the morals of society. Heroism was redefined to mean not only bravery in combat but courage in spiritual endeavors. The ability to become oneself regardless of established values led not only to creativity but concern for those less able to defend themselves and hence to new forms of communication. It is this sense of quest and conquer that gives these two decades their reputation as prime movers and their label as "found" generations.

In addition to his professorial duties at Santa Barbara Mr. Nash has written Wilderness and the American Mind, *Revised edition 1982,* American Environmentalism, *1989,* The Nervous Generation, *1970,* The Call of the Wild, *1970,* From These Beginnings, *1973 and* The Rights of Nature *1989.*

* * *

To be a professor at an American University twenty years ago was to feel the excitement that accompanies cultural challenge and also, I think, to sense the spirit of the 1920s. At my institution in Santa Barbara, California, the students burned the Bank of America, a man was killed in a bombing of our faculty club, tear gas and marshal law prevailed in the campus bedroom community called Isla Vista. There were excesses involved in all of this, but also enormous vigor and energy. Today, by way of contrast, the emphasis is on surf, sand, sex and, of course, jobs and the future, just as it was in the late 1940s and early 1950s. Today's students are much less interesting to teach. Whereas those in the late 60s were interested in saving the world, today's are more concerned with saving their own butts. The contrast serves to point out what was different about the 1960s and also, I think, about the 1920s.

My thesis here is that the 1920s and the 1960s were times of disillusionment among *some* Americans with *some* parts of the American tradition. I would further argue that this climate of disillusionment, criticism, and crisis was also a time of experimentation, questioning, creation and self-discovery. The 1920s and the 1960s were "lost" only in terms of the values they challenged and partially replaced. They were "found" in terms of new ones. There was a tendency toward escapism in these periods, but we should recognize that escape not only is flight from something, but also flight to something. We should recognize that alienation means not just turning away, but also release. When "all Gods are dead," as F. Scott Fitzgerald told us they were for his contemporaries, there is a chance to create new gods. I would in fact go so far as to venture a generalization that the most creative periods in the cultural history of man have been those characterized by criticism, change, crisis. As John Aldridge has said elsewhere in this book, it is necessary to break out of "smothering...conformity" in order to realize the fruits of "creative independence." I think the 1920s and the 1960s both did this, and I think that the sympathy that the 60s felt for the 20s recognizes this commonality.

For my sermon quotation as the Puritans used to call it, I wish to take a statement by that empressario of cheap paperback classics of literature, one Emanual Haldeman-Julius. Haldeman-Julius published no less than one hundred million five cent booklets in his Little Blue Book series in the nine years following 1919. He had to know something about popular taste to be so successful. In 1925, he said: "there is a tremendous awakening, a mental renaissance...the time is right for fearless and far-reaching projects. Let us not throw away this precious opportunity by allowing ourselves to be dulled with inaction by the cynics who believe all is lost." I like this idea of a "mental renaissance" because I think what happened transcended the Harlem Renaissance, to which Darwin Turner has applied the term, and actually extends to many sectors of culture throughout the United States in the 1920s. I think "mental renaissance" is also an apt term for characterizing the 1960s. Those students who burned the bank in Isla Vista, California may have broken the law, but they also broke out of the stultifying mediocrity and conformism that characterized their predecessors and their successors. These students of the 60s were also touched by the "mental renaissance" that is the concomitant of deep and searching questioning of their cultural values.

This thesis and this talk expands upon a book I wrote in 1970 entitled *The Nervous Generation: American Thought 1917 to 1930.* I wrote it because I was dissatisfied with the easy generalizations used to characterize the 1920s. I was interested to learn that the word "stereotype" was created by Walter Lippman in 1922 in his book *Public Opinion.* It is fitting that the word should be coined in the 20s because we have largely treated the decade in terms of stereotypes. Lippman calls a stereotype an intellectual crutch, a substitute for precise analysis and an excuse for not viewing individuals and historical eras singularly, as they actually are. I was unhappy because as I looked at the American 1920s, I saw a great many things that were not explained by such easy phrases as "lost generation" "jazz age," "roaring twenties," and by the adjectives cynical, disillusioned, irresponsible, debauched, nihilistic and bewildered. As I tried to look more deeply at the decade, I learned, to my surprise, that F. Scott Fitzgerald and Ernest Hemingway were not at all popular in a decade for which they were supposed to be spokesmen. I found that Zane Grey, Harold Bell Wright and Gene Stratton-Porter were the best selling authors. Their works appeared sixteen times on the best seller list in the 1920s. Fitzgerald and Hemingway's never made it at all. It was also interesting to learn from some of my older colleagues at the University of California about taste and reading habits in the 1920s. One distinguished professor of English who was about twenty years old in 1920 and presumably in the center of the lost generation, mentioned that he never heard of F. Scott Fitzgerald until some twelve years later when he began work on his doctorate in American literature and studied Fitzgerald as a classic. During the 1920s, he said, people read Zane Grey and Harold Bell Wright.

In *The Nervous Generation,* I first looked at the reputation of the 1920s taking as my guideline, the observation of Voltaire that history is only a pack of tricks we play on the dead. I found popularizers such as the journalist Frederick Lewis Allen using the stereotyped view of the 1920s and I expected as much. But I was surprised to find how pervasive it was among professional historians who should have known better. Almost everyone subscribed to the idea that World War I had come as a destructive force destroying the old idealistic American faith and precipitating a strange and tragic interregum called the 1920s. It required the shock of the Great Depression and World War II to jolt the nation back to more sensible and serious concerns. The problem, it seemed to me, was that few people took the 1920s seriously. Few tried to find out what contributions the period made to American thought and culture. Few were able to discuss the decade in any terms but those of what had preceded and followed it.

As I argued in *The Nervous Generation*, few Americans should be considered lost or alienated in the 1920s. Most went on as before, running the paper route and slopping the hogs. This was particularly true in popular culture where I looked at tastes in heroes, books, and religion as well as at certain popular causes or crusades. I found that Americans of the 1920s were remarkably old-fashioned. I concluded that the dislocations of the period produced not a less intense but a more intense clinging to old values and traditions. In this sense, I wasn't denying the generalization that World War I was disruptive; I was postulating a different result.

I also found that many intellectuals did indeed feel lost and alienated but here again, I challenged the stereotyped conclusion. It seemed to me that when someone is lost, lets say in a wilderness, he has the option of crawling into a hollow log and waiting for death. But there is also a compulsion that many would feel to try to get found or to find themselves. I think this latter pattern of behavior is more characteristic of intellectuals in the 1920s than is log-crawling. Many intellectuals resurrected or reinterpreted parts of the American faith. Some moved on to new modes of believing and thinking. The effect was as Haldeman-Julius said, a "mental renaissance." The 1920s was a conducive context for new thinking and in *The Nervous Generation* I reviewed it under several categories including attitude toward man, the impact of the war, ethical and aesthetic theory, democratic theory, democratic philosophy, and views of nation and of nature.

To illustrate what I was about further, let me expand upon my argument in the book with new material on Henry L. Mencken. I've come to see Mencken as extremely important because he seems to be the archetype of the cynical intellectual of the 1920s: brash, irreverent, iconoclastic, disrespectful—so his reputation goes. Here was a man, it is said, who scorned sacred beliefs, traditions and institutions. He seems to be nihilistic, alienated, and disillusioned. Mencken appears, to take a phrase from the 1950s, to be a rebel without a cause. And it is true that you can find Mencken saying that he would tow the Statue of Liberty beyond the three mile limit and sink it in the ocean. But to look again at Mencken is to see that in his view Statues of Liberty or their intellectual equivalents retarded individual freedom and intellectual freedom. He would tow the statues away, not the freedom. Actually Mencken was terribly concerned about keeping the real torch of liberty alive in the 1920s. And the point is that the 1920s cleared the air for the likes of Henry Lewis Mencken. In an atmosphere of cracked or crumbling beliefs Mencken and his mentality flourished. He relished in criticism; it was the context in which he did his best work. The disillusionment that followed World War I created for Mencken a golden opportunity, not for hedonism, cynicism, or philistinism, but for intellectual creativity. The old order was exposed and vulnerable. The flanks of traditional certainties were bared. Mencken lept to the attack, fangs bared. His attack had the object of not so much killing, but of new creation. Destruction is a prerequisite for reconstruction. The king is dead; long live the king. What Mencken represented was a kind of cultural clearing of trunks and underbrush before the seeds of a new culture could be planted. The clearing, to be sure, was not complete and some old ideas persisted very strongly in some quarters. But there was enough chopping and burning so that light could enter the forest and encourage the growth of men like Mencken.

Mencken was in the thick of the censorship issue in the 1920s. Frankness regarding sex was the crux of the issue because the suppression of overt sexuality in both behavior and literature had been one of the hallmarks of the genteel tradition prior to World War I. Discretion in this regard characterized the puritanical and allegedly innocent old, formal order. Conversely, free discussion of sex came to symbolize rebellion against the old values.

By the early 1920s several books appeared that addressed sex more explicitly. The names of Theodore Drieser, F. Scott Fitzgerald and Sinclair Lewis could be mentioned. But the most celebrated case involved James Branch Cabell's *Jurgen* (1920). Mencken defended this book as one of the best things about post-war American literature. But he was drawn into the censorship controversy most directly by an article entitled "Hatrack" that appeared in the April 1926 issue of Mencken's *American Mercury*. Hatrack was the name of a prostitute, and while the article would hardly rate more than a "PG" by modern standards, it enraged the conservative community. In Boston, the Reverend T. Frank Chase, the conservative leader of the Roman Catholic Watch and Ward Society and self-appointed guardian of American morality according to the criteria of the genteel tradition, moved to an attack on Mencken as he already had moved on Aldous Huxley, Sherwood Anderson and John Dos Passos. Mencken was enraged. He believed that American literature must be liberated as a prelude to the liberation of American life. By the old standards Mencken was indeed lost, a member of the lost generation. But he had new ones to expound concerning free expression, truthfulness, artistic integrity and honesty generally in American culture.

The "Hatrack" controversy set up one of those rare but delightful direct confrontations in the history of ideas comparable, for example, to the Scopes "monkey" trial. At 2 p.m. on April 5, 1926 Henry Mencken planned to sell the issue of the *American Mercury* containing the controversial article openly on the Boston Common. To anticipate a moment, this was also the place where countercultural radicals of the 1960s rallied. Mencken's customer by previous arrangement would be none other than Reverend T.R. Frank Chase. As the sale took place, police moved in and amidst the flashing bulbs of news photographers, booked Henry L. Mencken for violating the Massachusetts vice law. Mencken could have been subjected to two years of jail and a heavy fine, and he was nervous about the ensuing trial. The next day, April 6, he made a long speech defending the *American Mercury* as a serious, high-minded journal and defending the philosophy that openness was better than closing discussion with antiquated dogma. Mencken left the courtroom thinking he had lost the case, but on April 7 Judge James P. Parmenter dropped all charges. Mencken became an overnight liberal hero, just the way, for instance, Mario Savio did in the 1964 Berkely Free Speech Movement. That evening Mencken went to Harvard and received the applause of younger Americans receptive to his liberal thinking. Just as in the 1970s, the campuses of the 1920s were fertile ground for criticism of the old order.

The April 7 appearance at Harvard was the high point for Mencken. Chase, working through another court, eventually obtained an order barring the *American Mercury* from the U.S. Mail. Mencken did back down to the extent of deleting an article on "Sex and the College Girl" by Bernard DeVoto from the May 1926 issue of his journal. But his achievement should not be minimized. For a segment of American society Mencken focused discontent and held up new artistic ethics. He made the phrase "banned in Boston" a joke, using ridicule to denounce Chase and his colleagues just as he used it to put down William Jennings Bryan in the aftermath of the Scopes trial.

Mencken indeed was lost by old standards. Small town middle western papers continued to rail against the Sage of Baltimore. The *Mendota* [Illinois] *Bulletin* sentenced him "to a good spanking and . . . one year of the wholesome environment of a small Middle Western town." But in the newer emerging points of view Mencken was not lost, but found. One commentator called him "the only honestly free man in America." His alienation from the old standard was a goad to action, not a retreat to nihilistic despair. Mencken's criticism of America was constructive rather than destructive; he was concerned with getting the nation back to a recognition of the true meaning of freedom. This can also explain Mencken's well-known antipathy to democracy and his detestation of the common man as a "boobus americanus." Next to this one must read Mencken's statement "how can any man be a Democrat who is sincerely a Democrat?" It is possible to disagree with Henry Mencken's conclusions but not, I think, with the fact that he was trying for new values and that he found the intellectual atmosphere of the 1920s ideal for this attempt.

It is not hard to draw parallels between the 1920s and the. The reason is that in both periods significant sections of American society raised searching questions about the dominant culture. Some of these critics became disillusioned, even alienated. This rebellious posture was productive in both eras of some of the most creative years of the 20th century.

Take the concept of youth. Both the twenties and the sixties, it seems to me, were times when youth was recognized as having separate and distinct interests, often counter to those of older, established people. The phrase "younger generation" was invented in the 1920s. Previously youth had been regarded as small adults, midget Horatio Alger businessmen carrying attache cases. Their aspirations were thought to be precisely those of the adult community. But in the 1920s, and again in the 1960s, it became apparent that the values of youth were not synonymous with those of adults. The generation gap appeared. The popular press of the twenties was full of "the youth problem" and descriptions of "wild" and "flaming" youth. After 1929, there was a hiatus during which youth was forgotten amidst heavier concerns of depression and world war. But in the late 1950s and 1960s we saw the same spurt of identification of a younger age group that we had following World War I. The key phrase in the latter period was "teen." *Seventeen Magazine* began publication in 1945 and the word "teenager" became widely used in imitation magazines and in columns. "Juvenile delinquency" dominated the press and young people began to identify "our kind" of dancing and music. In time they did the same with ideas and values.

Music figured prominently in defining the younger generations under consideration. In the 1920s, it was, of course jazz; in the 1950s and 60s, rock 'n' roll. Both were highly emotional, intense, authentic and in sharp contrast to the soothing, structured, easy-listening music preferred by the older generation.

To assess the meaning of music in the defiance of youth let's stand outside a Hibbing, Minnesota motion picture theater in 1955 and watch a short chubby-faced Jewish boy emerge from a screening of "Blackboard Jungle." The plot, concerning juvenile delinquents, was intriguing to him containing, as it did, the idea of defiance of the adult order. But Bobby Zimmerman particularly related to the movie's theme song. "Rock Around The Clock" done by a group called Bill Haley and His Comets. As he walks away from the theater, we see him turn excitedly to his companion and exclaim: "hey, that's our music, that's written for us!" Later, under the name of Bob Dylan, the Hibbing teenager rejected his family and his culture, spearheading the cult of defiance that electrified the 1960s.

Both jazz and rock 'n' roll carried a connotation of rebellion. Significantly the very movie Dylan had seen featured a scene in which an English teacher's prized collection of swing records were systematically destroyed by bop-crazed teenagers in a symbol of the generational clash. More than music was at stake. The adult emphasis on success, progress, competition, and organization was under fire. Both jazz and rock, significantly, originated among black Americans, long critical of the mainstream of America and its values. When younger white Americans began to relate to black music they placed themselves in touch with an easier, freer, less inhibited form of culture. The implications were far-reaching. Chuck Berry, for example, in 1957 in a song "School Days" talked about deliverance from the days of old. School was the prime teenage authority symbol and song constituted a mocking of the institution and also, as Berry's lyrics developed, of golden rules. Interestingly a favorite saying of Henry L. Mencken was Jerome N. Frank's remark that "the Golden Rule is that there is no Golden Rule."

At early rock 'n' roll concerts in the late 1950s, just as at jazz parties in the 1920s there was an enormous release on the part of young people. They seemed to be physically, through their dancing and aesthetic enjoyment of the music, rejecting older ideas and older values. It was clear, at any rate, that the grown-up generation in both periods looked upon the youth music as subversive. In the 1920s Henry Ford took upon himself the task of attempting to order American taste and morals as he had industrial production. He was a constant opponent of jazz. The new music clashed squarely with his ruralism and Bible belt morality. In 1921 Ford struck out angrily at "the waves upon waves of musical slush that invade decent parlors and sent the young people of this generation imitating the drivel of morons." He referred to "the mush, the slush, the sly suggestion, the abandoned sensuousness of sliding notes." Jazz, in Ford's mind, was linked to the whole loosening of morals and other values in the 1920s. he referred to the music as "monkey talk, jungle squeals, grunts and squeaks, and gasps suggestive of cave love."

We can find much the same thing said about rock 'n' roll thirty years later. The critics of Elvis Presley resembled Henry Ford. In September 1956, when Presley performed on Ed Sullivan's, "Talk of The Town" television show before an estimated 54 million people, the cameras were ordered to show Elvis only from the waist up for fear of the public response to Elvis' gyrating pelvis. When Presley and other early rock 'n' roll artists went on tour they were frequently confronted with warrants for their arrest on the grounds of "impairing the morals of minors." It is certain that parents had the same concerns about rock 'n' roll in the 1950s as they did about jazz in the 1920s. It was more than just not understanding the music; they also perceived it as a threat. One magazine writer put it very well: "rock 'n' roll is background music in the war between the generations." Or we might turn to Jerry Rubin's statement "the revolution began with rock 'n' roll."

One of the reasons for Rubin's remark was the realization that both jazz and rock 'n' roll implicitly, and sometimes explicitly, criticized many of the most important values and concerns of the adult world. In the 1950s and 60s this criticism was often gathered together under, in California, what was called the "hang loose" ethic. It clashed directly with the priorities of the workaday world. Surf music that impacted so hugely on American popular culture about 1963 is a case in point. The Beach Boys made clear they were "on safari to stay," that there would be an endless summer. "Tell the teacher I'm surfing, surfing U.S.A.," they sang. Articulated here was a lifestyle revolution against adult standards that emphasized school, college, jobs, and success—indeed against the whole Protestant work ethic. Booze, in the 1920s, and pot, and later acid, in the 1960s were an aid in cultural defiance. In time, of course, the rebellious pose became politicized in the songs of Bob Dylan and the countercultural crusades of the 1960s. The 60s, in this sense, went further than the 20s, but both began in the seed-bed of disillusionment with established values and both were furthered by music.

Frankness in discussion and in enjoyment of sex was central in the generation gap. Parents of the 1920s, as we have seen, tried to keep sex under the rug; so did their counterparts of the 1950s and 1960s. Youth, on the other hand, celebrated sex. I think it is significant that the last topless scene in a motion picture prior to the 1960s was *Ben Hur* in 1926. It was not until the sixties that a new wave of openness brought breasts back to the screen. There were other indications. Comedians of the late 1950s and early 1960s such as Lenny Bruce, carried on Henry L. Mencken's crusade against censorship, with the same implications, I think, of opening American culture. Bruce was one of the so-called "sick" comedians. It is possible to argue that he had no reverence for anything. But in the view of his followers it was society that was sick and the comedian the only sane and healthy mind around. Bruce, like Mencken, should be seen as a moralist with a strong sense of human dignity and a hate of the social conventions that destroyed it. Bruce on stage freely used words like "motherfucker" and was criticized for being "dirty." His well-known arrest and trial followed his deliberate use of "cocksucker" in defiance of a local ordinance. But at one point, he responded "you can't do anything with anybody's body to make it dirty to me. You can do only one thing to make it dirty—kill it. Hiroshima was dirty." Mencken, I think, would have agreed. And in Bruce's reference to Hiroshima was a not-too-veiled attack on the whole system of American ethics and politics. A few years later a similar attack was leveled on the Vietnam War.

Lenny Bruce died on August 3, 1966 of a drug overdose, but became something of a martyr to Americans who sensed in him, as they did in Mencken, a freer and bolder spirit. In his humor Bruce was defining new frontiers of candor and interpersonal relations. He was one of the "counterculture's" founding fathers.

The 1960s used this term and its antipode, "establishment", frequently. They also fit the 1920s, although that era preferred, as Elizabeth Stephenson has suggested, "Babbits" and "bohemians." The point is that both the counterculture and the bohemians were out there at the fringes of American culture questioning and challenging, doubting and trying to find alternate guidelines to their lives, their politics, and their art. In the process, they helped inspire two of the most exciting and creative periods in American history.

One of the efforts of dissenters in the 1920s and 1960s concerned the identification of a new style of heroism. It was so unlike the old style that most observers would say that the new heroes were not heroes at all, but, rather, anti-heroes. I prefer the phrase "anti-hero heroes." The primary characteristic of this new type of hero was that he was a rebel. His life embodied a cult of defiance, of doubting. He was unsuccessful by the old criteria; he didn't conquer things, he didn't win. Indeed he was often a total failure. But the old definitions of heroism, both in the 20s and 60s appeared to have increasingly little relevance to what some Americans thought was important. They didn't square with reality as perceived. In *The Nervous*

Generation I argued that despair, disillusionment and defeat in the 20s became the bricks for constructing a new existential metaphysics. The existential hero, if we are to believe Kierkegaard, Camus, and Sarte, is no hero at all in the traditional sense. He does not win, he does not conquer or change the world. What he does is confront, unblinkingly, the meaninglessness of existence and the inevitability of human failure. He must, above all things, be himself, be authentic. And this almost always, involves a rejection of society. Consequently, the existential hero is cast in the role of rebel. He defies. He is "lost," but in an effort to find himself.

The idea of being part of a lost generation was very important to the existentially-oriented heroic posture of the 1920s and the 1960s. Intellectuals of these periods wanted to believe that they were lost, and they wanted others to believe it. It was philosophically desirable to effect a disillusioned posture, because being lost helped create existential situations of their lives. The alienated stance was a deliberate artistic construct, an attempt not to deny all values, but to create a setting in which radically new and existential values could be formulated.

Ernest Hemingway at first rejected the label "lost generation" when Gertrude Stein applied it to him in 1921. He tells us in *A Moveable Feast* "the hell with her lost generation talk and all the dirty, easy labels. It's a lot of rot," But Hemingway gradually changed his mind. It was his genius to see that the war experience and the lost generation concept had aesthetic and ethical possibilities, and when he published his first novel, *The Sun Also Rises* (1926), he selected the Stein label as his lead quotation. And the themes of alienation and futility that pervade the book are very much in keeping with its implications. Jake Barnes, Brett Ashley and their crowd are heroes, not in the sense of attaining glory, but in the sense of confronting the inevitable human failure with courage and grace. It is abundantly clear that people like this were outsiders in the sense of being disassociated from traditional society and traditional values.

The same challenge to traditional patterns of heroism occurred in the 1950s and 1960s and inspired some of the most creative aspects of that era. Roots appear in the roles of Humphrey Bogart where heroism stems not from conforming to, but disdaining the establishment. The generation which formed the counterculture in the 1960s also went to school on motion pictures like *High Noon* (1952) in which Gary Cooper defends an essentially unworthy society for personal reasons. Similarly Alan Ladd in *Shane* (1953) and Richard Boone as Paladin, in *Have Gun Will Travel* (1957), were often cast in roles opposed to the establishment. They might support society but they did so on their own terms. They were never a part of it, and they never sacrificed their individuality. "There are times," said Brett Maverick in 1957 "when a man must rise above principle." So much for the old values.

In literature one of the major expressions was the 1951 characterization of Holden Caulfield in J. D. Salinger's *The Catcher in the Rye.* Society was "phoney," life was absurd in the existential sense, and a protagonist like Caulfield never wins. But many leaders of the 1960s "related to him."

Similarly they related to James Dean during his short, but meteoric rise to popularity in the mid-1950s. Dean personified the cult of defiance and when, perhaps, he, took his own life on September 30, 1955 in a blazing auto crash in California, he anticipated the suicide of Ernest Hemingway a few years later. For both men, I think, suicide was the ultimate existential gesture.

At this time, to be sure, the defiance was raw and unfocused. When Marlon Brando was asked in "The Wild Ones," "What are you against?", he responded "What have you got?" In the winter of 1960 a young man emerged from Minnesota, just as F. Scott Fitzgerald had done a generation earlier, who would help channel the energies of rebels without causes. We have already met Bob Dylan. He was untraditional in values, in dress, in his attitude toward the nation, its past, and its traditional success criteria. Dylan was one who led the way in posing searching questions about the system and the place of the individual in it. After a brief fling at attempting to change the world, Dylan also led the way back to an internalization of peace and freedom. The result was a withdrawal. The 1920s called it, "expatriation." The meccas of the sixties were no longer Paris but, Taos and Humbolt County, California. Greenwich Village was a point in common. The 1970s didn't know San Francisco's Haight, Ashbury. There seems to me a great similarity between the sad young people of the 1920s and the 1960s. They caught a glimpse of a better America, better at least than Babbit and Coolidge or Willie Loman and Nixon and they tried to change the American dream.

For the final assessment, we might return to Henry L. Mencken who once observed that "the liberation of the human mind has best been furthered by gay fellows who heaved dead cats into sanctuaries and then went roistering down the highways of the world." Mencken and his colleagues heaved cats and so did the counterculture. The establishments of both eras labeled the cat heavers irresponsible, a lost generation. A second look tends to reveal them as perhaps more "found" than their detractors like to concede.

Contributors

John W. Aldridge, Professor of English at the University of Michigan, is the author of a number of critical books on contemporary literature. He also contributes essays and reviews to *The New York Times Book Review, One American Scholar, Sewauee Review*, and other periodicals.

Malcolm Cowley, his contributions to literary history, critical evaluation, and personal reminiscence include *Blue Juniata* (1929); *Exile's Return* (1934; Rev. 1951); *The Literary Situation* (1954); *A Second Flowering: Works and Days of the Lost Generation* (1973); *And I Worked At the Writer's Trade: Chapters of Literary History, 1918-1978* (1978). Notwithstanding this partial and selective list of literary credentials, Cowley managed an active membership in the National Institute of Arts and Letters (serving as its President from 1956-1959, and from 1962-1965). He also served as Chancellor of the more selective American Academy of Arts and Letters. Malcolm Cowley died in 1989. His impressive literary legacy survives.

Patricia Erens is Professor at Rosary College, Illinois, she has written four books: *The Films of Shirley MacLaine, Sexual Stratagems: The World of Women in Film, The Film Career of Akira Kurosawa* and *The Jew in American Cinema*. She has contributed numerous articles to leading film magazines.

Norman H. Hostetler graduated cum laude with a B.A. in Humanities at Kansas State University in 1960. He received his M.A. (1965) and Ph.D. in English (1973) from The University of Pennsylvania. Since 1973 he has been at The University of Nebraska-Lincoln, where he is now Associate Professor of English.

Alfred Kazin after receiving his M.A. at Columbia University in 1938, Kazin has held posts at such distinguished universities as Harvard, Smith College, Amherst College, New York University, Princeton, University of California, State University of New York at Stony Brook, and Cambridge. He has served as literary editor of *The New Republic* and *Fortune Magazine*. Mr. Kazin's studies of American prose include the classic *On Native Grounds*, 1942, *F. Scott Fitzgerald; The Man and His Work*, 1951, *The Statue of Theodore Dreiser*, 1955, *Melville, Moby Dick*, 1956, *The Inmost Leaf*, 1955, and *Starting Out in the Thirties*, 1965.

Edward Lueders is Professor of English and University Professor at the University of Utah in Salt Lake City. He has published widely as a social historian *Carl Van Vechten & the Twenties*, 1955 a literary biographer *Carl Van Vechten*, 1965, an editor *College and Adult Reading List of Books in Literature & the Fine Arts*, 1961, a poet-anthologist *Reflections on a Gift of Watermelon Pickle*, 1966, an essayist and nature writer *The Clam Lake Papers*, 1979, and a novelist *The Wake of the General Bliss*, 1989. In his latest book, he is moderator and editor of *Writing Natural History: Dialogues with Authors* 1989. He also plays cocktail and dinner hour piano (light jazz, show tunes, etc.) at the resort areas of Snowbird and Alta in the canyons above Salt Lake City.

Lawrence E. Mintz since taking his PhD. at Michigan State University in 1969, Professor Mintz has earned an international reputation in the field of American humor. Professor Mintz's edited collection of essays, *Humor in America*, was published by Greenwood Press (1988), and he has published several articles, chapters in books, and reviews and presented conference papers on American popular literature, television, comic strips, and many aspects of humor. He is on the advisory board of the *Journal of Popular Culture*. He is a professor of American Studies at the University of Maryland.

Ralph Von Treschow Napp, a highly respected practicing psychologist associated with Winston-Salem State University studied Freudian psychoanalysis at the University of Munich from 1951 until 1957. His numerous publication, including a book entitled *Breaking Down the Barrier*, have led to considerable and diverse expertise in such interrelated subjects as sociology, American studies, and modern history.

Roderick Nash is Professor of History and Environmental History at the University of California Santa Barbara. He has written *Wilderness and the American Mind* (1982) and *The Rights of Nature* (1989). The present essay is based in part on *The Nervous Generation: American Thought, 1917 to 1930* (1970) which will be reissued by Ivon P. Dee, Inc. in 1990.

John W. Parker taught English at the University of Nevada, Columbia, Kentucky-Wesleyan College, George Peabody College, and Methodist College in North Carolina. He served as Chairman of the Department of English at both Kentucky-Wesleyan and Methodist College. In 1963, he became Professor of English at the University of South Florida.

Elizabeth Stevenson's *Babbits and Bohemians, The American 1920's* established her as one of America's leading cultural historians. While serving as Assistant Dean of Emory University, she has written biographies and critical studies of Henry James, Henry Adams, and Lafcadio Hearn.

Amos St. Germain is on the faculty of Wentworth Institute of Technology where he is Professor and Head of the Department of Humanities and Social Sciences. He is the author of numerous essays on American Culture and holds a B.A. in History from Fordham University, an M.A. in American Studies from Purdue University, and Ph.D. in American Civilization from the University of Iowa.

Darwin T. Turner is Professor of English and Chair of African-American World Studies at the University of Iowa. He has served as President of the Iowa Humanities Board, has been elected to the Board of Directors of the Federation of State Humanities Councils, and has published a Norton Critical edition of *Cane*.

Philip Young. After his *Ernest Hemingway*, 1952, he published several other works on the writer, some of them very widely translated. Since changing the subject, he has published a collection of shorter pieces called *Three Bags Full: Essays in American Fiction* (1972), a book on exiled Loyalist American women, *Revolutionary Ladies* (1977), which won a prize in American history, and *Hawthorne's Secret: An Un-Told Tale* (1984). He is now writing a book tentatively called *Melville's Fiction and The Family Stamp*.